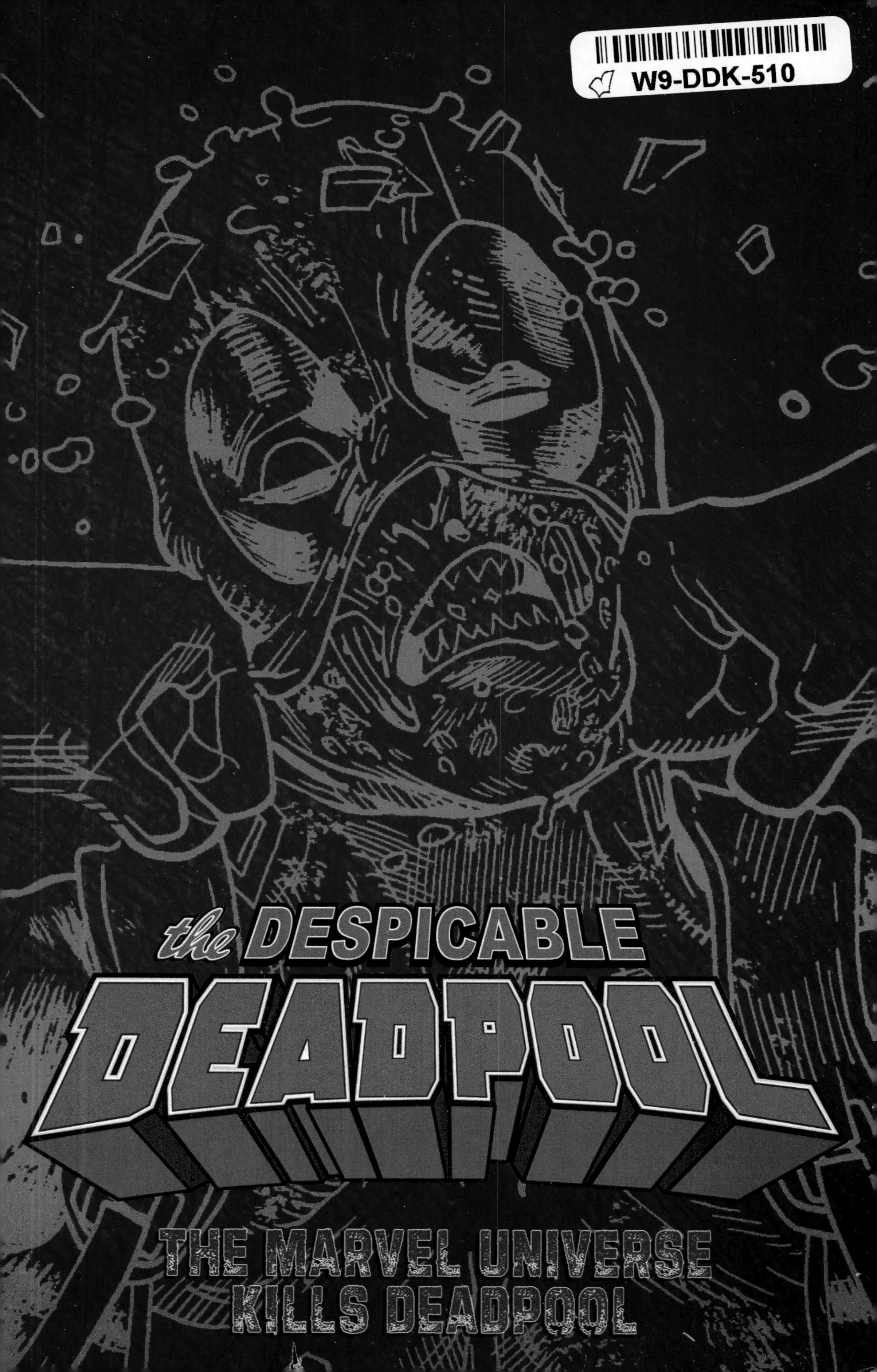
the DESPICABLE
DEADPOOL
THE MARVEL UNIVERSE
KILLS DEADPOOL

the DESPICABLE DEADPOOL

THE MARVEL UNIVERSE KILLS DEADPOOL

WRITER
Gerry Duggan

DESPICABLE DEADPOOL #297–299

PENCILER
Mike Hawthorne

INKER
Terry Pallot

COLORIST
Jordie Bellaire

DESPICABLE DEADPOOL #300

PENCILERS
Scott Koblish, Matteo Lolli & Mike Hawthorne

INKERS
Scott Koblish, Matteo Lolli, Terry Pallot, Craig Yeung & Mike Hawthorne

COLORISTS
Nick Filardi, Ruth Redmond & Jordie Bellaire

Special thanks to David B. Cooper

LETTERER
VC's Joe Sabino

COVER ART
Mike Hawthorne & Nathan Fairbairn

ASSISTANT EDITOR
Annalise Bissa

EDITOR
Jordan D. White

DEADPOOL CREATED BY ROB LIEFELD & FABIAN NICIEZA

COLLECTION EDITOR JENNIFER GRÜNWALD
ASSISTANT EDITOR CAITLIN O'CONNELL
ASSOCIATE MANAGING EDITOR KATERI WOODY
EDITOR, SPECIAL PROJECTS MARK D. BEAZLEY

VP PRODUCTION & SPECIAL PROJECTS JEFF YOUNGQUIST
SVP PRINT, SALES & MARKETING DAVID GABRIEL
BOOK DESIGNER ADAM DEL RE

EDITOR IN CHIEF C.B. CEBULSKI
CHIEF CREATIVE OFFICER JOE QUESADA
PRESIDENT DAN BUCKLEY
EXECUTIVE PRODUCER ALAN FINE

DESPICABLE DEADPOOL VOL. 3: THE MARVEL UNIVERSE KILLS DEADPOOL. Contains material originally published in magazine form as DESPICABLE DEADPOOL #297-300. First printing 2018. ISBN 978-1-302-91039-6. Published by MARVEL WORLDWIDE, INC., a subsidiary of MARVEL ENTERTAINMENT, LLC. OFFICE OF PUBLICATION: 135 West 50th Street, New York, NY 10020. Copyright © 2018 MARVEL No similarity between any of the names, characters, persons, and/or institutions in this magazine with those of any living or dead person or institution is intended, and any such similarity which may exist is purely coincidental. **Printed in the U.S.A.** DAN BUCKLEY, President, Marvel Entertainment; JOHN NEE, Publisher; JOE QUESADA, Chief Creative Officer; TOM BREVOORT, SVP of Publishing; DAVID BOGART, SVP of Business Affairs & Operations, Publishing & Partnership; DAVID GABRIEL, SVP of Sales & Marketing, Publishing; JEFF YOUNGQUIST, VP of Production & Special Projects; DAN CARR, Executive Director of Publishing Technology; ALEX MORALES, Director of Publishing Operations; DAN EDINGTON, Managing Editor; SUSAN CRESPI, Production Manager; STAN LEE, Chairman Emeritus. For information regarding advertising in Marvel Comics or on Marvel.com,

297

"The Marvel Universe Kills Deadpool"

Part One

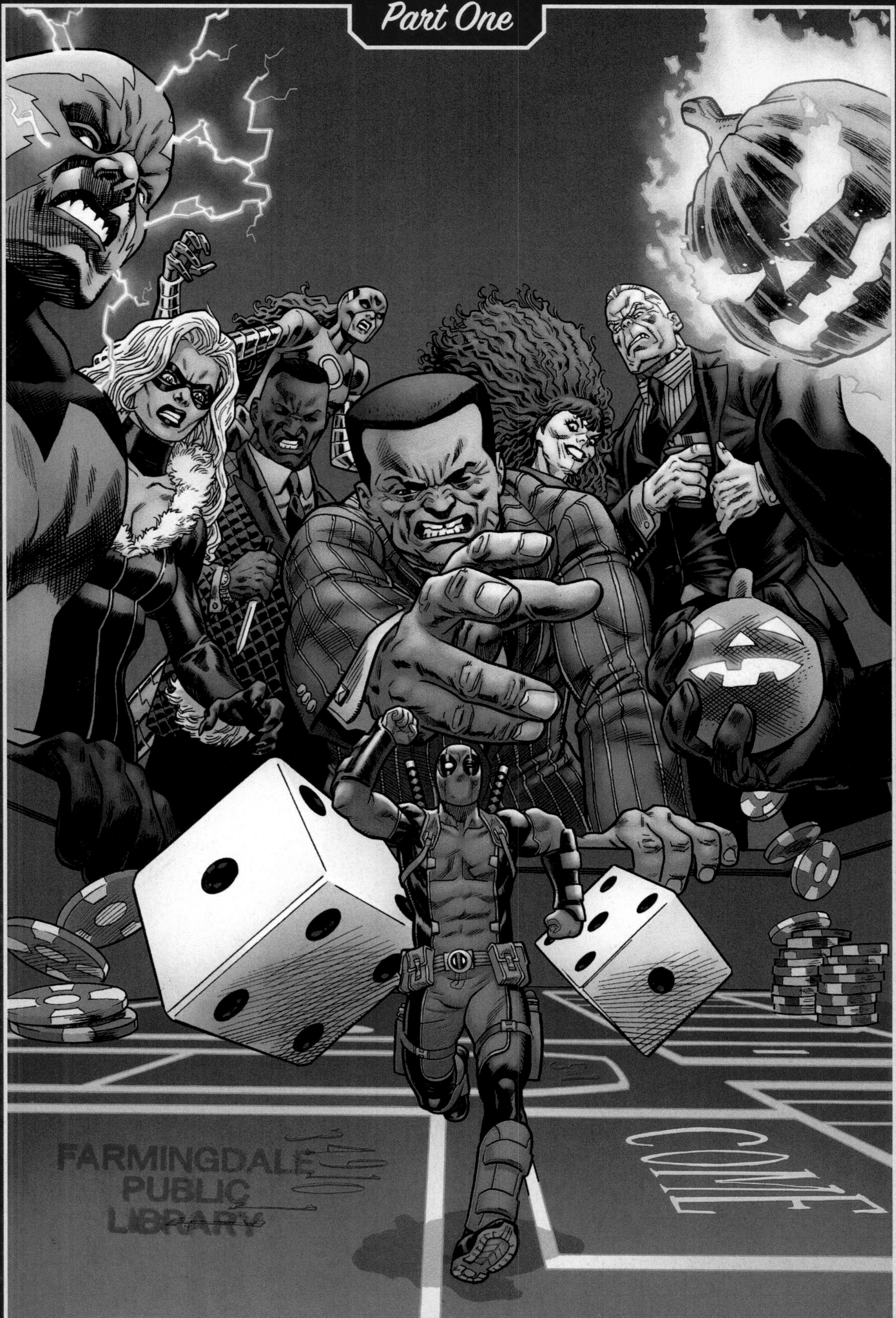
COME

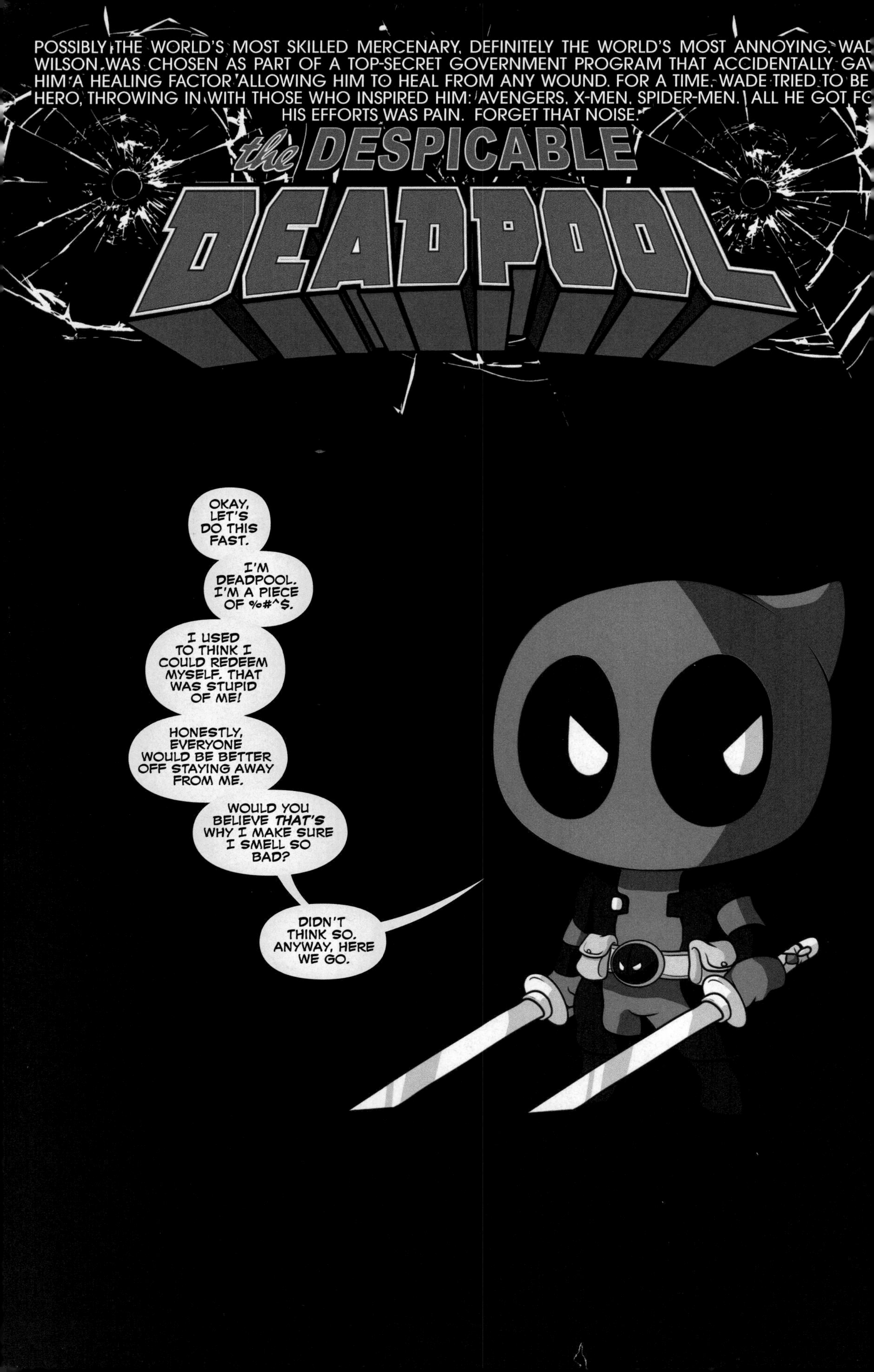

POSSIBLY THE WORLD'S MOST SKILLED MERCENARY, DEFINITELY THE WORLD'S MOST ANNOYING, WAD WILSON WAS CHOSEN AS PART OF A TOP-SECRET GOVERNMENT PROGRAM THAT ACCIDENTALLY GAV HIM A HEALING FACTOR ALLOWING HIM TO HEAL FROM ANY WOUND. FOR A TIME, WADE TRIED TO BE HERO, THROWING IN WITH THOSE WHO INSPIRED HIM: AVENGERS. X-MEN. SPIDER-MEN. ALL HE GOT FO HIS EFFORTS WAS PAIN. FORGET THAT NOISE.
the DESPICABLE DEADPOOL
OKAY, LET'S DO THIS FAST.
I'M DEADPOOL. I'M A PIECE OF %#^$.
I USED TO THINK I COULD REDEEM MYSELF. THAT WAS STUPID OF ME!
HONESTLY, EVERYONE WOULD BE BETTER OFF STAYING AWAY FROM ME.
WOULD YOU BELIEVE THAT'S WHY I MAKE SURE I SMELL SO BAD?
DIDN'T THINK SO. ANYWAY, HERE WE GO.

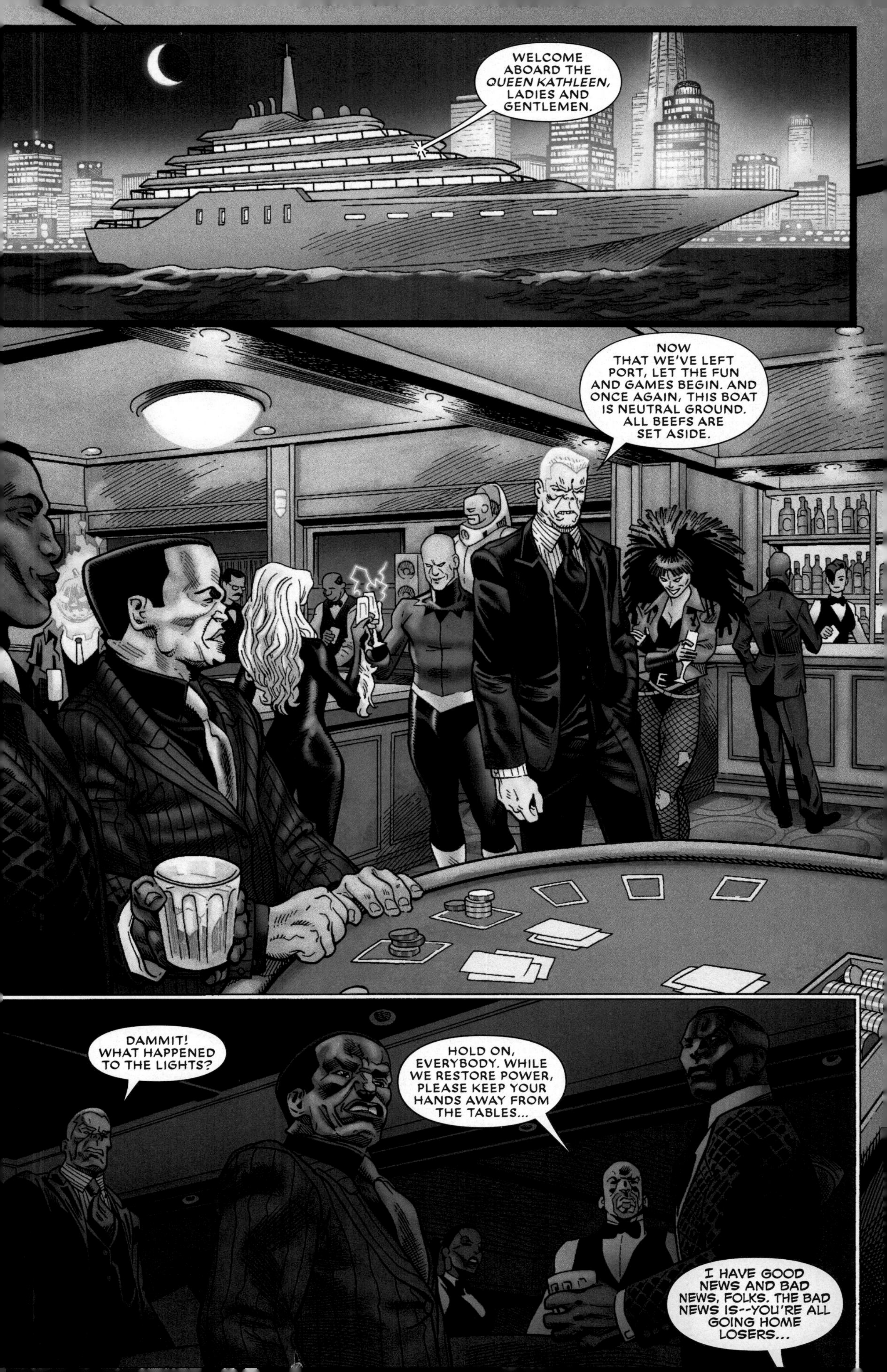

WELCOME ABOARD THE *QUEEN KATHLEEN,* LADIES AND GENTLEMEN.
NOW THAT WE'VE LEFT PORT, LET THE FUN AND GAMES BEGIN. AND ONCE AGAIN, THIS BOAT IS NEUTRAL GROUND. ALL BEEFS ARE SET ASIDE.
DAMMIT! WHAT HAPPENED TO THE LIGHTS?
HOLD ON, EVERYBODY. WHILE WE RESTORE POWER, PLEASE KEEP YOUR HANDS AWAY FROM THE TABLES...
I HAVE GOOD NEWS AND BAD NEWS, FOLKS. THE BAD NEWS IS--YOU'RE ALL GOING HOME LOSERS...

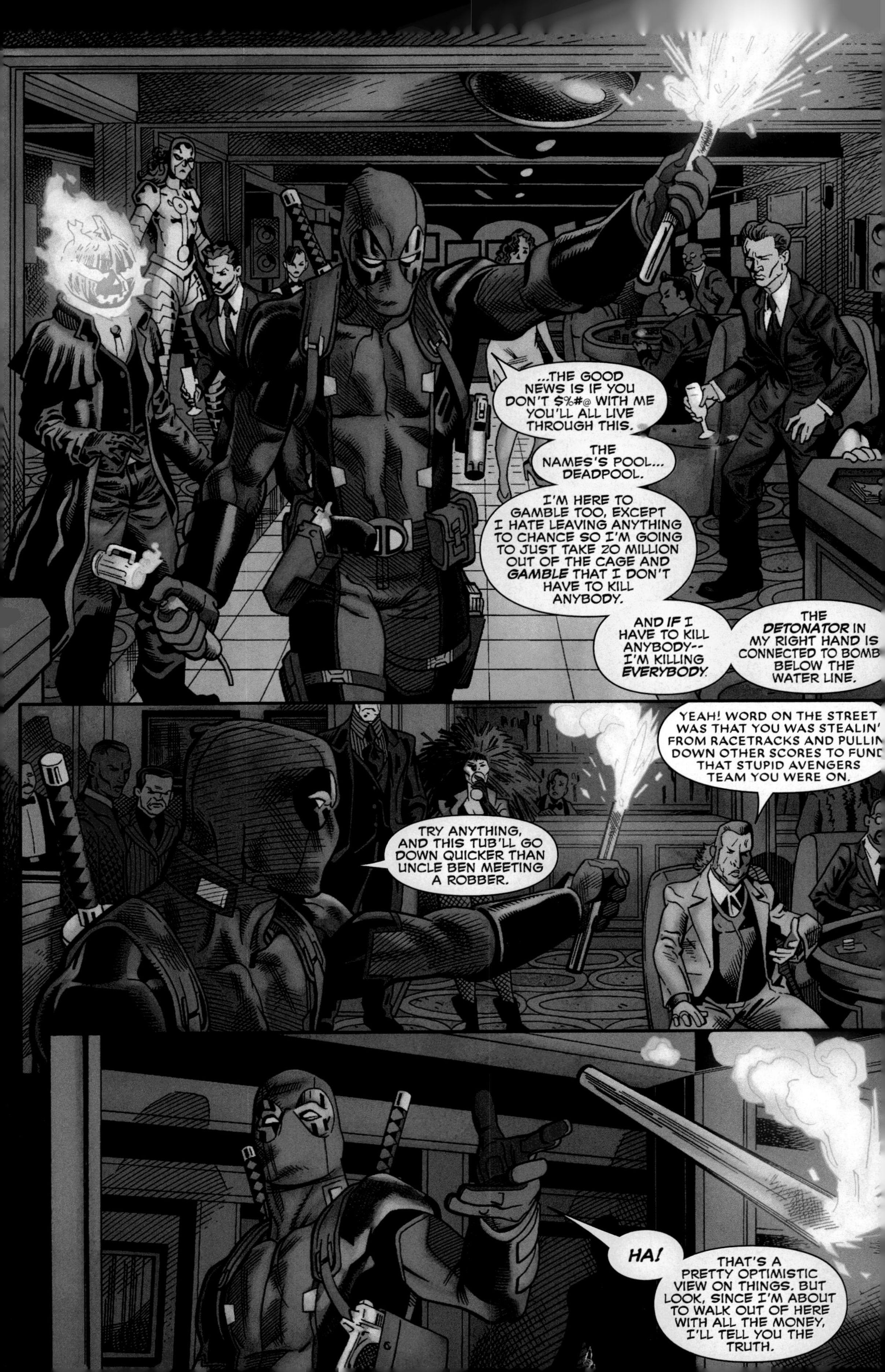
...THE GOOD NEWS IS IF YOU DON'T $%#@ WITH ME YOU'LL ALL LIVE THROUGH THIS.
THE NAMES'S POOL... DEADPOOL.
I'M HERE TO GAMBLE TOO, EXCEPT I HATE LEAVING ANYTHING TO CHANCE SO I'M GOING TO JUST TAKE 20 MILLION OUT OF THE CAGE AND GAMBLE THAT I DON'T HAVE TO KILL ANYBODY.
AND IF I HAVE TO KILL ANYBODY-- I'M KILLING EVERYBODY.
THE DETONATOR IN MY RIGHT HAND IS CONNECTED TO BOMB BELOW THE WATER LINE.
TRY ANYTHING, AND THIS TUB'LL GO DOWN QUICKER THAN UNCLE BEN MEETING A ROBBER.
YEAH! WORD ON THE STREET WAS THAT YOU WAS STEALIN' FROM RACETRACKS AND PULLIN DOWN OTHER SCORES TO FUND THAT STUPID AVENGERS TEAM YOU WERE ON.
HA!
THAT'S A PRETTY OPTIMISTIC VIEW ON THINGS. BUT LOOK, SINCE I'M ABOUT TO WALK OUT OF HERE WITH ALL THE MONEY, I'LL TELL YOU THE TRUTH.

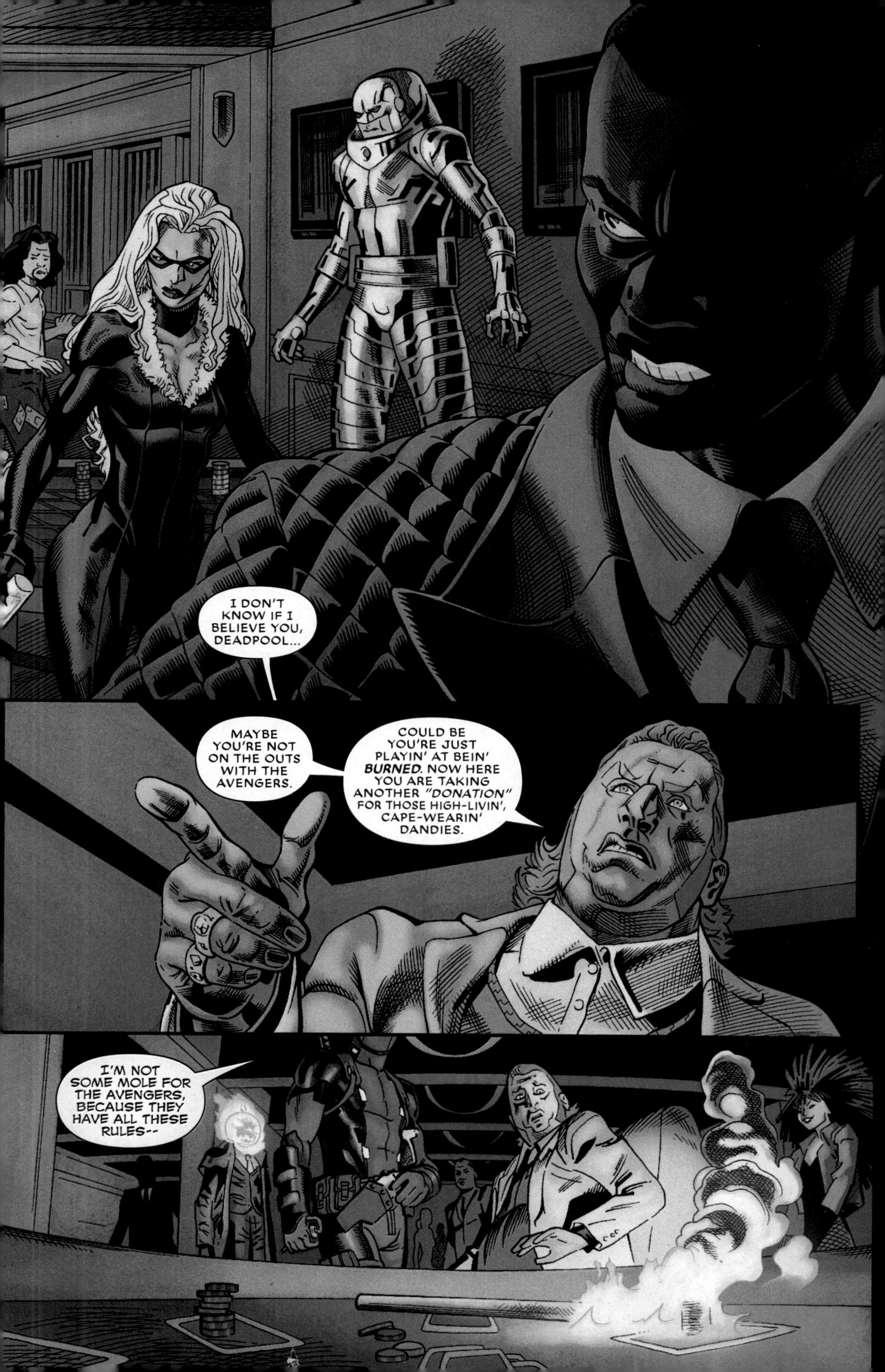
I DON'T KNOW IF I BELIEVE YOU, DEADPOOL...
MAYBE YOU'RE NOT ON THE OUTS WITH THE AVENGERS.
COULD BE YOU'RE JUST PLAYIN' AT BEIN' ***BURNED.*** NOW HERE YOU ARE TAKING ANOTHER *"DONATION"* FOR THOSE HIGH-LIVIN', CAPE-WEARIN' DANDIES.
I'M NOT SOME MOLE FOR THE AVENGERS, BECAUSE THEY HAVE ALL THESE RULES--

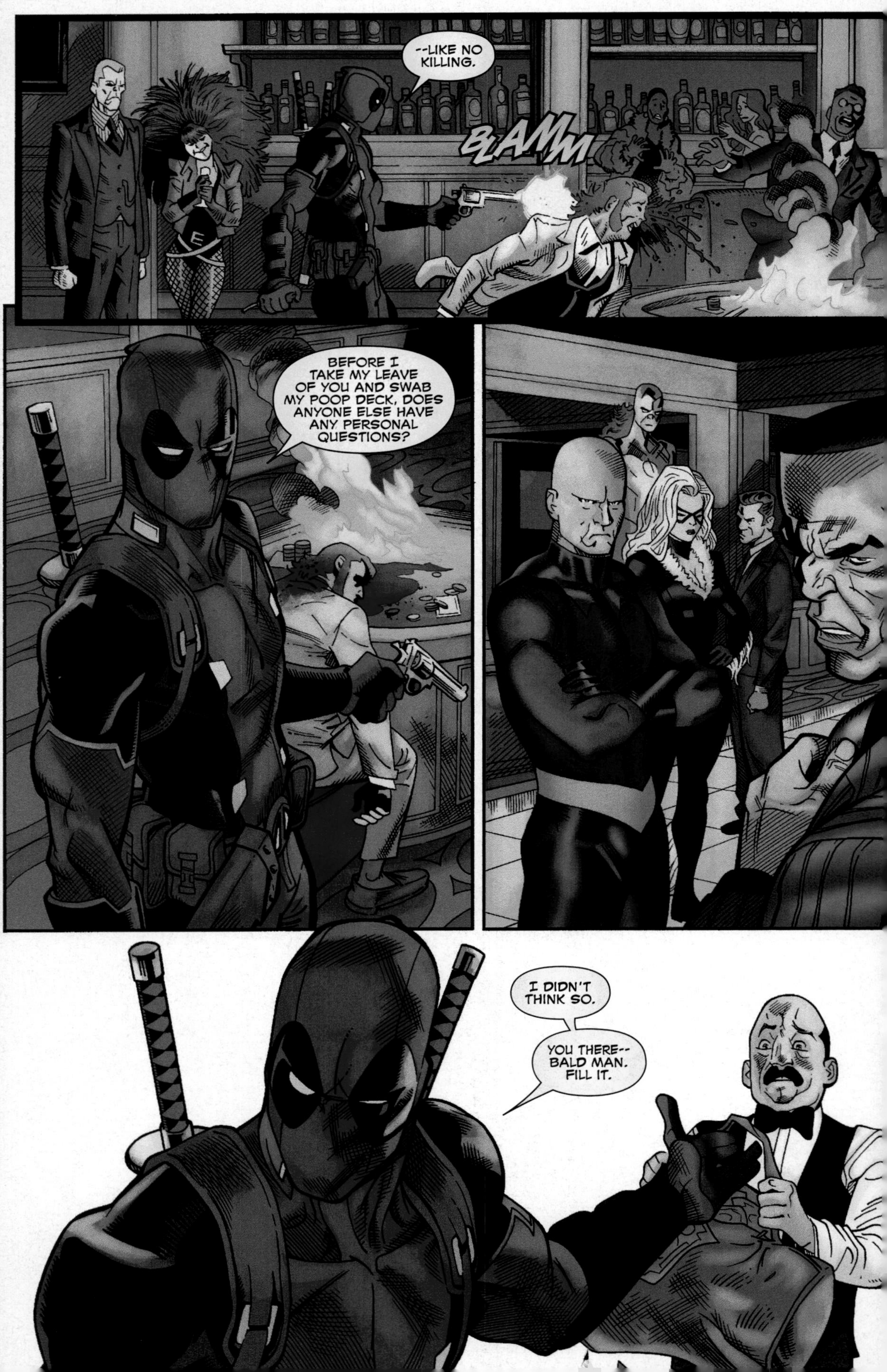
--LIKE NO KILLING.
BLAMM
BEFORE I TAKE MY LEAVE OF YOU AND SWAB MY POOP DECK, DOES ANYONE ELSE HAVE ANY PERSONAL QUESTIONS?
I DIDN'T THINK SO.
YOU THERE-- BALD MAN. FILL IT.

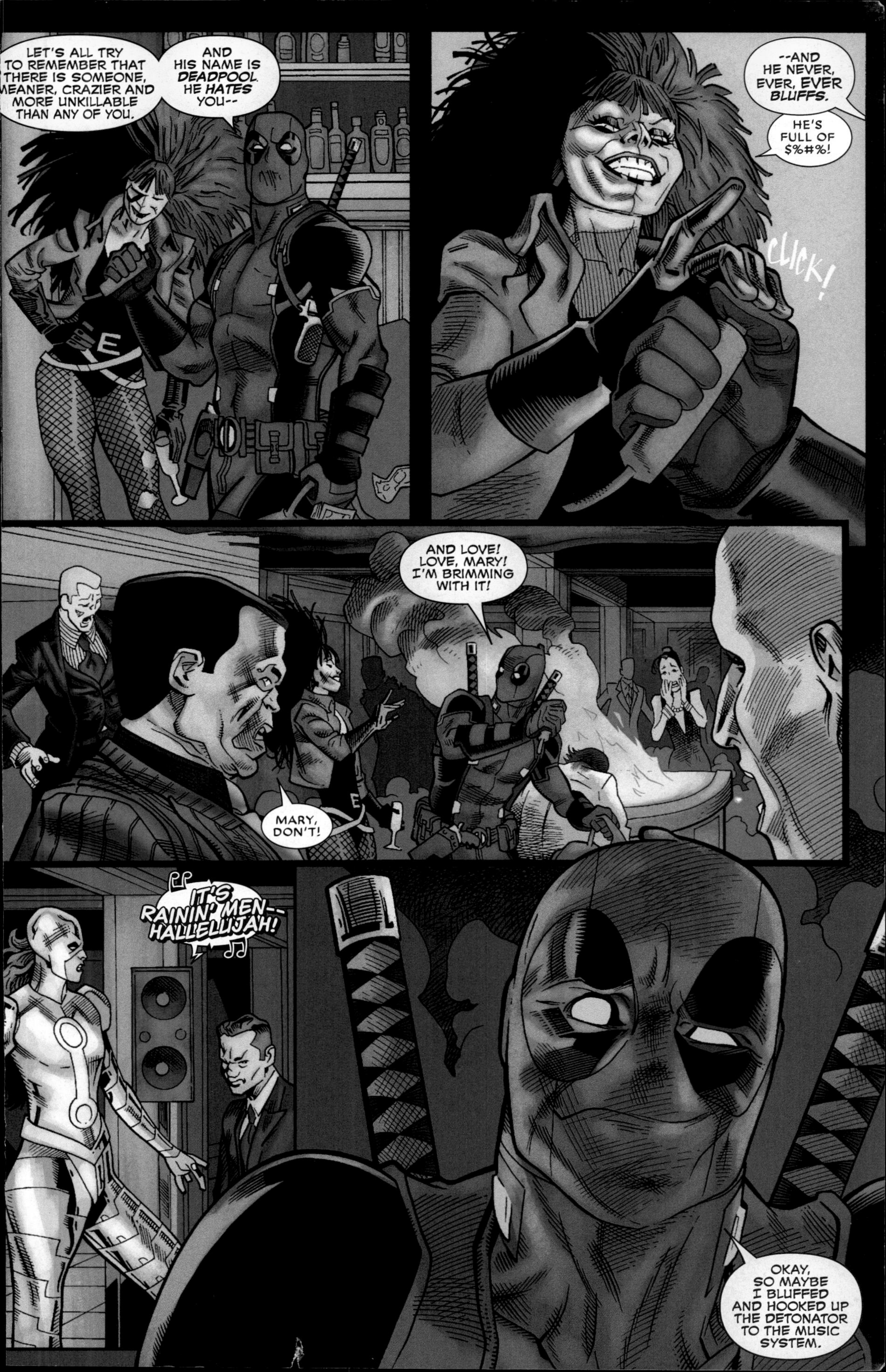
LET'S ALL TRY TO REMEMBER THAT THERE IS SOMEONE, MEANER, CRAZIER AND MORE UNKILLABLE THAN ANY OF YOU.
AND HIS NAME IS DEADPOOL. HE HATES YOU--
--AND HE NEVER, EVER, EVER BLUFFS.
HE'S FULL OF $%#%!
CLICK!
AND LOVE! LOVE, MARY! I'M BRIMMING WITH IT!
MARY, DON'T!
IT'S RAININ' MEN-- HALLELUJAH!
OKAY, SO MAYBE I BLUFFED AND HOOKED UP THE DETONATOR TO THE MUSIC SYSTEM.

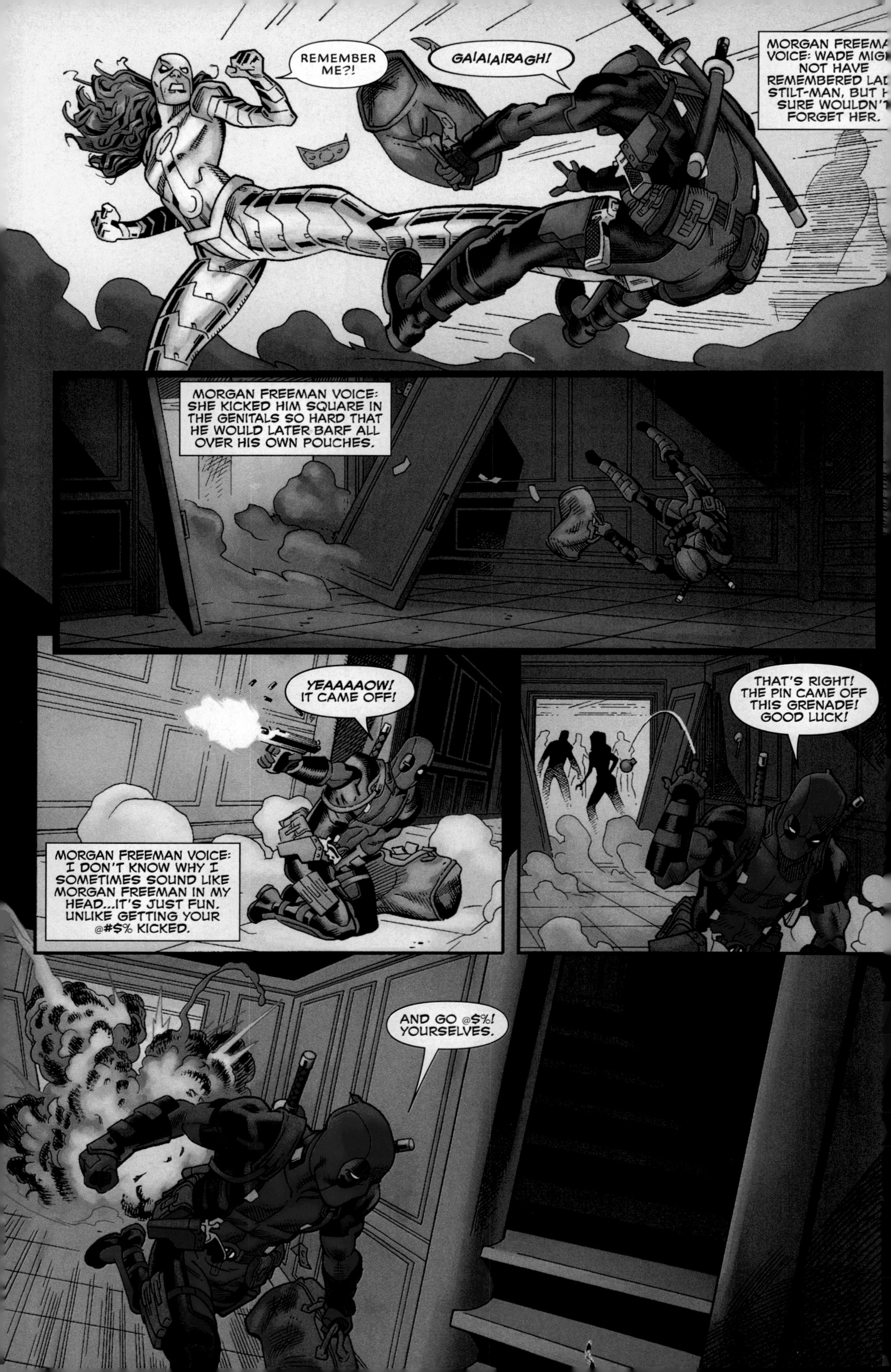
REMEMBER ME?!
GA!A!A!RAGH!
MORGAN FREEMA VOICE: WADE MIGH NOT HAVE REMEMBERED LAD STILT-MAN, BUT H SURE WOULDN'T FORGET HER.
MORGAN FREEMAN VOICE: SHE KICKED HIM SQUARE IN THE GENITALS SO HARD THAT HE WOULD LATER BARF ALL OVER HIS OWN POUCHES.
YEAAAAOW! IT CAME OFF!
MORGAN FREEMAN VOICE: I DON'T KNOW WHY I SOMETIMES SOUND LIKE MORGAN FREEMAN IN MY HEAD...IT'S JUST FUN. UNLIKE GETTING YOUR @#$% KICKED.
THAT'S RIGHT! THE PIN CAME OFF THIS GRENADE! GOOD LUCK!
AND GO @$%! YOURSELVES.

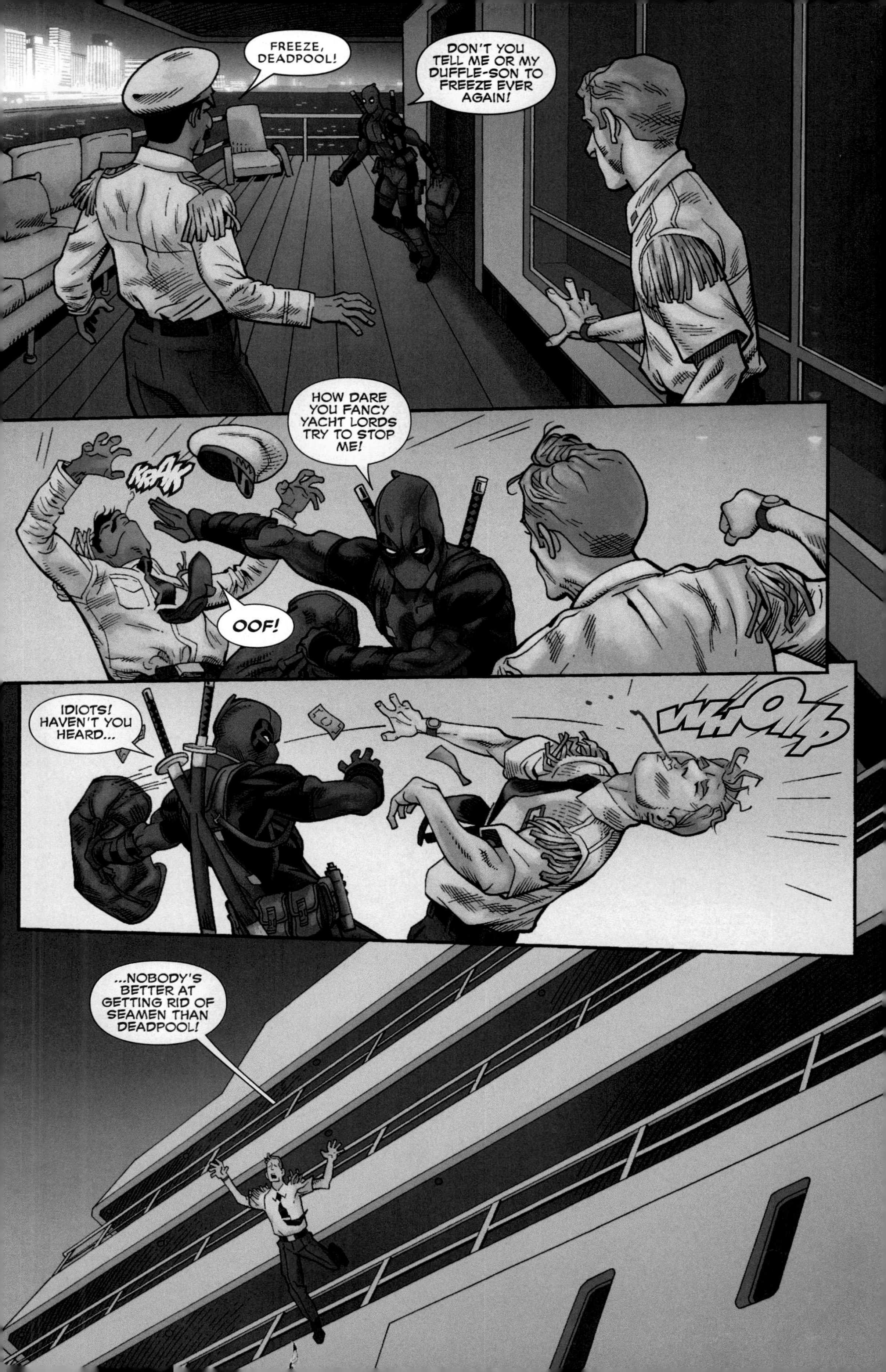
FREEZE, DEADPOOL!
DON'T YOU TELL ME OR MY DUFFLE-SON TO FREEZE EVER AGAIN!
HOW DARE YOU FANCY YACHT LORDS TRY TO STOP ME!
KRAK
OOF!
IDIOTS! HAVEN'T YOU HEARD...
WHOMP
...NOBODY'S BETTER AT GETTING RID OF SEAMEN THAN DEADPOOL!

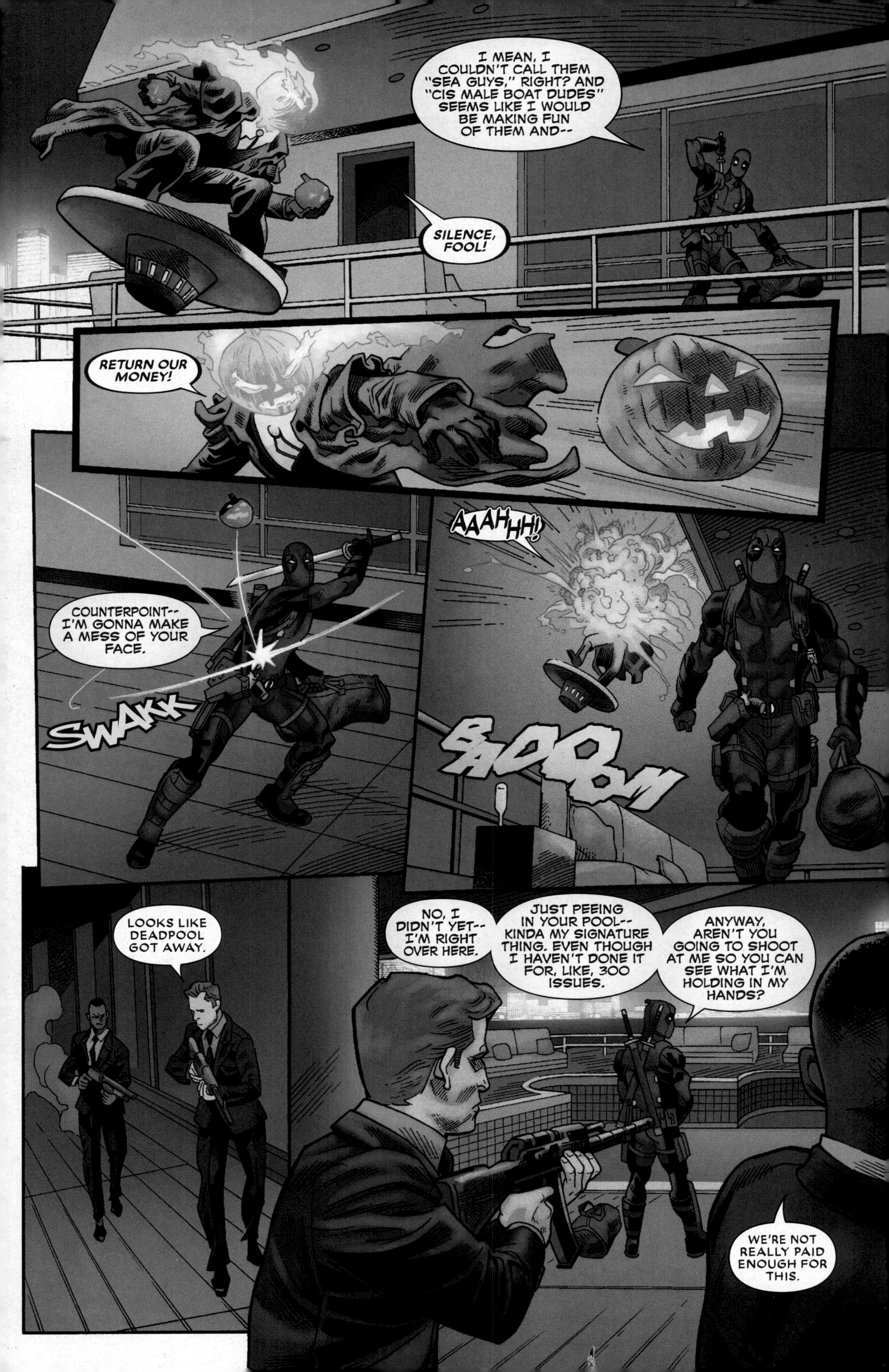
I MEAN, I COULDN'T CALL THEM "SEA GUYS," RIGHT? AND "CIS MALE BOAT DUDES" SEEMS LIKE I WOULD BE MAKING FUN OF THEM AND--
SILENCE, FOOL!
RETURN OUR MONEY!
COUNTERPOINT-- I'M GONNA MAKE A MESS OF YOUR FACE.
SWAKK
AAAHHH!
BOOOM
LOOKS LIKE DEADPOOL GOT AWAY.
NO, I DIDN'T YET-- I'M RIGHT OVER HERE.
JUST PEEING IN YOUR POOL-- KINDA MY SIGNATURE THING. EVEN THOUGH I HAVEN'T DONE IT FOR, LIKE, 300 ISSUES.
ANYWAY, AREN'T YOU GOING TO SHOOT AT ME SO YOU CAN SEE WHAT I'M HOLDING IN MY HANDS?
WE'RE NOT REALLY PAID ENOUGH FOR THIS.

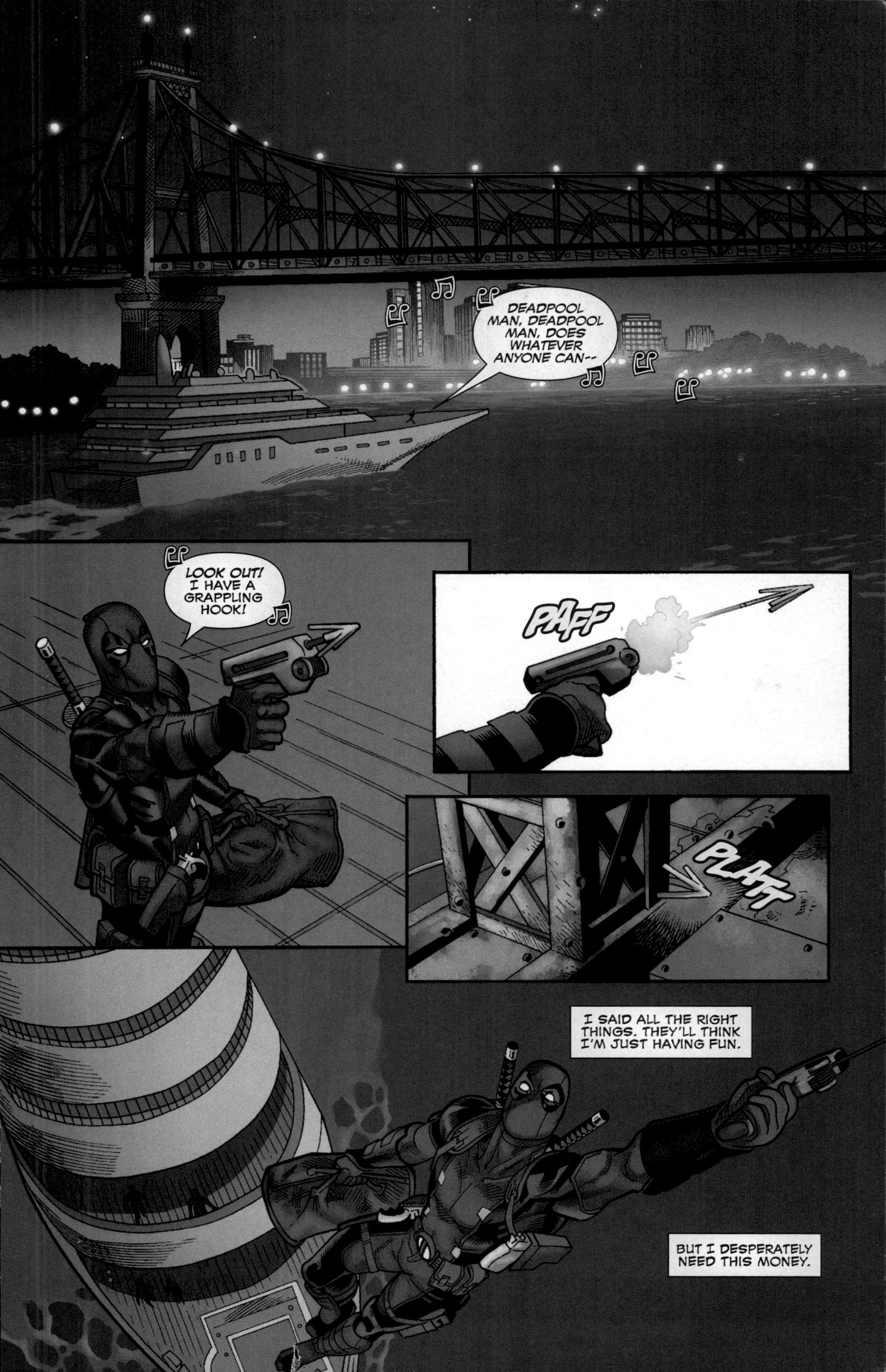
DEADPOOL MAN, DEADPOOL MAN, DOES WHATEVER ANYONE CAN--
LOOK OUT! I HAVE A GRAPPLING HOOK!
PAFF
PLATT
I SAID ALL THE RIGHT THINGS. THEY'LL THINK I'M JUST HAVING FUN.
BUT I DESPERATELY NEED THIS MONEY.

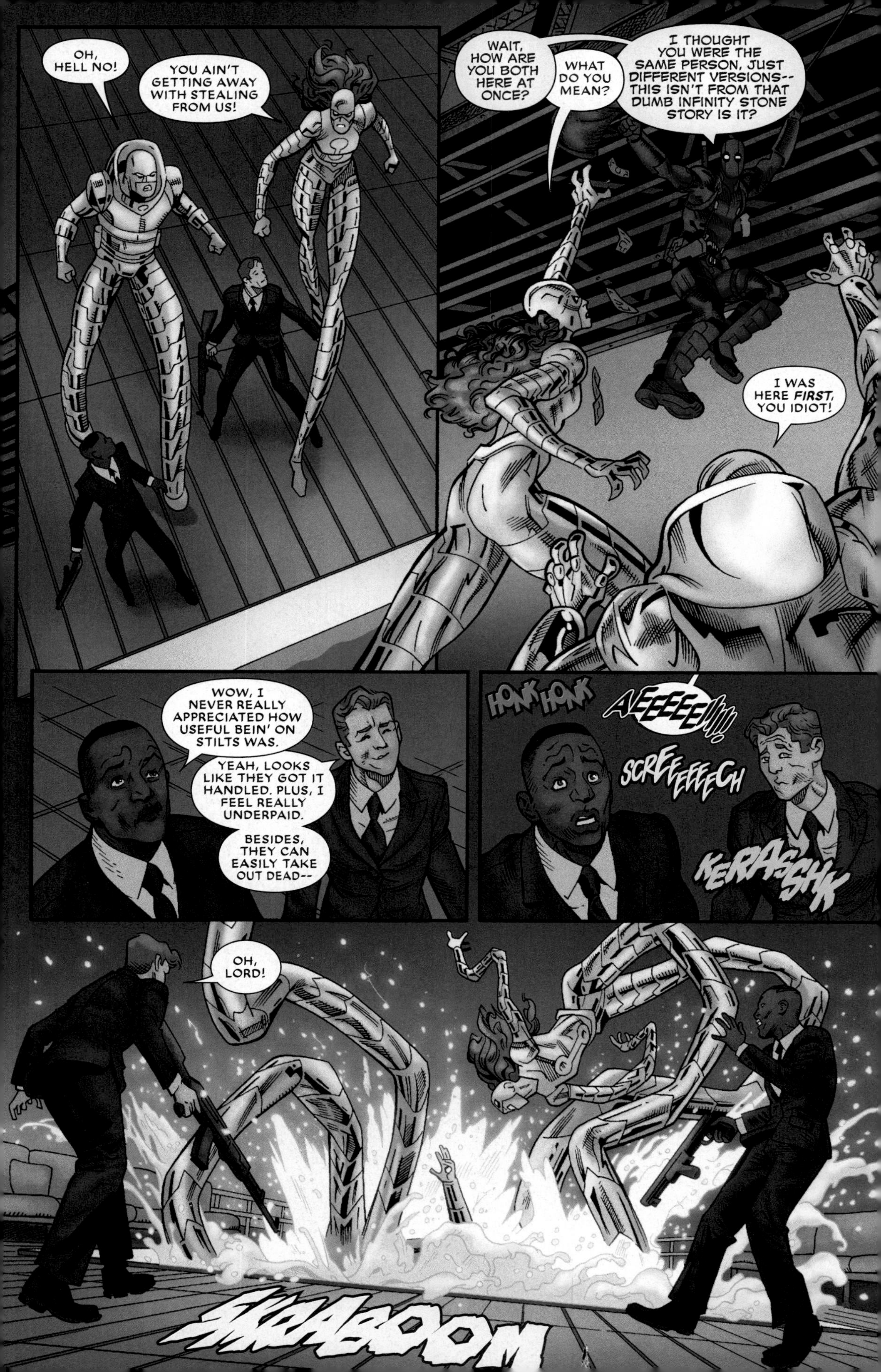
OH, HELL NO!
YOU AIN'T GETTING AWAY WITH STEALING FROM US!
WAIT, HOW ARE YOU BOTH HERE AT ONCE?
WHAT DO YOU MEAN?
I THOUGHT YOU WERE THE SAME PERSON, JUST DIFFERENT VERSIONS-- THIS ISN'T FROM THAT DUMB INFINITY STONE STORY IS IT?
I WAS HERE FIRST, YOU IDIOT!
WOW, I NEVER REALLY APPRECIATED HOW USEFUL BEIN' ON STILTS WAS.
YEAH, LOOKS LIKE THEY GOT IT HANDLED. PLUS, I FEEL REALLY UNDERPAID.
BESIDES, THEY CAN EASILY TAKE OUT DEAD--
HONK HONK
AEEEEE!!!!
SCREEEEEECH
KERASSHK
OH, LORD!
SKRABOOM

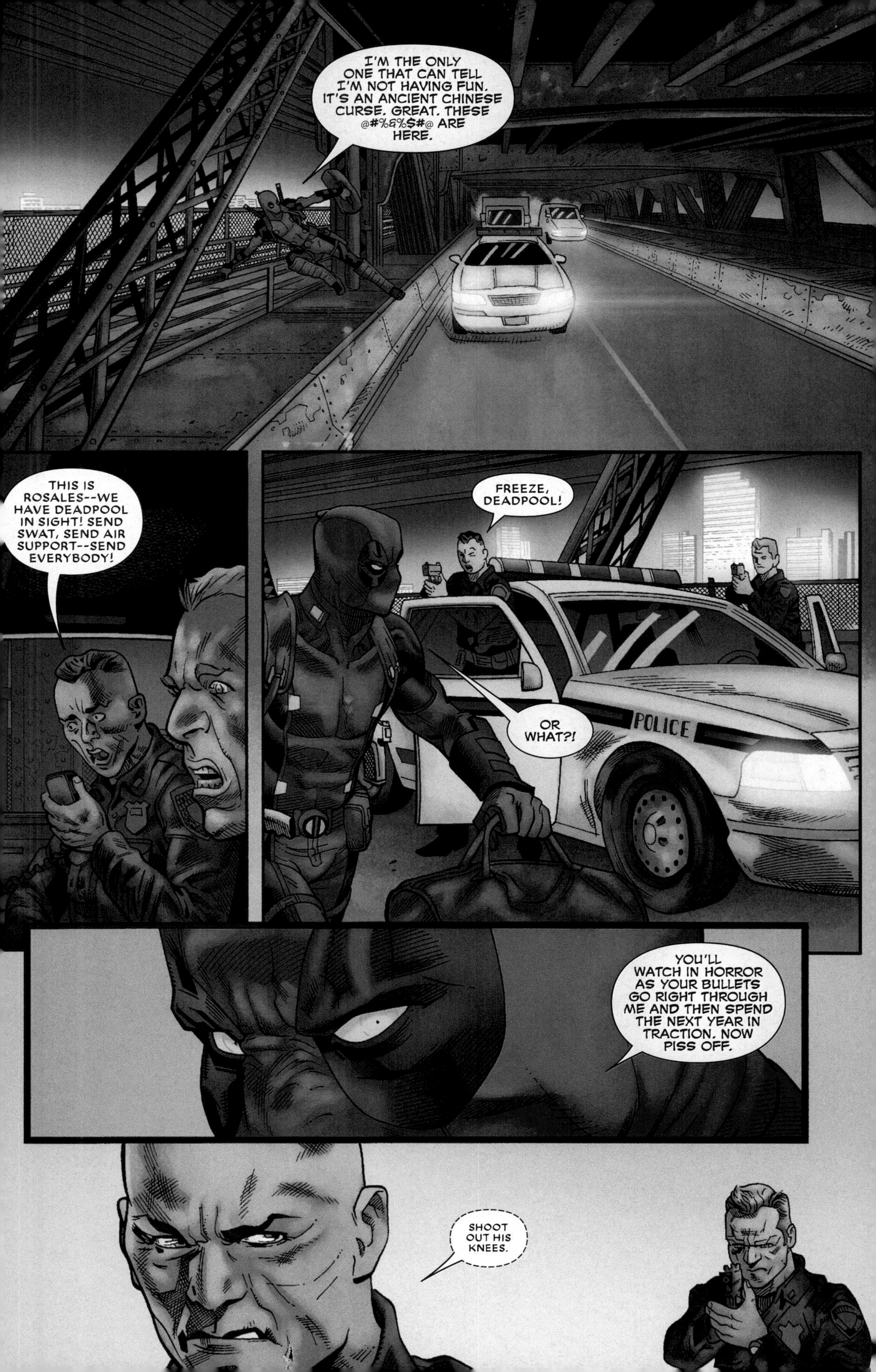
I'M THE ONLY ONE THAT CAN TELL I'M NOT HAVING FUN. IT'S AN ANCIENT CHINESE CURSE. GREAT. THESE @#%&%$#@ ARE HERE.
THIS IS ROSALES--WE HAVE DEADPOOL IN SIGHT! SEND SWAT, SEND AIR SUPPORT--SEND EVERYBODY!
FREEZE, DEADPOOL!
OR WHAT?!
POLICE
YOU'LL WATCH IN HORROR AS YOUR BULLETS GO RIGHT THROUGH ME AND THEN SPEND THE NEXT YEAR IN TRACTION. NOW PISS OFF.
SHOOT OUT HIS KNEES.

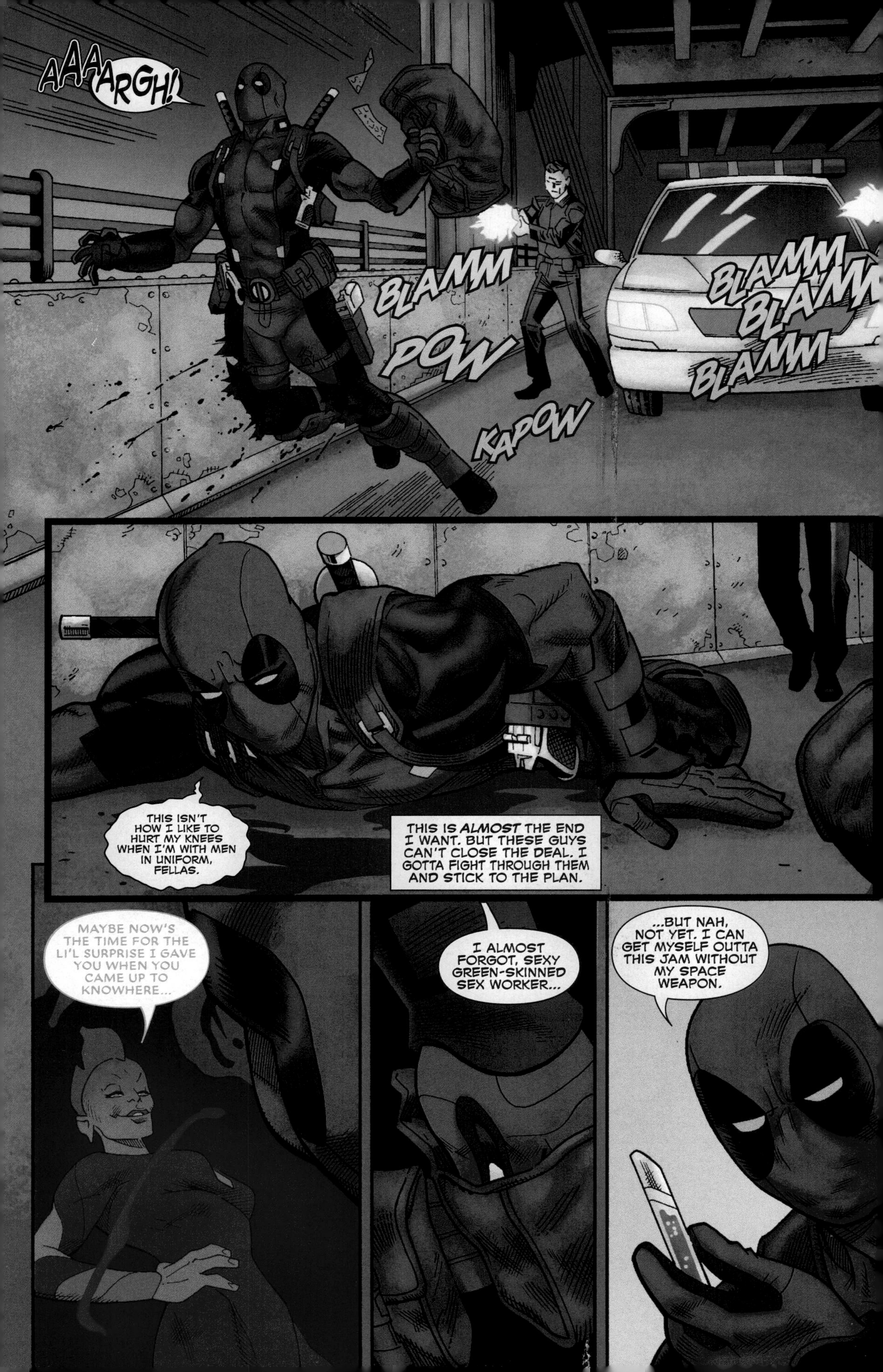
AAAARGH!
BLAMM
POW
KAPOW
BLAMM
BLAMM
BLAMM
THIS ISN'T HOW I LIKE TO HURT MY KNEES WHEN I'M WITH MEN IN UNIFORM, FELLAS.
THIS IS *ALMOST* THE END I WANT. BUT THESE GUYS CAN'T CLOSE THE DEAL. I GOTTA FIGHT THROUGH THEM AND STICK TO THE PLAN.
MAYBE NOW'S THE TIME FOR THE LI'L SURPRISE I GAVE YOU WHEN YOU CAME UP TO KNOWHERE...
I ALMOST FORGOT, SEXY GREEN-SKINNED SEX WORKER...
...BUT NAH, NOT YET. I CAN GET MYSELF OUTTA THIS JAM WITHOUT MY SPACE WEAPON.

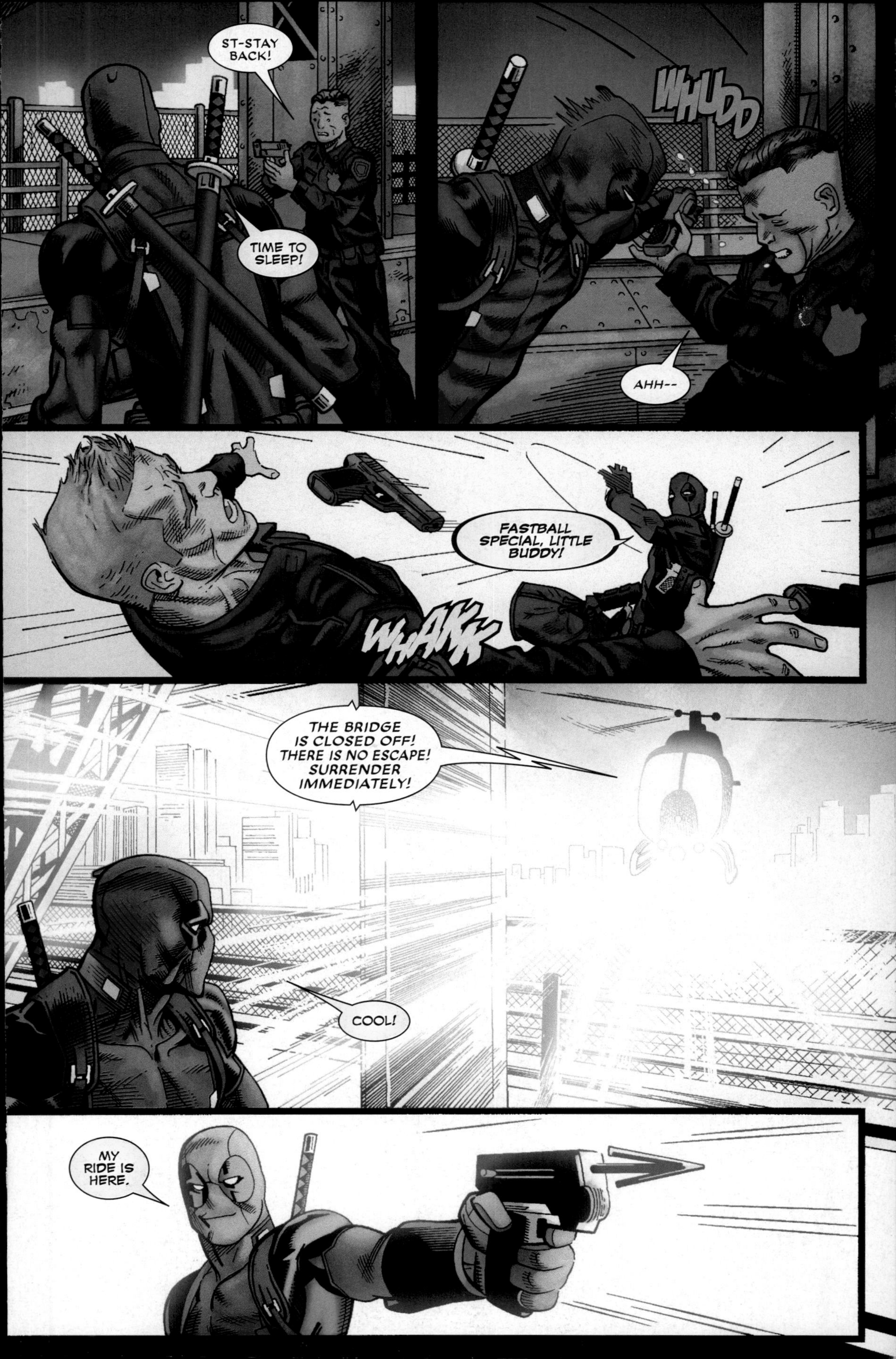
ST-STAY BACK!
TIME TO SLEEP!
WHUDD
AHH--
FASTBALL SPECIAL, LITTLE BUDDY!
WHAKK
THE BRIDGE IS CLOSED OFF! THERE IS NO ESCAPE! SURRENDER IMMEDIATELY!
COOL!
MY RIDE IS HERE.

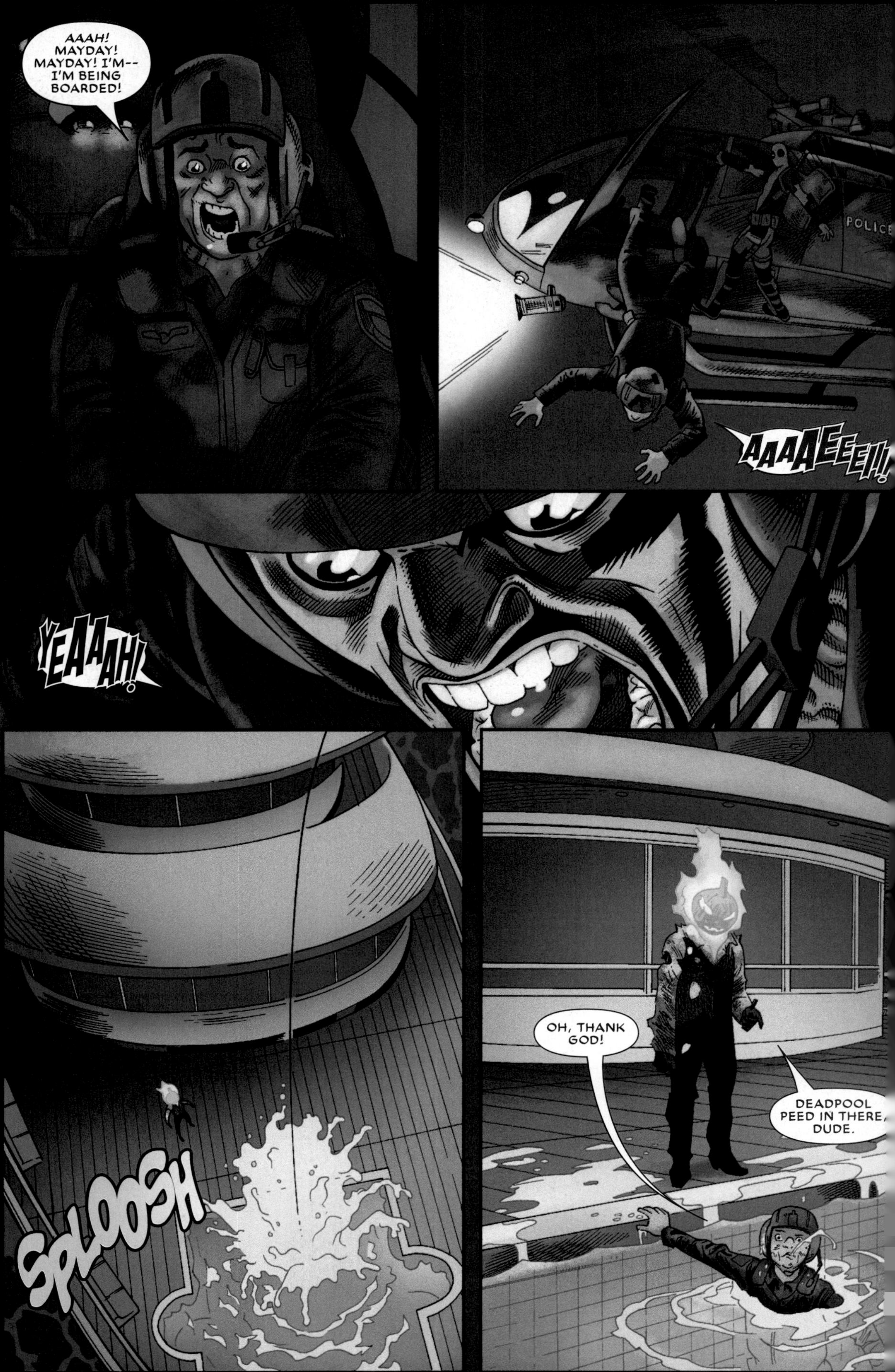
AAAH! MAYDAY! MAYDAY! I'M-- I'M BEING BOARDED!
POLICE
AAAAEEEII!!
YEAAAAH!!
SPLOOSH
OH, THANK GOD!
DEADPOOL PEED IN THERE, DUDE.

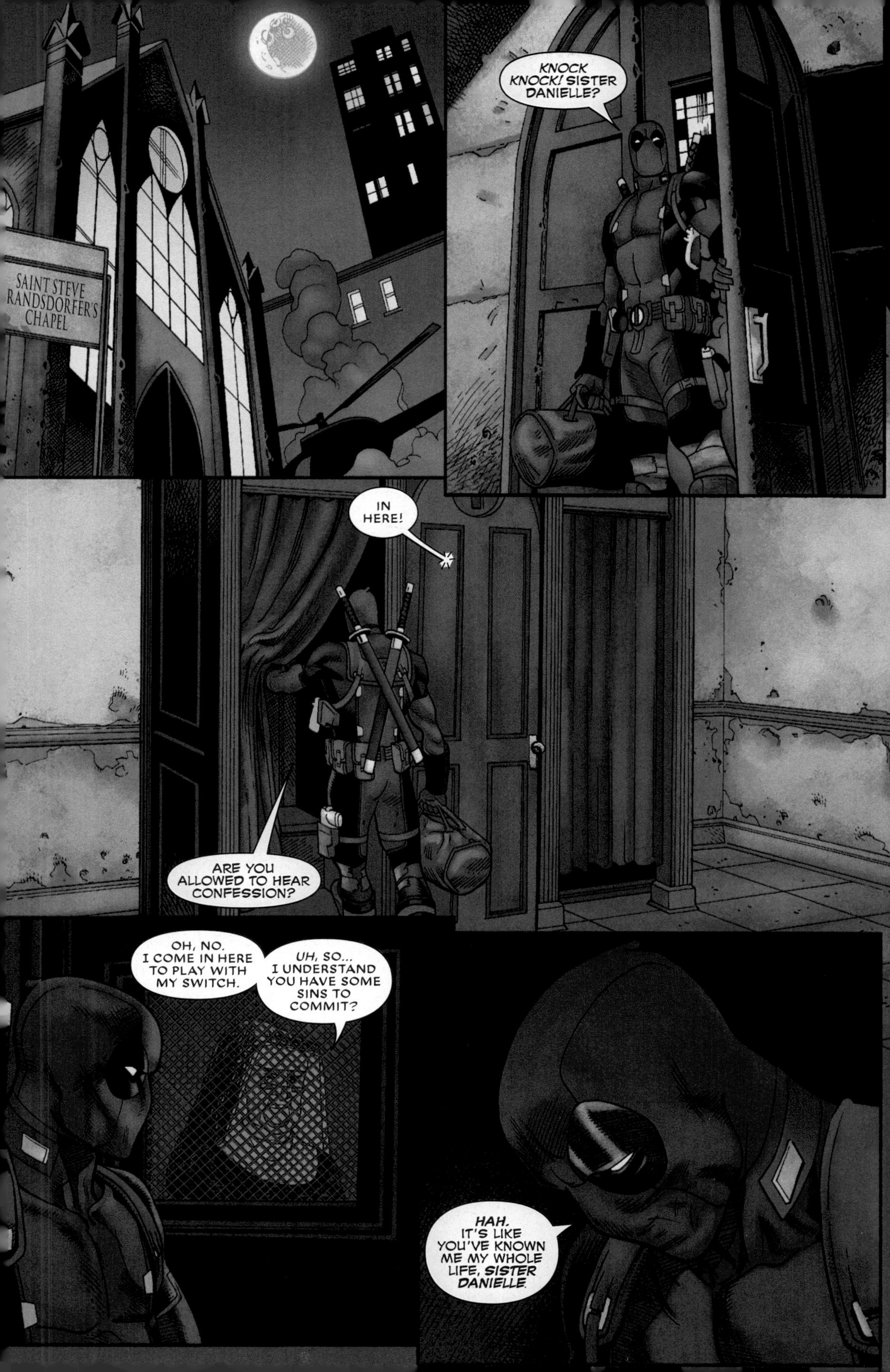
SAINT STEVE RANDSDORFER'S CHAPEL
KNOCK KNOCK! SISTER DANIELLE?
IN HERE!
ARE YOU ALLOWED TO HEAR CONFESSION?
OH, NO. I COME IN HERE TO PLAY WITH MY SWITCH.
UH, SO... I UNDERSTAND YOU HAVE SOME SINS TO COMMIT?
HAH. IT'S LIKE YOU'VE KNOWN ME MY WHOLE LIFE, SISTER DANIELLE.

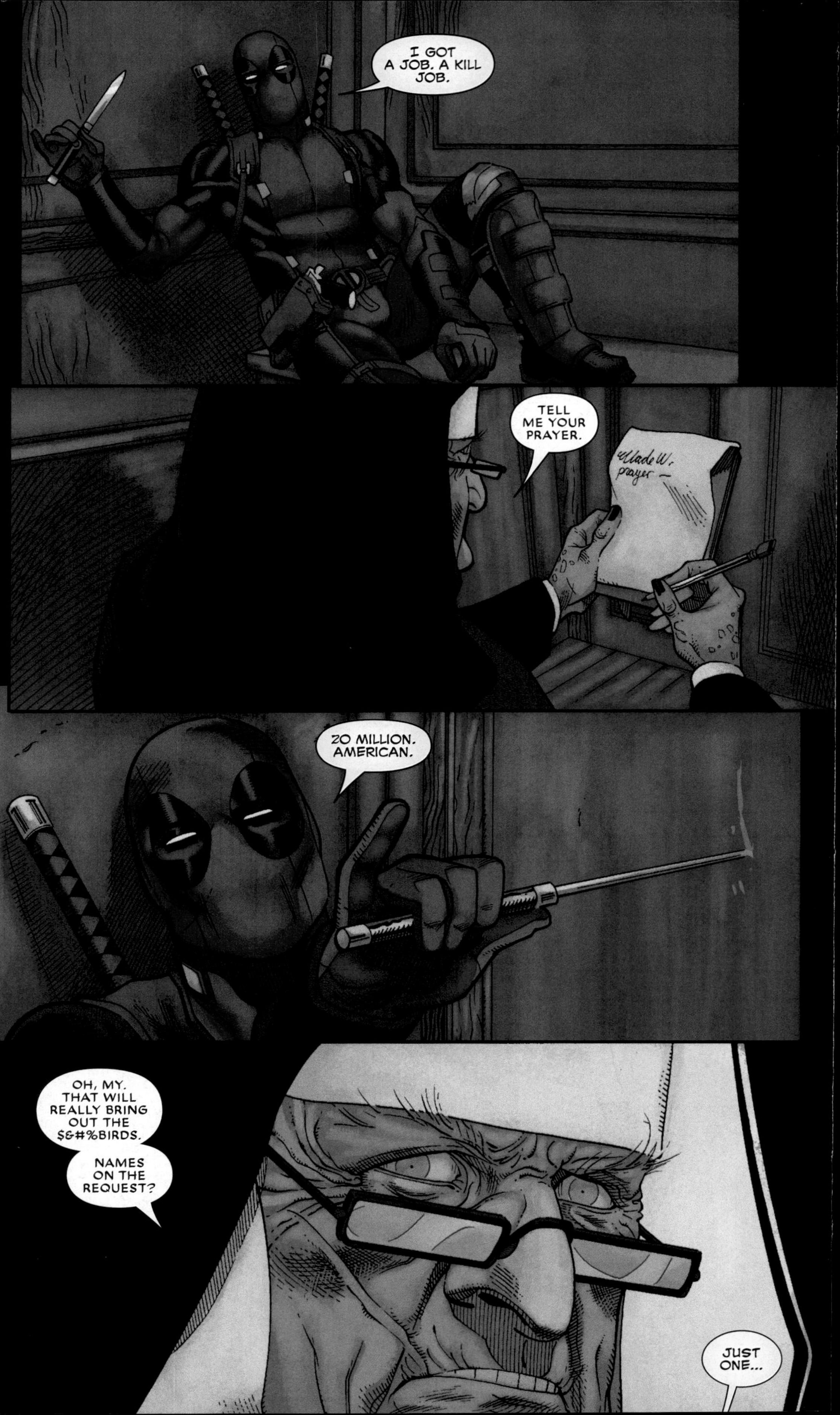

I GOT A JOB. A KILL JOB.
TELL ME YOUR PRAYER.
20 MILLION. AMERICAN.
OH, MY. THAT WILL REALLY BRING OUT THE $&#%BIRDS.
NAMES ON THE REQUEST?
JUST ONE...

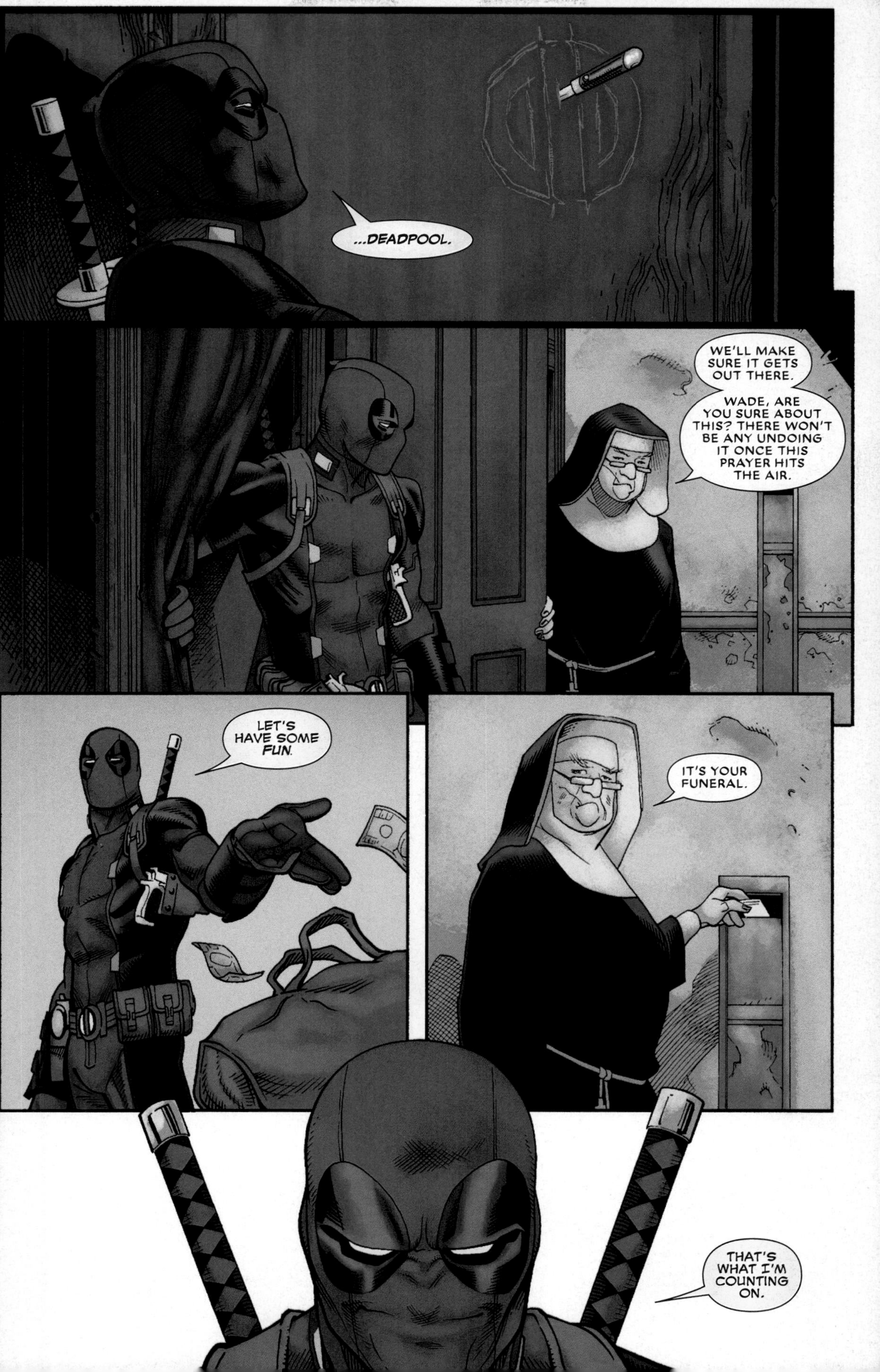
...DEADPOOL.
WE'LL MAKE SURE IT GETS OUT THERE.
WADE, ARE YOU SURE ABOUT THIS? THERE WON'T BE ANY UNDOING IT ONCE THIS PRAYER HITS THE AIR.
LET'S HAVE SOME FUN.
IT'S YOUR FUNERAL.
THAT'S WHAT I'M COUNTING ON.

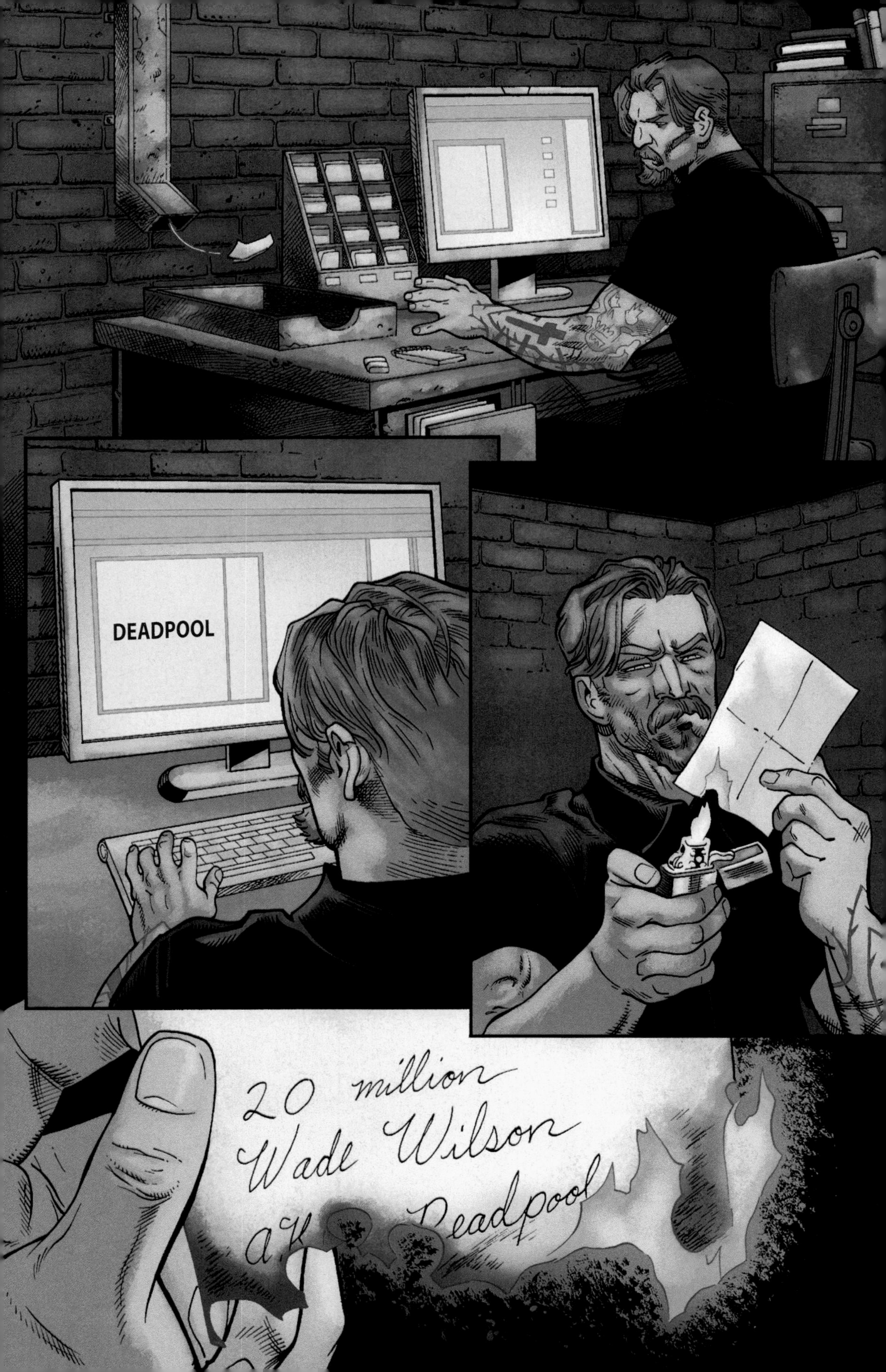
DEADPOOL
20 million
Wade Wilson
aka Deadpool

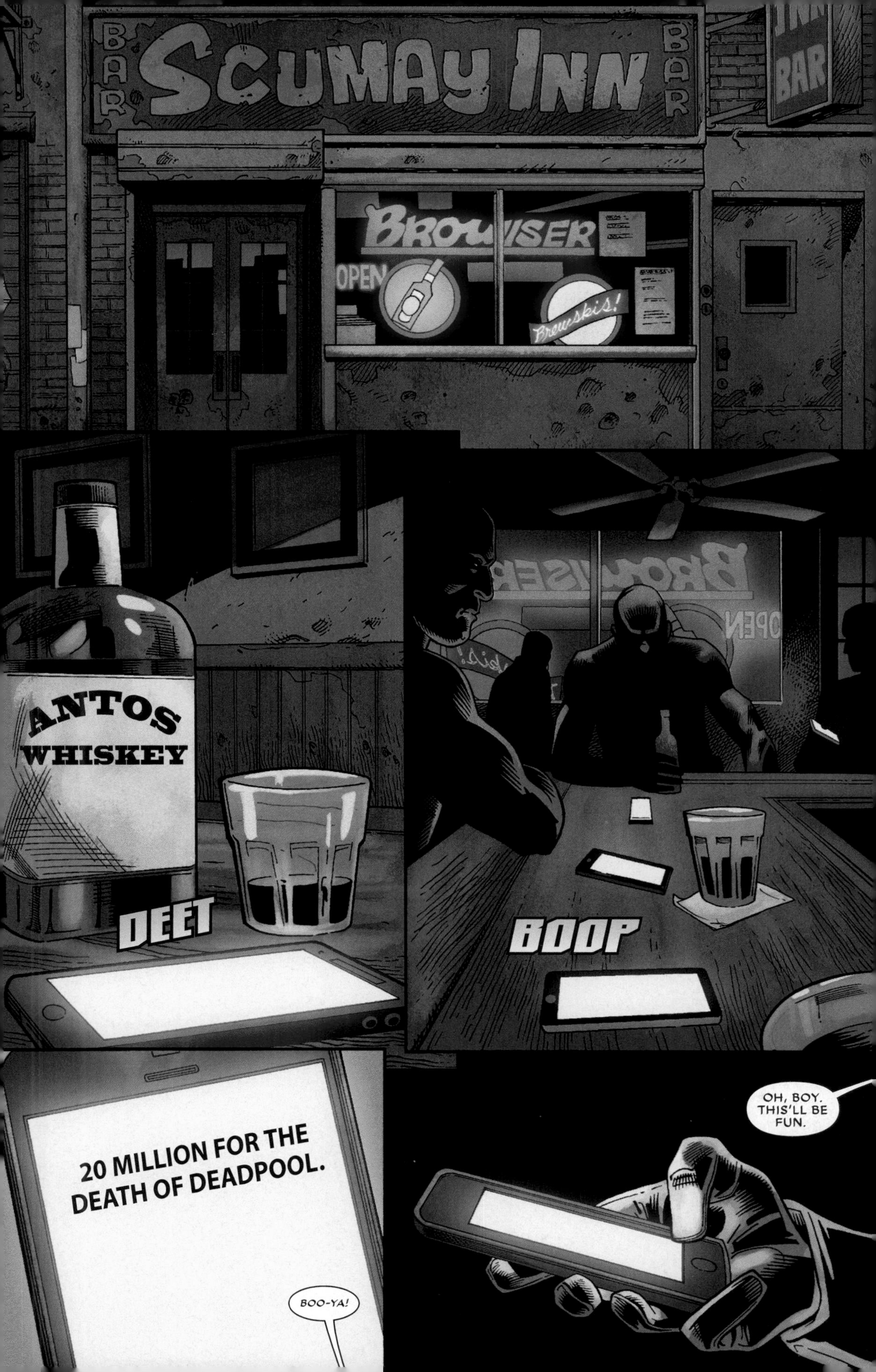
BAR
SCUMAY INN
BAR
INN
BAR
BROWSER
OPEN
Brewskis!
ANTOS
WHISKEY
DEET
BOOP
20 MILLION FOR THE DEATH OF DEADPOOL.
BOO-YA!
OH, BOY. THIS'LL BE FUN.

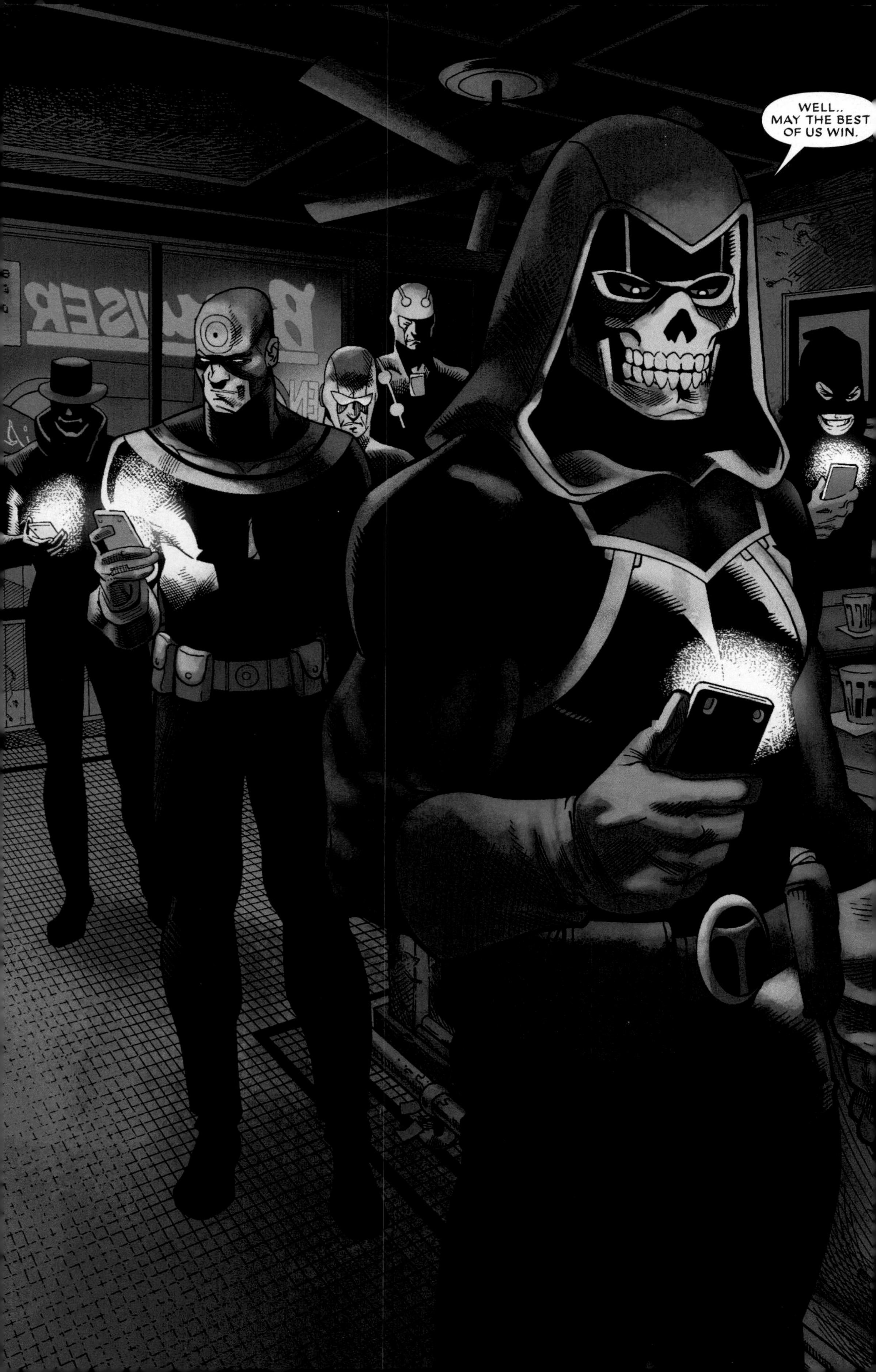
WELL.. MAY THE BEST OF US WIN.

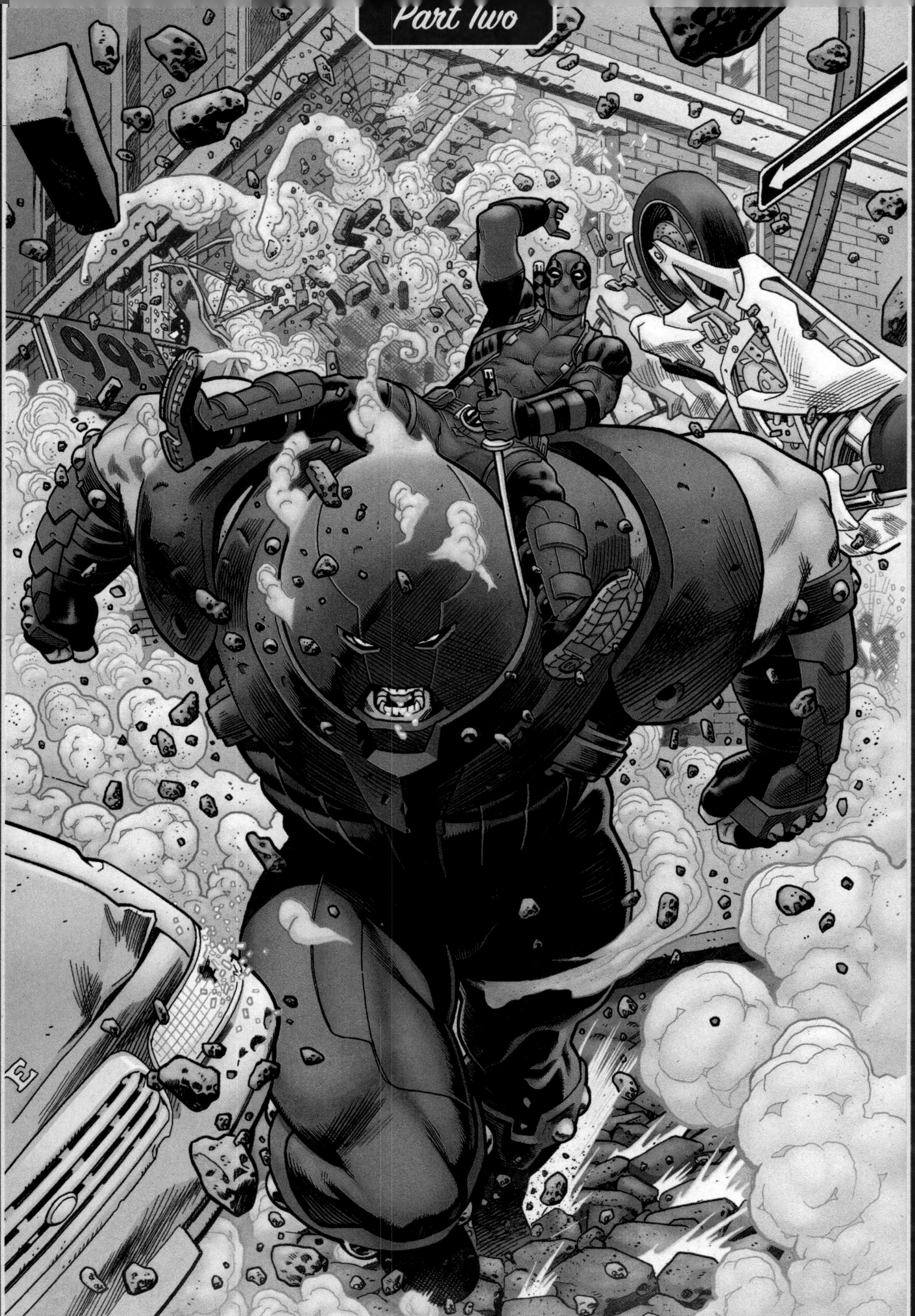
Part Two

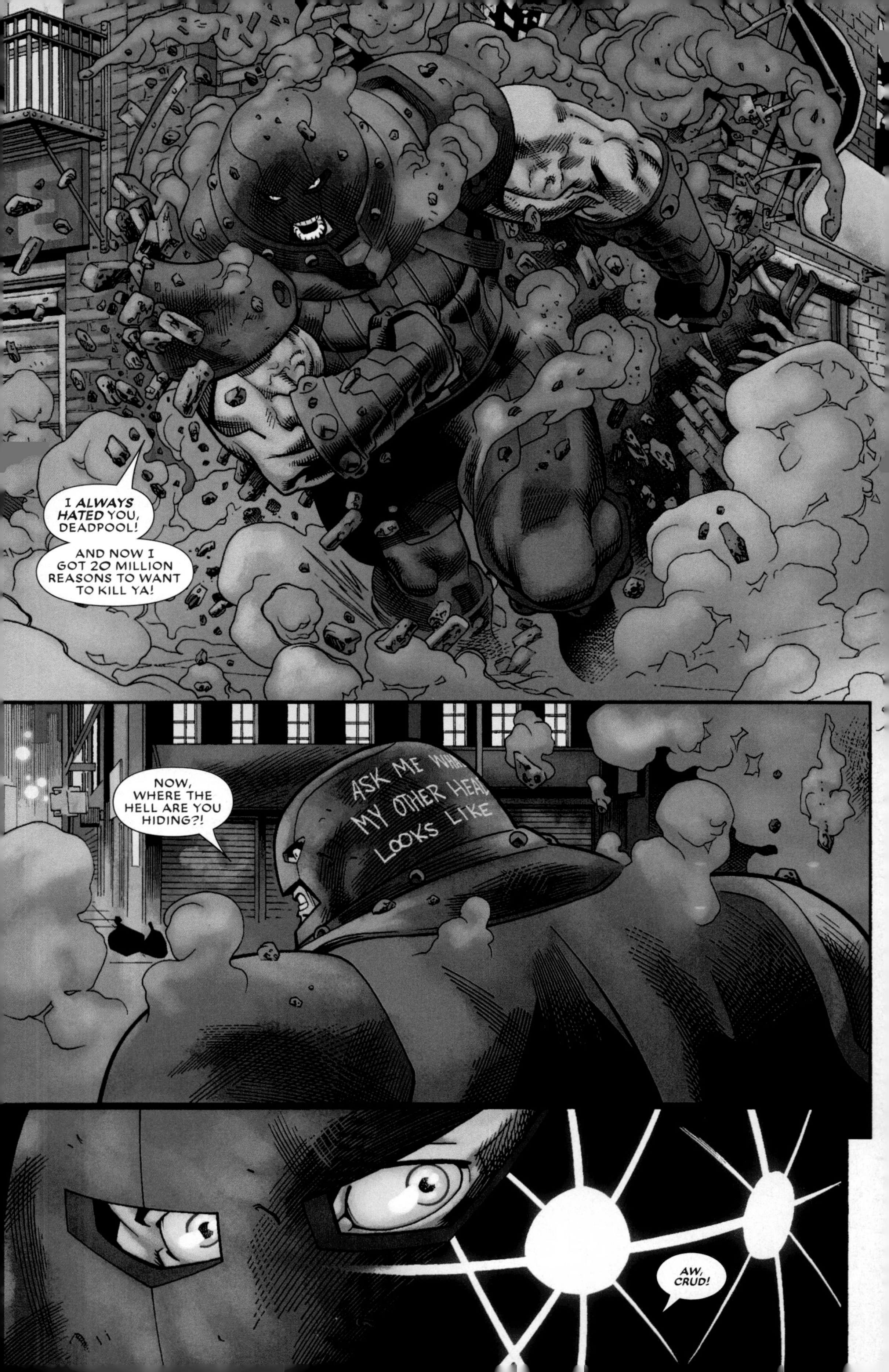
I ALWAYS HATED YOU, DEADPOOL!
AND NOW I GOT 20 MILLION REASONS TO WANT TO KILL YA!
NOW, WHERE THE HELL ARE YOU HIDING?!
ASK ME WHAT MY OTHER HEAD LOOKS LIKE
AW, CRUD!

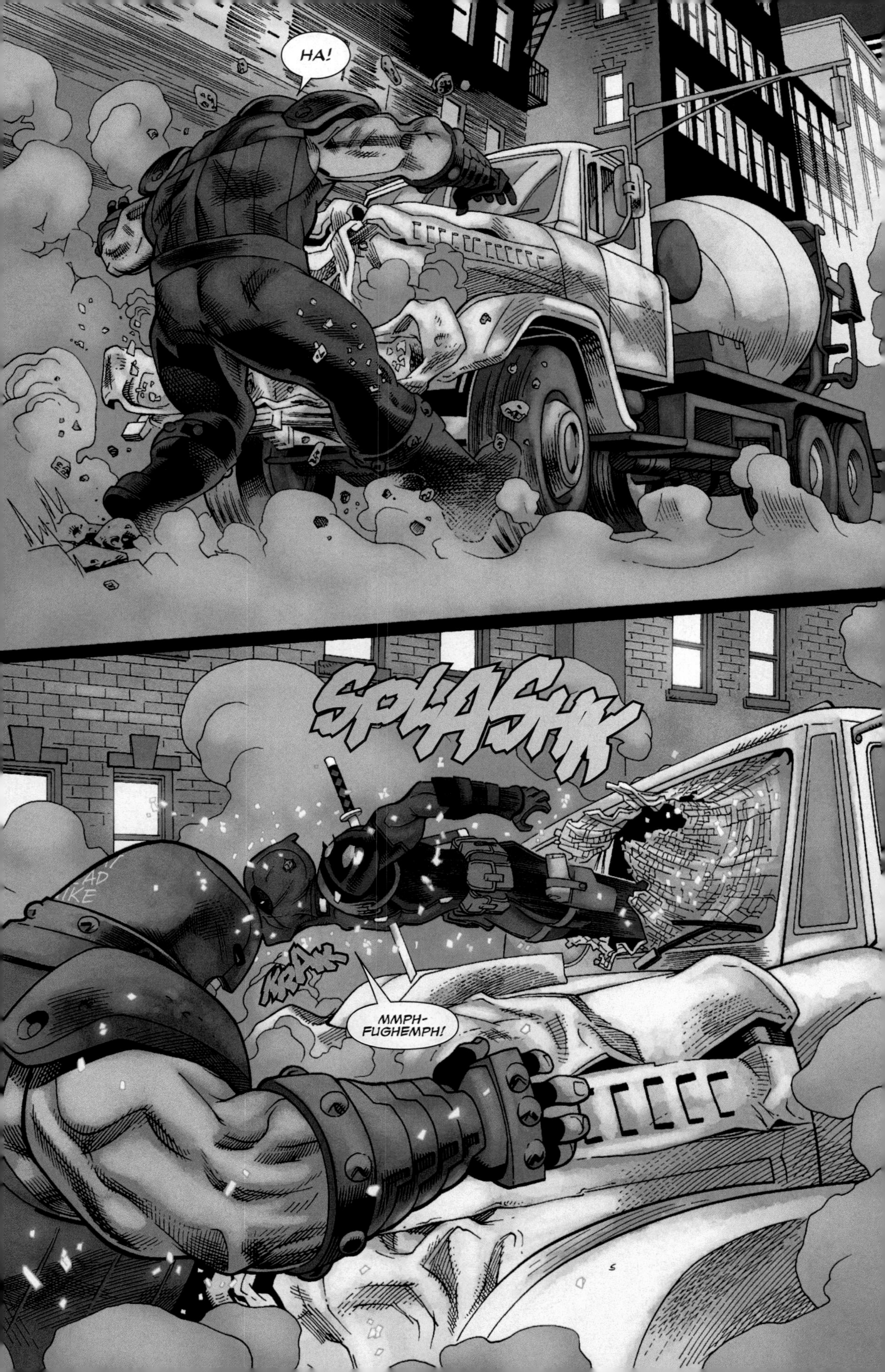
HA!
SPLASHK
KRAK
MMPH-
FUGHEMPH!

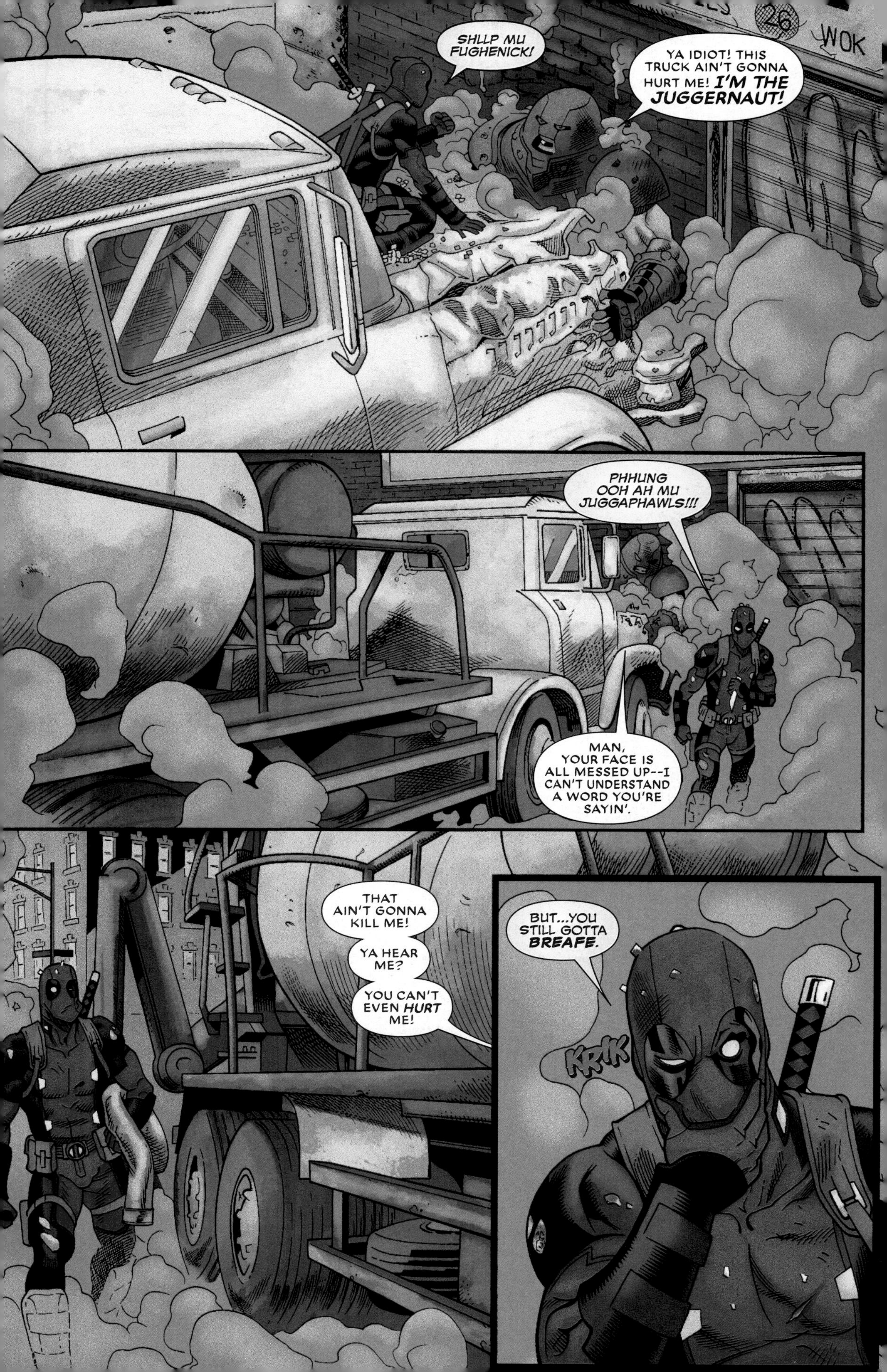
26
WOK
SHLLP MU FUGHENICK!
YA IDIOT! THIS TRUCK AIN'T GONNA HURT ME! I'M THE JUGGERNAUT!
PHHUNG OOH AH MU JUGGAPHAWLS!!!
MAN, YOUR FACE IS ALL MESSED UP--I CAN'T UNDERSTAND A WORD YOU'RE SAYIN'.
THAT AIN'T GONNA KILL ME!
YA HEAR ME?
YOU CAN'T EVEN HURT ME!
BUT...YOU STILL GOTTA BREAFE.
KRIK

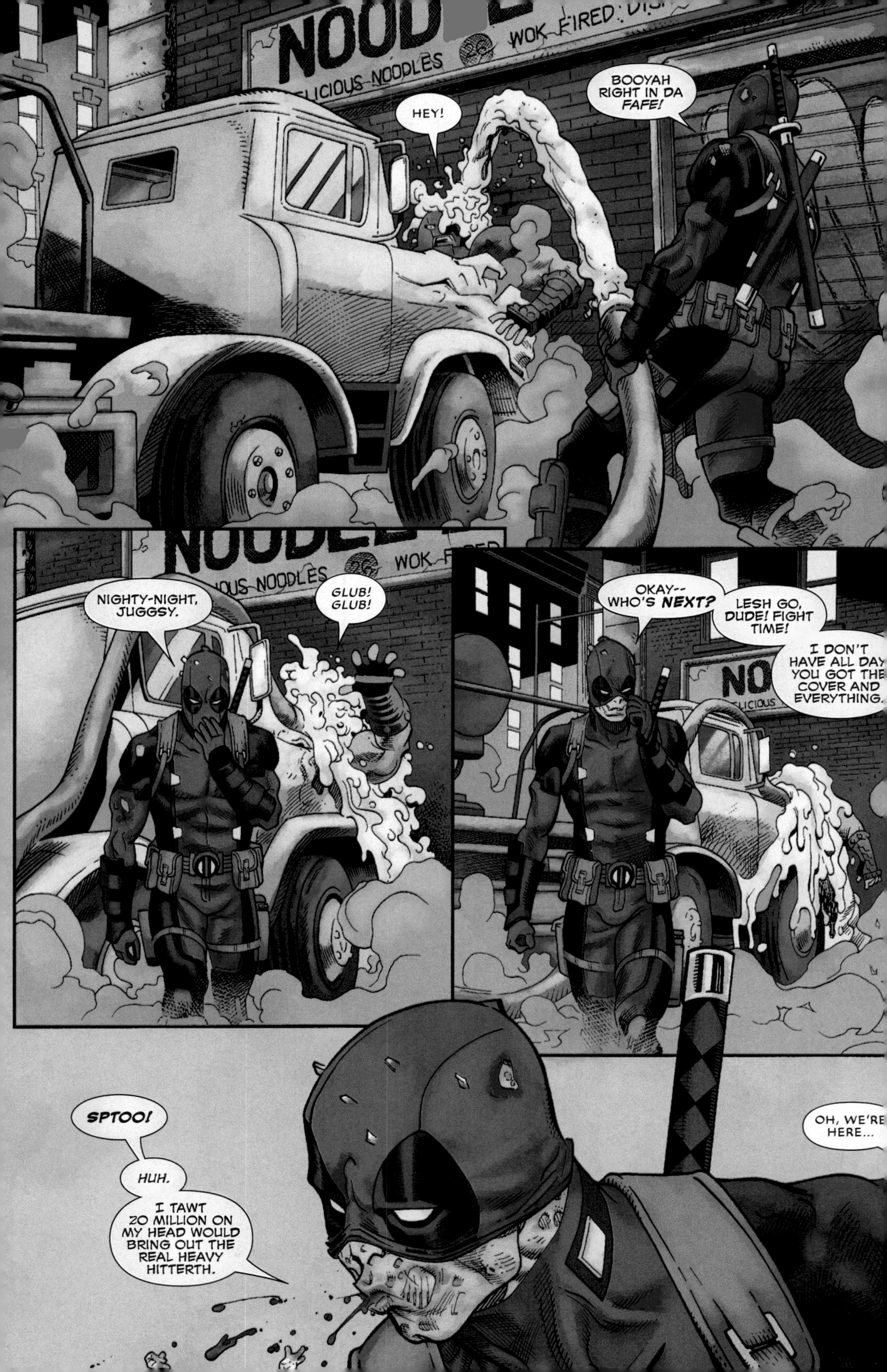
NOOD
ELICIOUS NOODLES
WOK FIRED
HEY!
BOOYAH RIGHT IN DA FAFE!
NIGHTY-NIGHT, JUGGSY.
GLUB! GLUB!
OKAY-- WHO'S NEXT?
LESH GO, DUDE! FIGHT TIME!
I DON'T HAVE ALL DAY YOU GOT THE COVER AND EVERYTHING.
SPTOO!
HUH.
I TAWT 20 MILLION ON MY HEAD WOULD BRING OUT THE REAL HEAVY HITTERTH.
OH, WE'RE HERE...

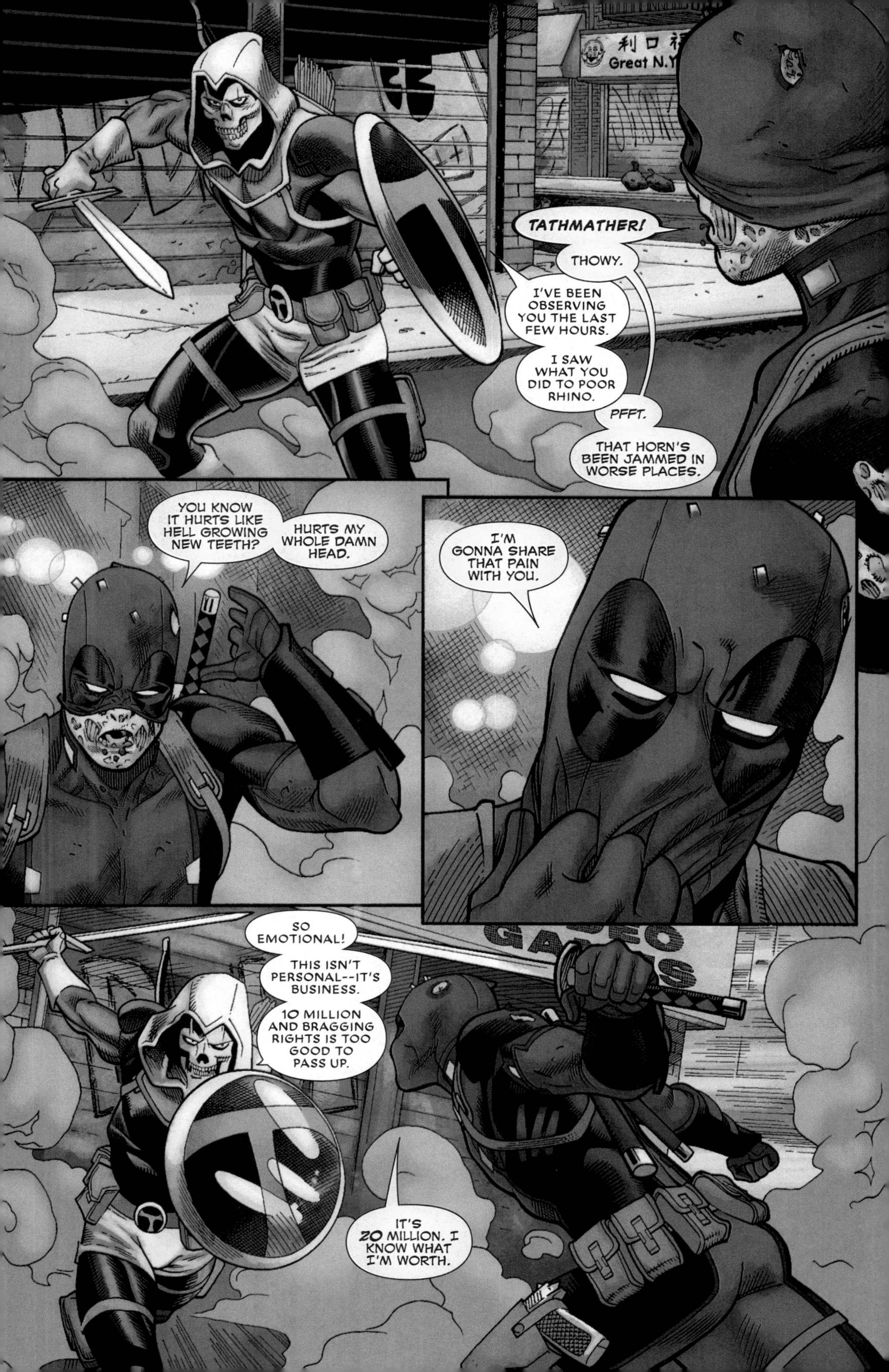
利口福
Great N.Y.
TATHMATHER!
THOWY.
I'VE BEEN OBSERVING YOU THE LAST FEW HOURS.
I SAW WHAT YOU DID TO POOR RHINO.
PFFT.
THAT HORN'S BEEN JAMMED IN WORSE PLACES.
YOU KNOW IT HURTS LIKE HELL GROWING NEW TEETH?
HURTS MY WHOLE DAMN HEAD.
I'M GONNA SHARE THAT PAIN WITH YOU.
SO EMOTIONAL!
THIS ISN'T PERSONAL--IT'S BUSINESS.
10 MILLION AND BRAGGING RIGHTS IS TOO GOOD TO PASS UP.
IT'S 20 MILLION. I KNOW WHAT I'M WORTH.

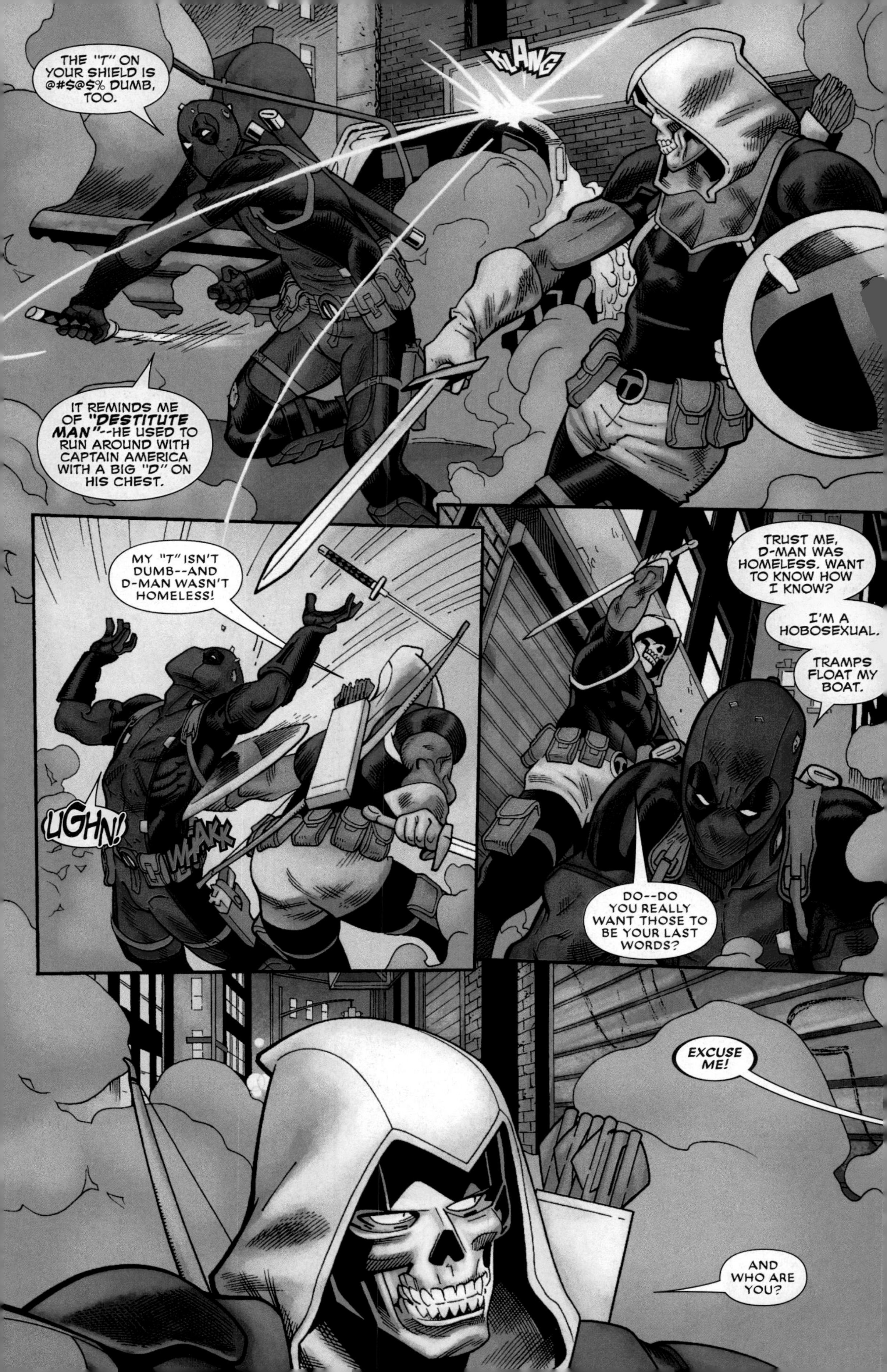
THE "T" ON YOUR SHIELD IS @#$@$% DUMB, TOO.
KLANG
IT REMINDS ME OF "DESTITUTE MAN"--HE USED TO RUN AROUND WITH CAPTAIN AMERICA WITH A BIG "D" ON HIS CHEST.
MY "T" ISN'T DUMB--AND D-MAN WASN'T HOMELESS!
UGHN!
WHAKK
TRUST ME, D-MAN WAS HOMELESS. WANT TO KNOW HOW I KNOW?
I'M A HOBOSEXUAL.
TRAMPS FLOAT MY BOAT.
DO--DO YOU REALLY WANT THOSE TO BE YOUR LAST WORDS?
EXCUSE ME!
AND WHO ARE YOU?

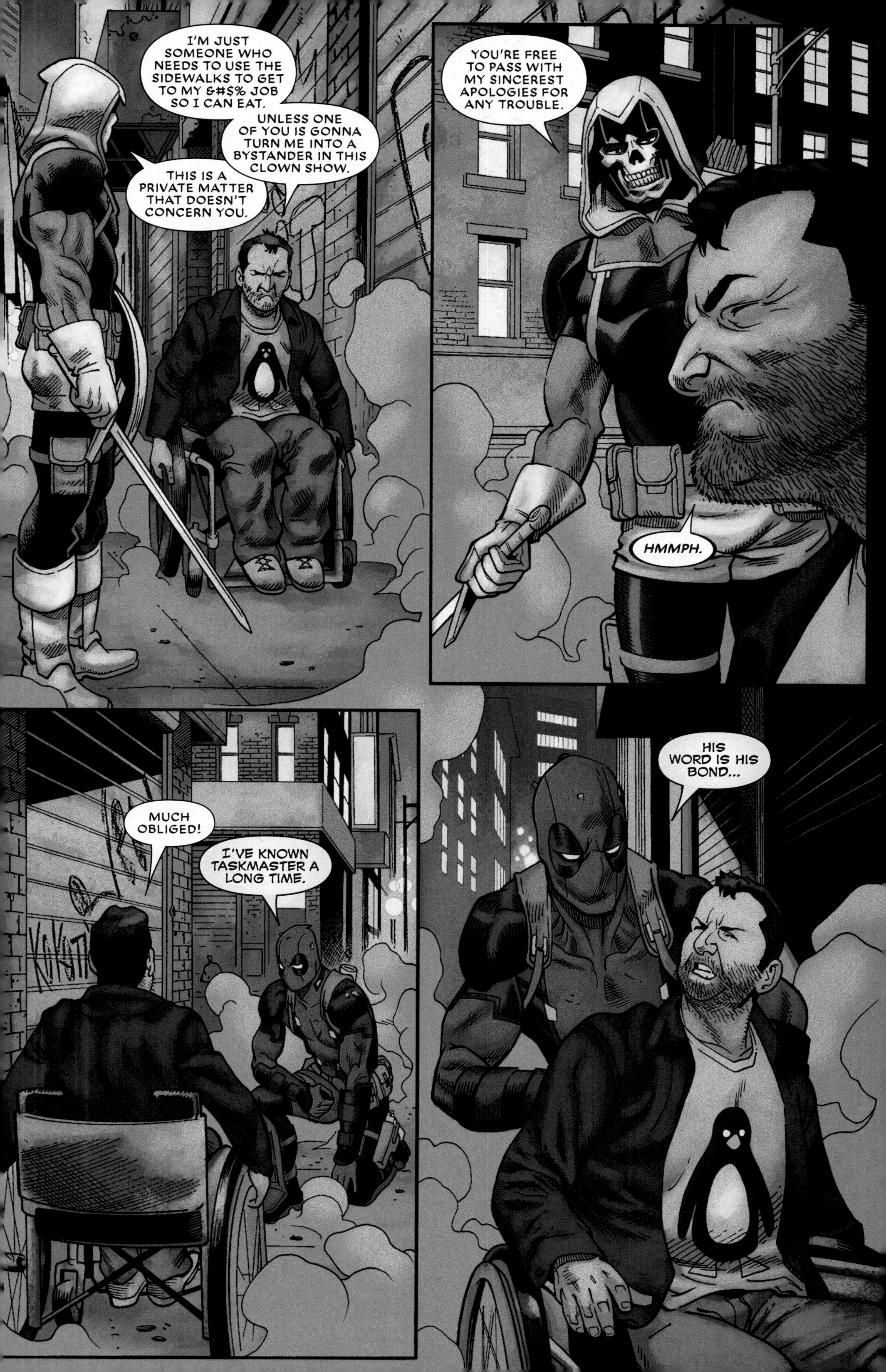
I'M JUST SOMEONE WHO NEEDS TO USE THE SIDEWALKS TO GET TO MY &#$% JOB SO I CAN EAT.
UNLESS ONE OF YOU IS GONNA TURN ME INTO A BYSTANDER IN THIS CLOWN SHOW.
THIS IS A PRIVATE MATTER THAT DOESN'T CONCERN YOU.
YOU'RE FREE TO PASS WITH MY SINCEREST APOLOGIES FOR ANY TROUBLE.
HMMPH.
MUCH OBLIGED!
I'VE KNOWN TASKMASTER A LONG TIME.
HIS WORD IS HIS BOND...

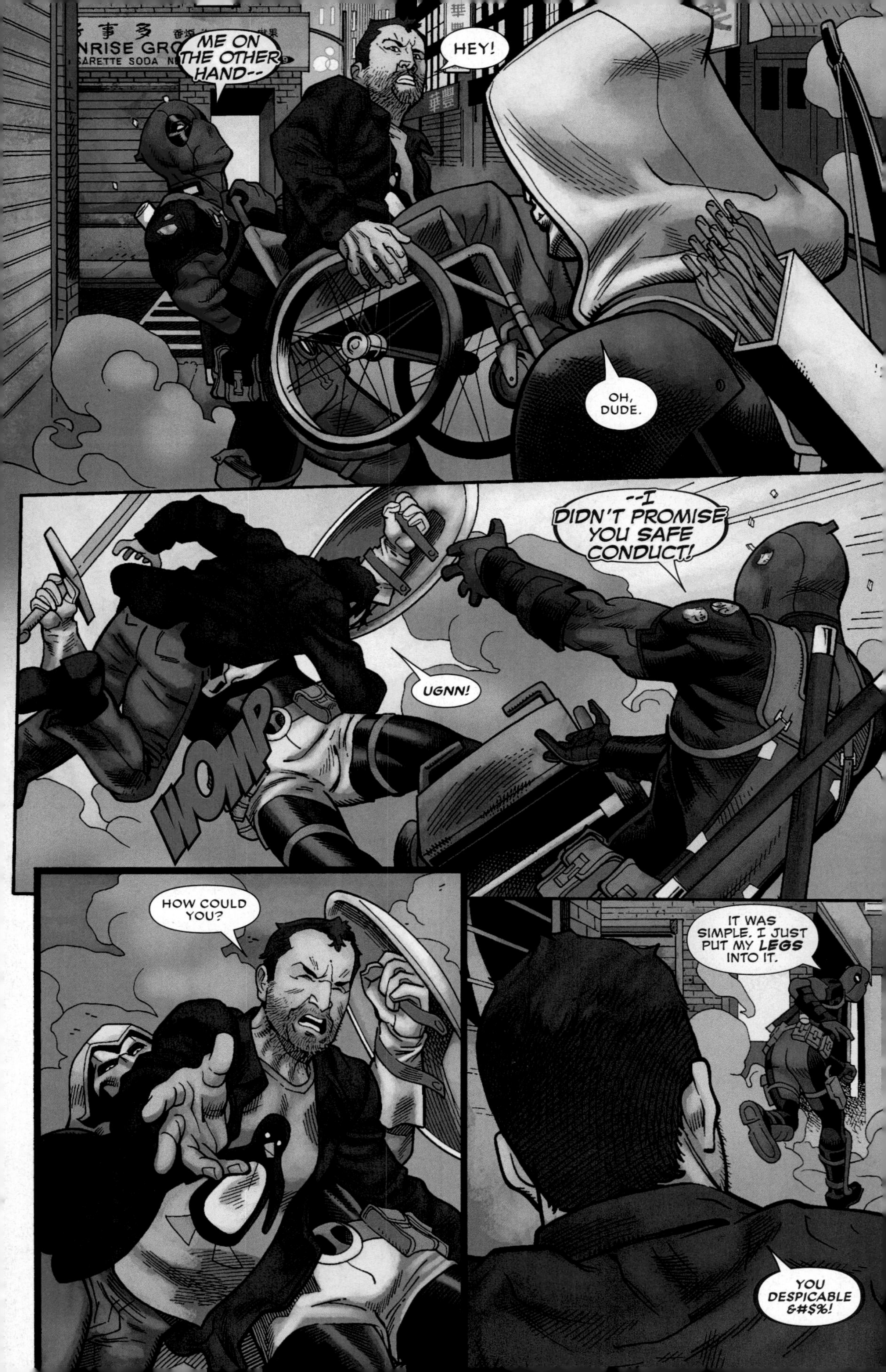
SUNRISE GRO
GARETTE SODA
ME ON THE OTHER HAND--
HEY!
OH, DUDE.
--I DIDN'T PROMISE YOU SAFE CONDUCT!
UGNN!
WOMP
HOW COULD YOU?
IT WAS SIMPLE. I JUST PUT MY LEGS INTO IT.
YOU DESPICABLE &#$%!

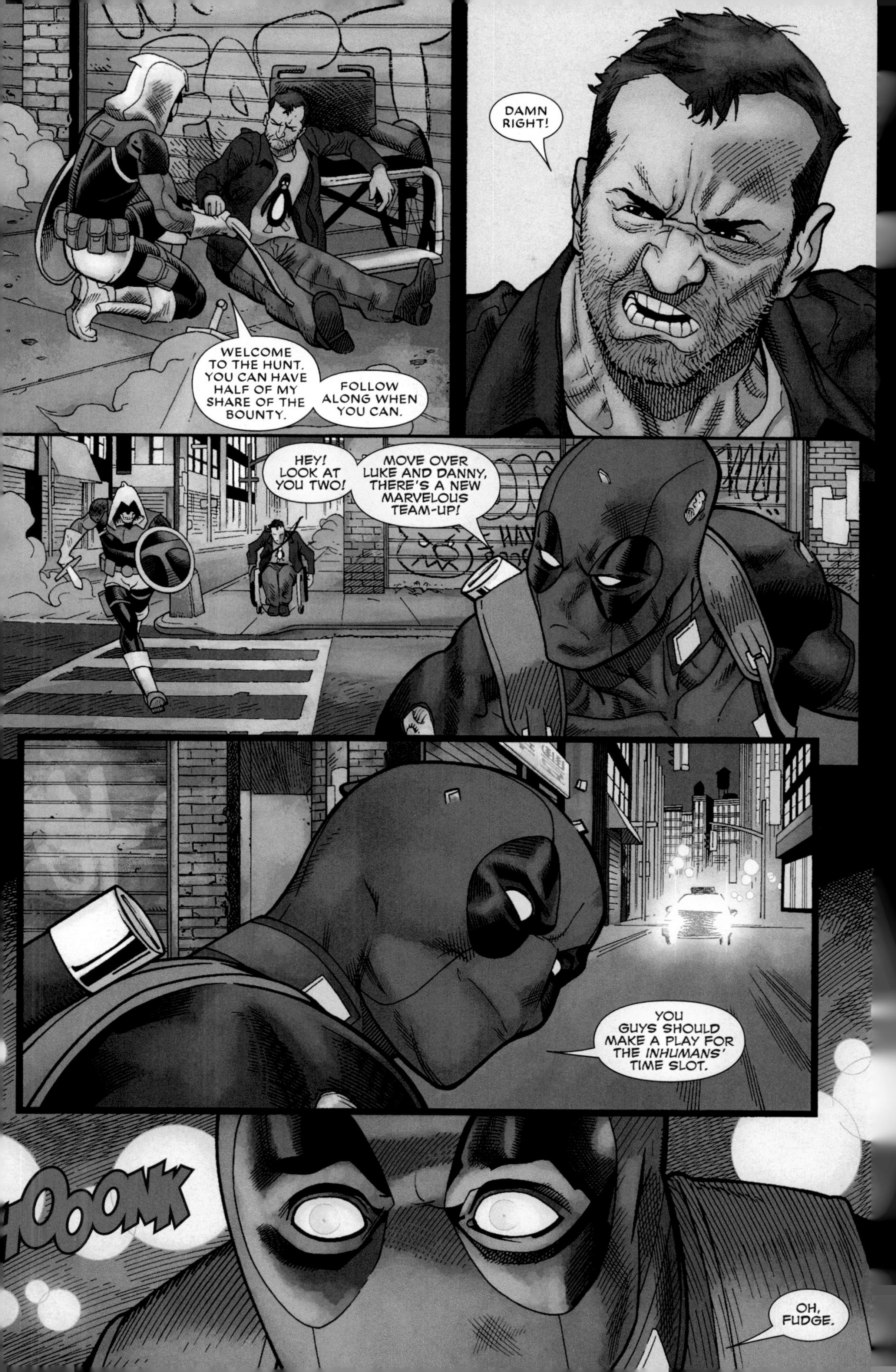

WELCOME TO THE HUNT. YOU CAN HAVE HALF OF MY SHARE OF THE BOUNTY.
FOLLOW ALONG WHEN YOU CAN.
DAMN RIGHT!
HEY! LOOK AT YOU TWO!
MOVE OVER LUKE AND DANNY, THERE'S A NEW MARVELOUS TEAM-UP!
YOU GUYS SHOULD MAKE A PLAY FOR THE *INHUMANS'* TIME SLOT.
HOOONK
OH, FUDGE.

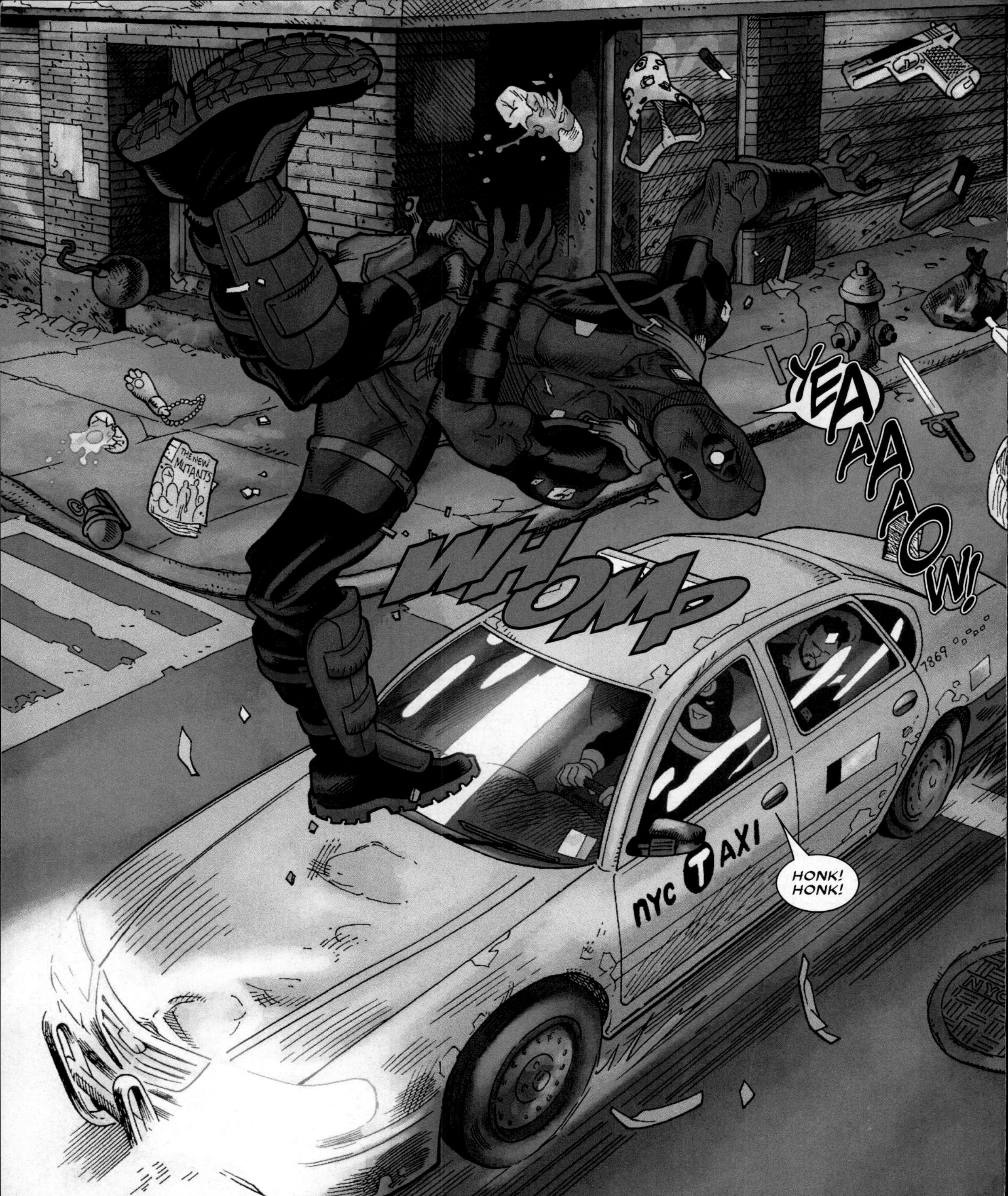
WHOMP
YEAAAAAOW!
HONK! HONK!
NYC TAXI
THE NEW MUTANTS
7869
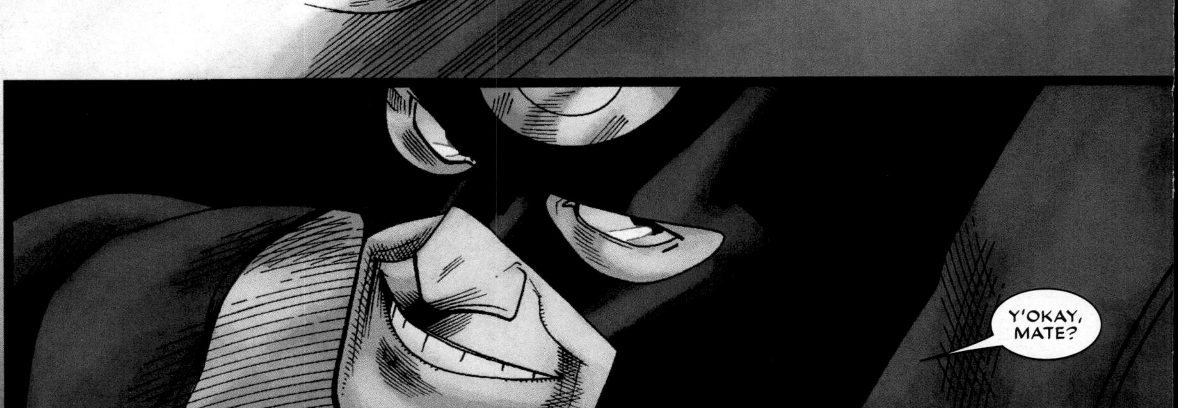
Y'OKAY, MATE?

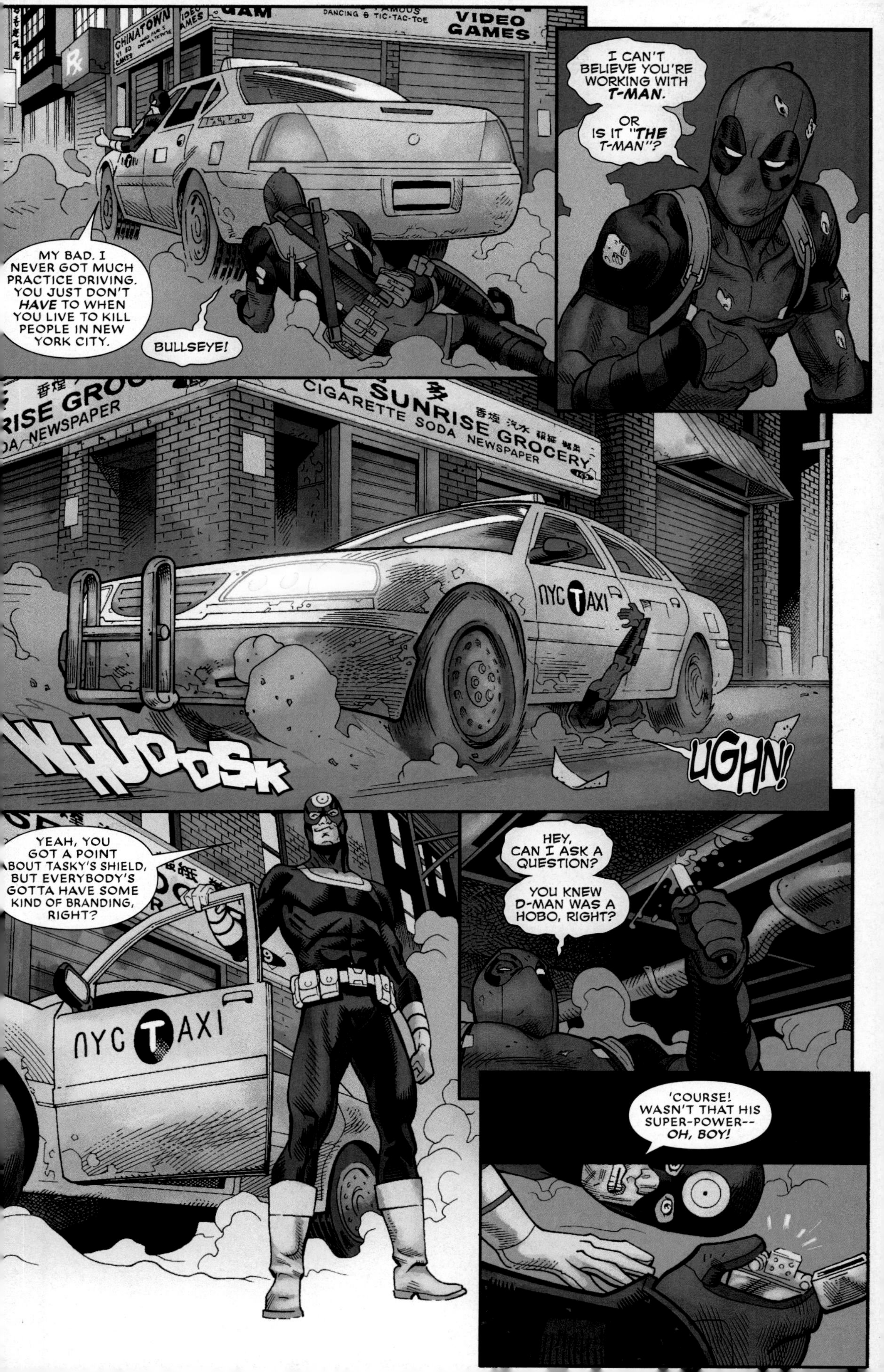
CHINATOWN VIDEO GAMES
DANCING & TIC-TAC-TOE
VIDEO GAMES
MY BAD. I NEVER GOT MUCH PRACTICE DRIVING. YOU JUST DON'T *HAVE* TO WHEN YOU LIVE TO KILL PEOPLE IN NEW YORK CITY.
BULLSEYE!
I CAN'T BELIEVE YOU'RE WORKING WITH *T-MAN*.
OR IS IT *"THE T-MAN"*?
SUNRISE GROCERY
CIGARETTE SODA NEWSPAPER
NYC TAXI
WHUOOSK
UGHN!
YEAH, YOU GOT A POINT ABOUT TASKY'S SHIELD, BUT EVERYBODY'S GOTTA HAVE SOME KIND OF BRANDING, RIGHT?
NYC TAXI
HEY, CAN I ASK A QUESTION?
YOU KNEW D-MAN WAS A HOBO, RIGHT?
'COURSE! WASN'T THAT HIS SUPER-POWER-- *OH, BOY!*

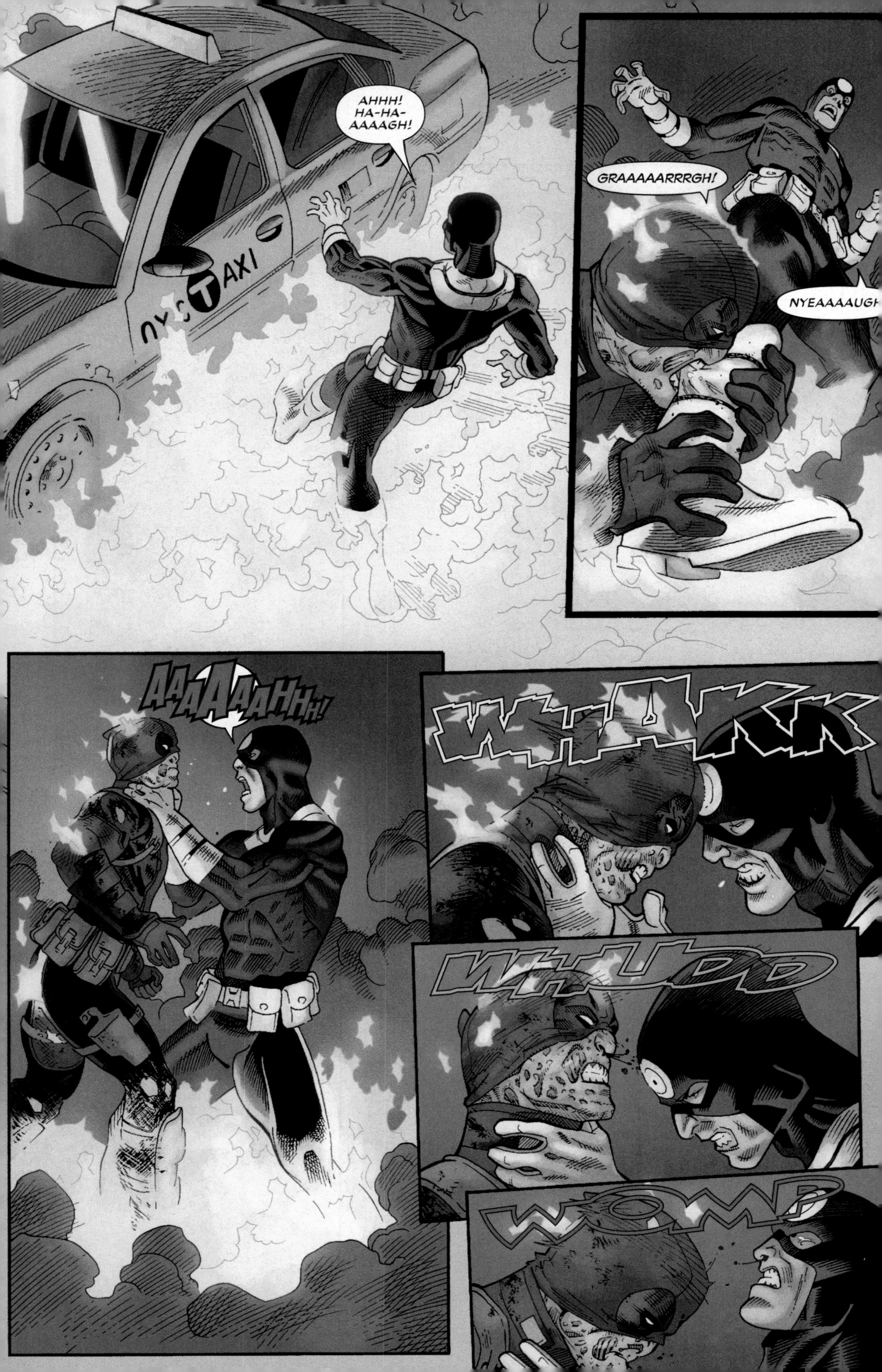
AHHH! HA-HA-AAAAGH!
GRAAAAAARRRGH!
NYEAAAAUGH
AAAAAAHHH!
WHAKK
WHUDD

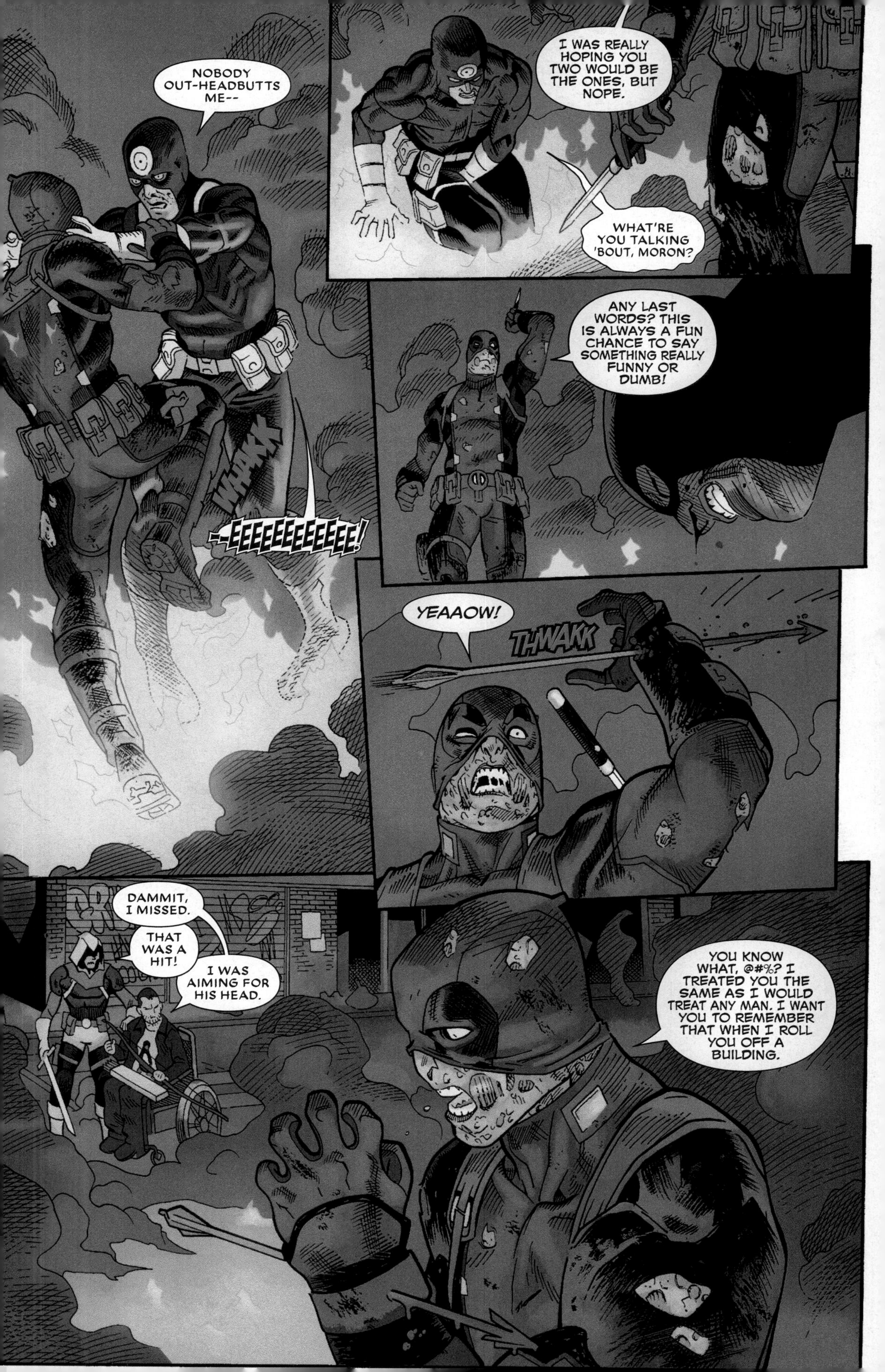
NOBODY OUT-HEADBUTTS ME--
WHAKK
--EEEEEEEEEEEE!
I WAS REALLY HOPING YOU TWO WOULD BE THE ONES, BUT NOPE.
WHAT'RE YOU TALKING 'BOUT, MORON?
ANY LAST WORDS? THIS IS ALWAYS A FUN CHANCE TO SAY SOMETHING REALLY FUNNY OR DUMB!
YEAAOW!
THWAKK
DAMMIT, I MISSED.
THAT WAS A HIT!
I WAS AIMING FOR HIS HEAD.
YOU KNOW WHAT, @#%? I TREATED YOU THE SAME AS I WOULD TREAT ANY MAN. I WANT YOU TO REMEMBER THAT WHEN I ROLL YOU OFF A BUILDING.

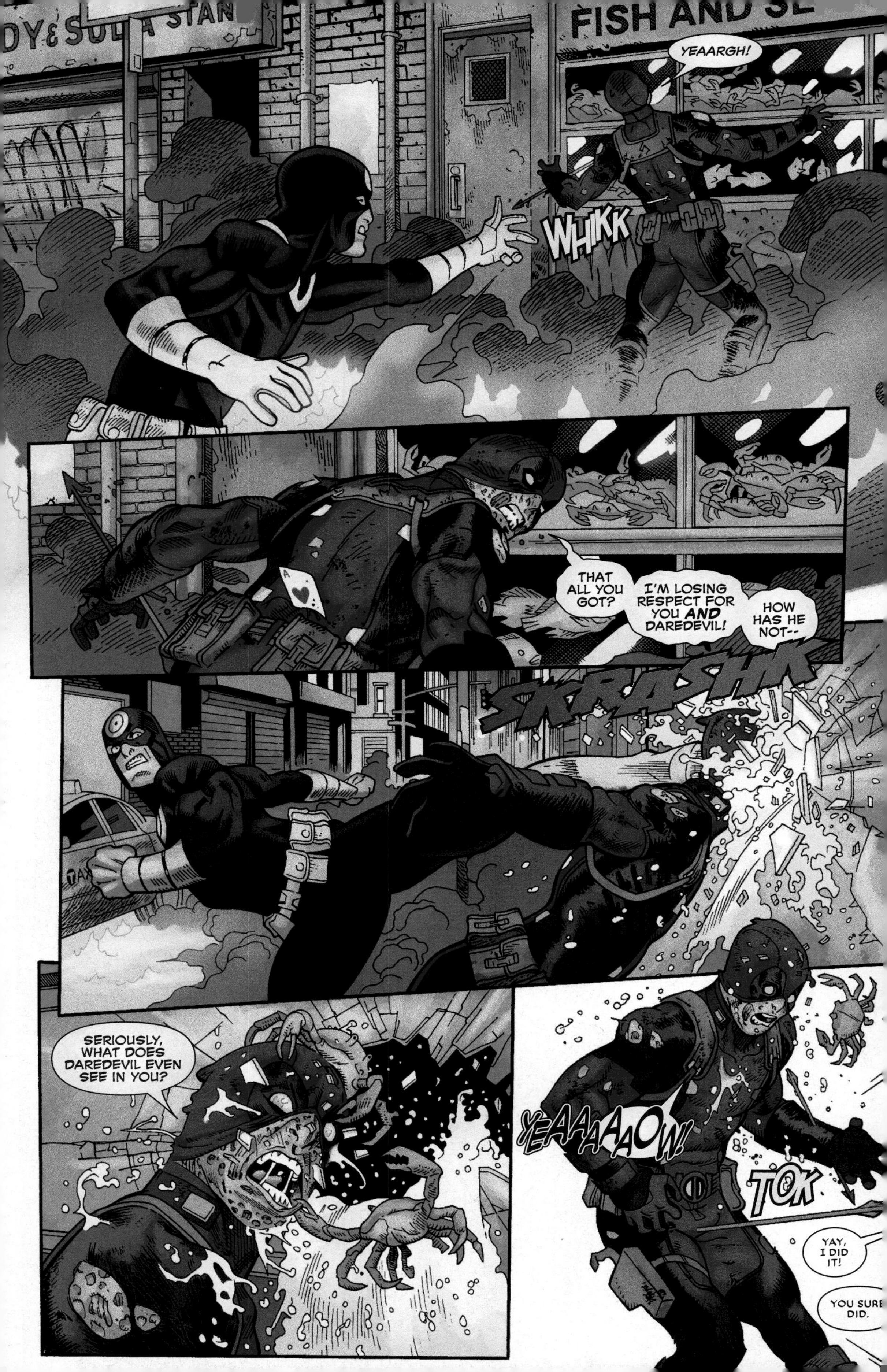
FISH AND SE
YEAARGH!
WHIKK
THAT ALL YOU GOT?
I'M LOSING RESPECT FOR YOU AND DAREDEVIL!
HOW HAS HE NOT--
SKRASHK
SERIOUSLY, WHAT DOES DAREDEVIL EVEN SEE IN YOU?
YEAAAAAAOW!
TOK
YAY, I DID IT!
YOU SURE DID.

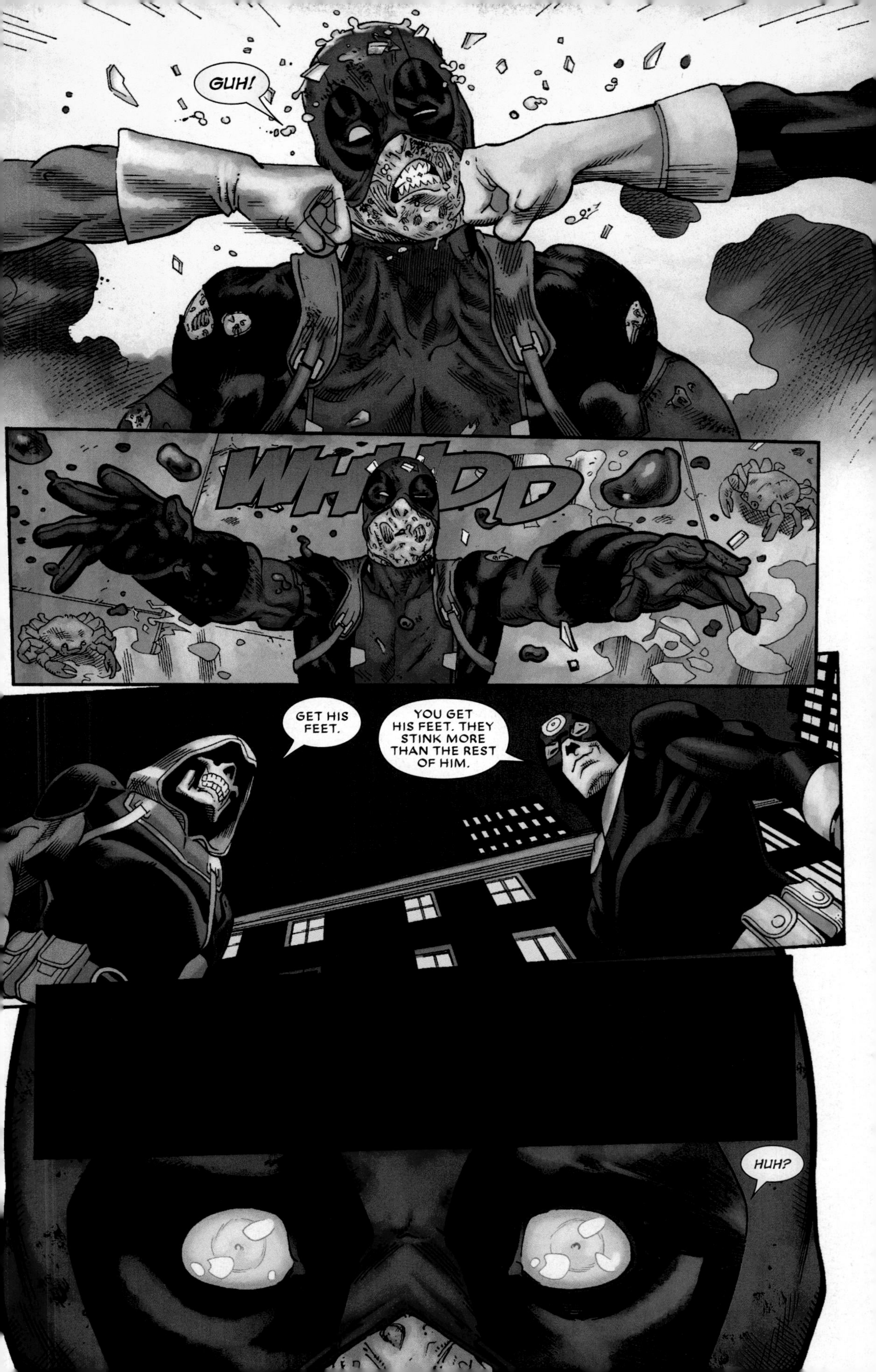
GUH!
WHUDD
GET HIS FEET.
YOU GET HIS FEET. THEY STINK MORE THAN THE REST OF HIM.
[redacted]
HUH?

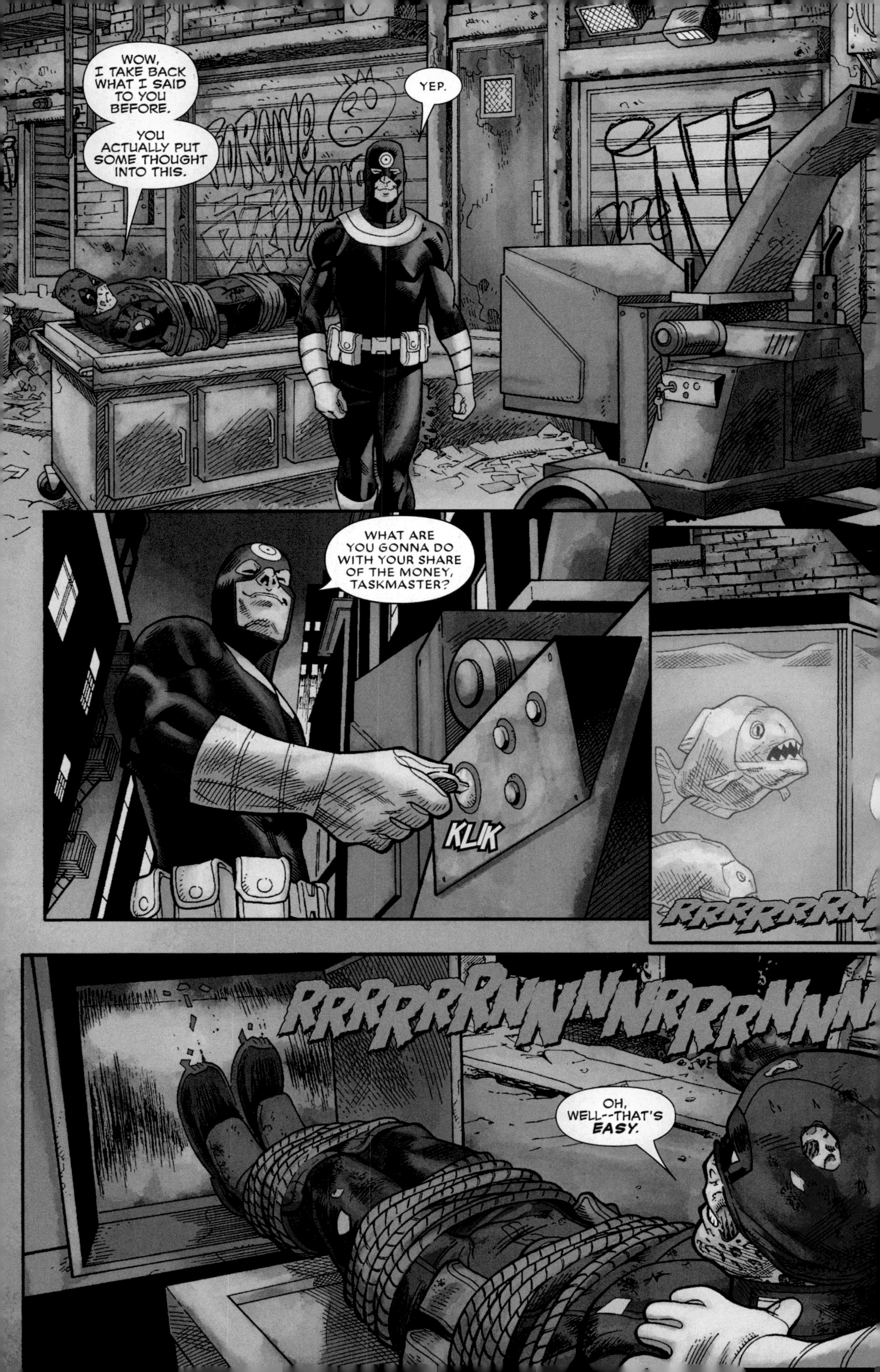
WOW, I TAKE BACK WHAT I SAID TO YOU BEFORE.
YOU ACTUALLY PUT SOME THOUGHT INTO THIS.
YEP.
WHAT ARE YOU GONNA DO WITH YOUR SHARE OF THE MONEY, TASKMASTER?
KLIK
RRRRRRRN
RRRRRRNNNNRRRRNNN
OH, WELL--THAT'S EASY.

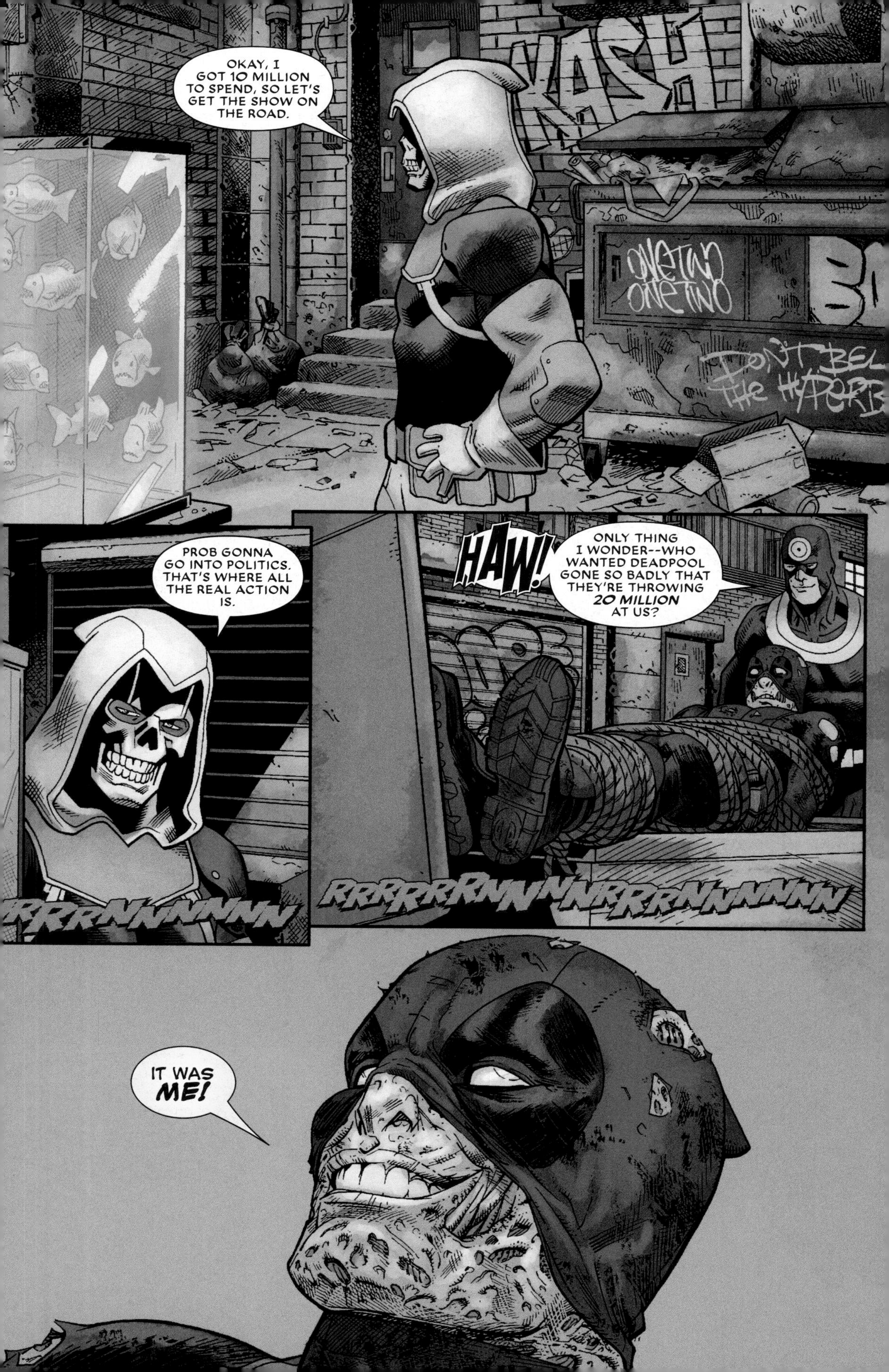
OKAY, I GOT 10 MILLION TO SPEND, SO LET'S GET THE SHOW ON THE ROAD.
PROB GONNA GO INTO POLITICS. THAT'S WHERE ALL THE REAL ACTION IS.
RRRRNNNNNNN
HAW!
ONLY THING I WONDER--WHO WANTED DEADPOOL GONE SO BADLY THAT THEY'RE THROWING *20 MILLION* AT US?
RRRRRRNNNNNRRRRNNNNNNN
IT WAS **ME!**

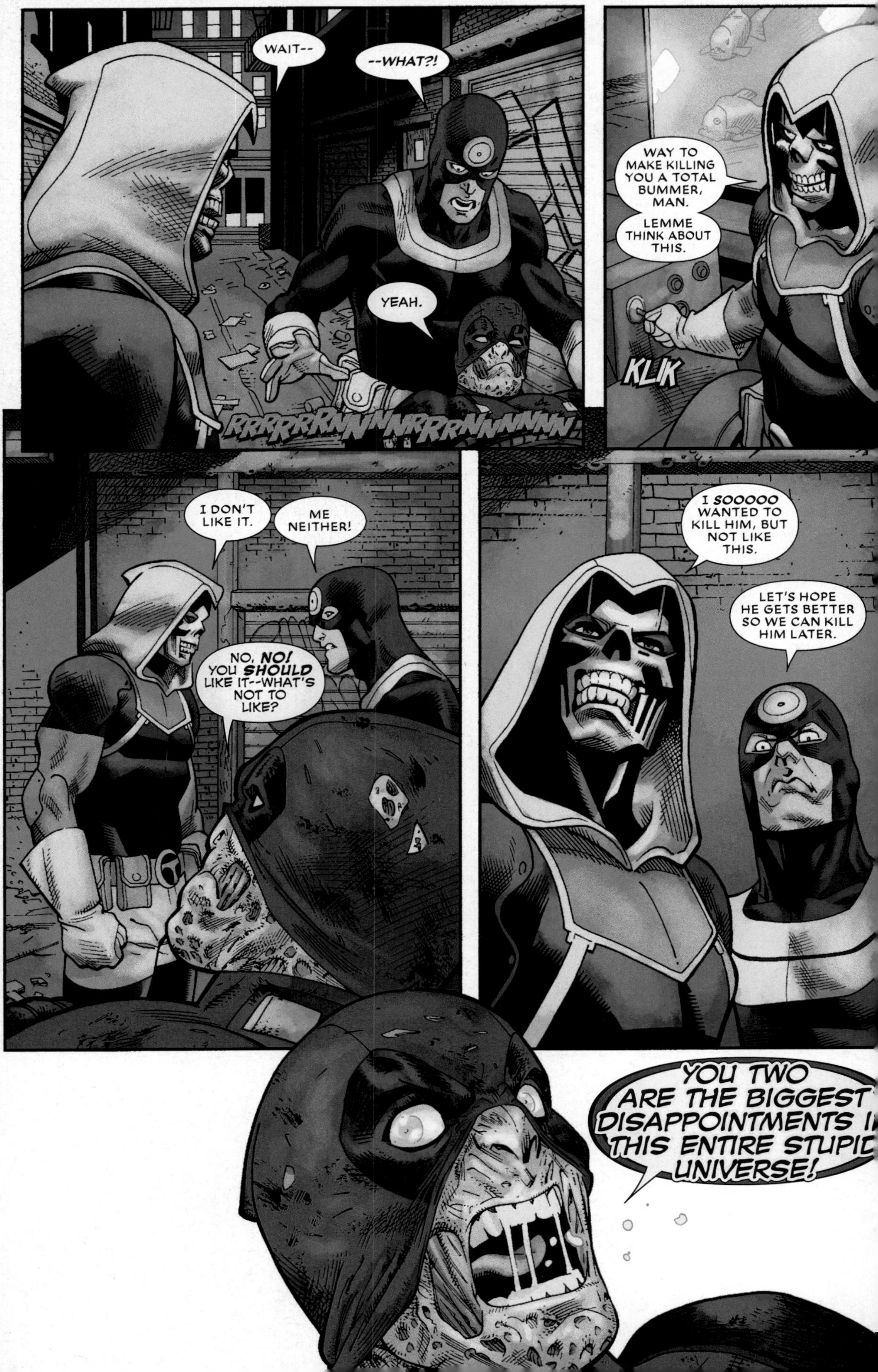
WAIT--
--WHAT?!
YEAH.
RRRRRRNNNNRRRNNNNNN
WAY TO MAKE KILLING YOU A TOTAL BUMMER, MAN.
LEMME THINK ABOUT THIS.
KLIK
I DON'T LIKE IT.
ME NEITHER!
NO, NO! YOU SHOULD LIKE IT--WHAT'S NOT TO LIKE?
I SOOOOO WANTED TO KILL HIM, BUT NOT LIKE THIS.
LET'S HOPE HE GETS BETTER SO WE CAN KILL HIM LATER.
YOU TWO ARE THE BIGGEST DISAPPOINTMENTS I THIS ENTIRE STUPID UNIVERSE!

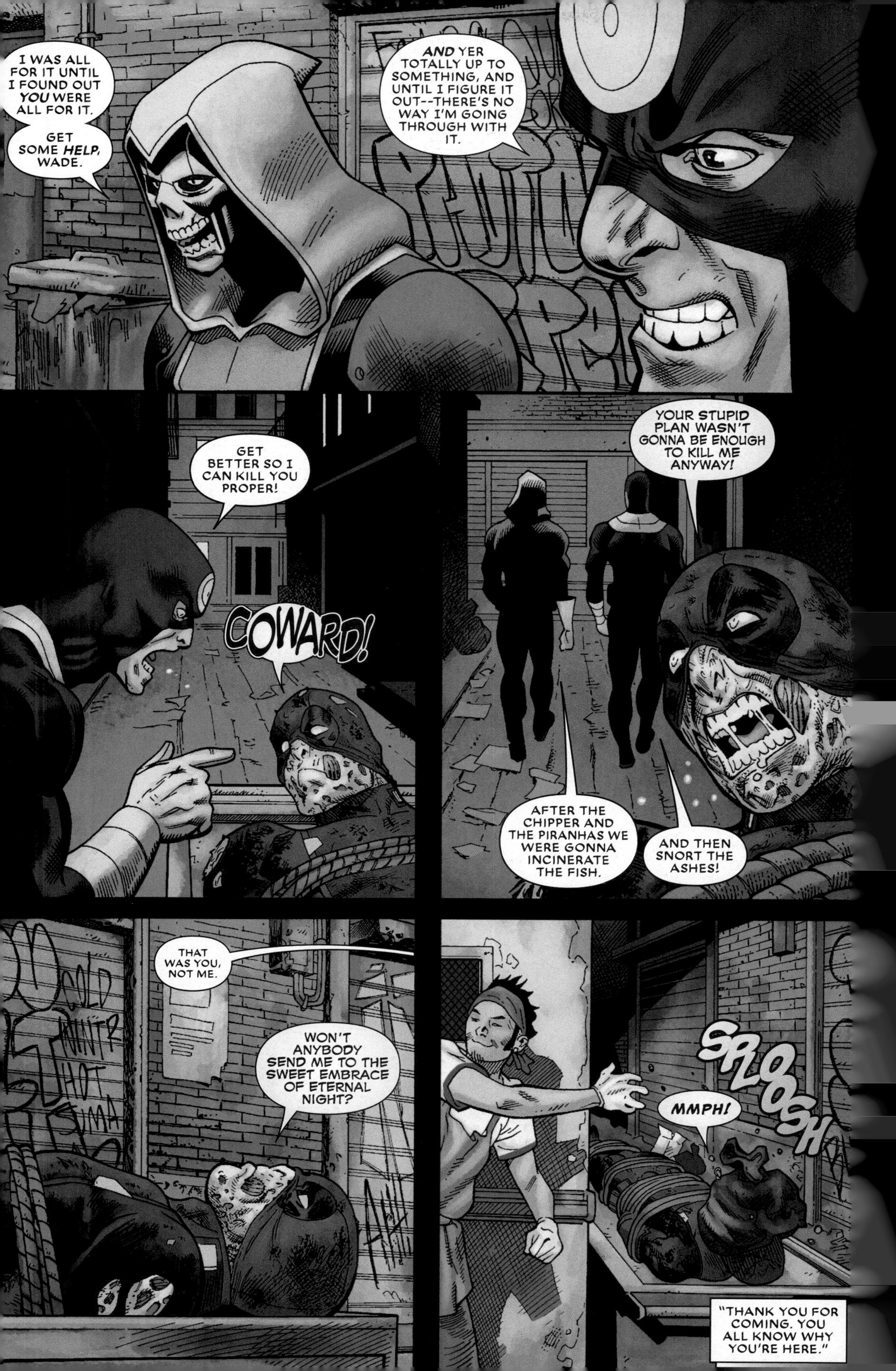
I WAS ALL FOR IT UNTIL I FOUND OUT YOU WERE ALL FOR IT.
GET SOME HELP, WADE.
AND YER TOTALLY UP TO SOMETHING, AND UNTIL I FIGURE IT OUT--THERE'S NO WAY I'M GOING THROUGH WITH IT.
GET BETTER SO I CAN KILL YOU PROPER!
COWARD!
YOUR STUPID PLAN WASN'T GONNA BE ENOUGH TO KILL ME ANYWAY!
AFTER THE CHIPPER AND THE PIRANHAS WE WERE GONNA INCINERATE THE FISH.
AND THEN SNORT THE ASHES!
THAT WAS YOU, NOT ME.
WON'T ANYBODY SEND ME TO THE SWEET EMBRACE OF ETERNAL NIGHT?
SPLOOSH
MMPH!
"THANK YOU FOR COMING. YOU ALL KNOW WHY YOU'RE HERE."

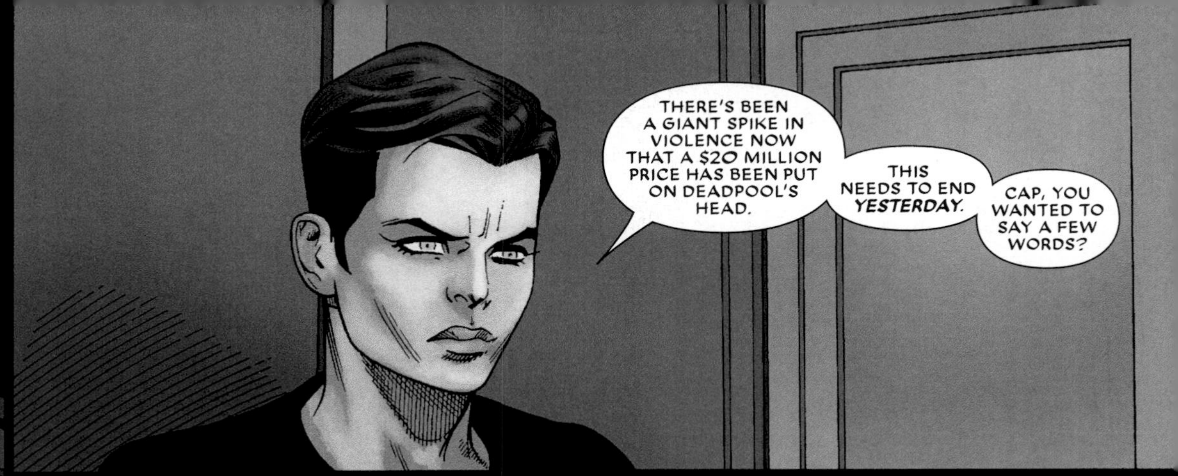
THERE'S BEEN A GIANT SPIKE IN VIOLENCE NOW THAT A $20 MILLION PRICE HAS BEEN PUT ON DEADPOOL'S HEAD.
THIS NEEDS TO END *YESTERDAY*.
CAP, YOU WANTED TO SAY A FEW WORDS?
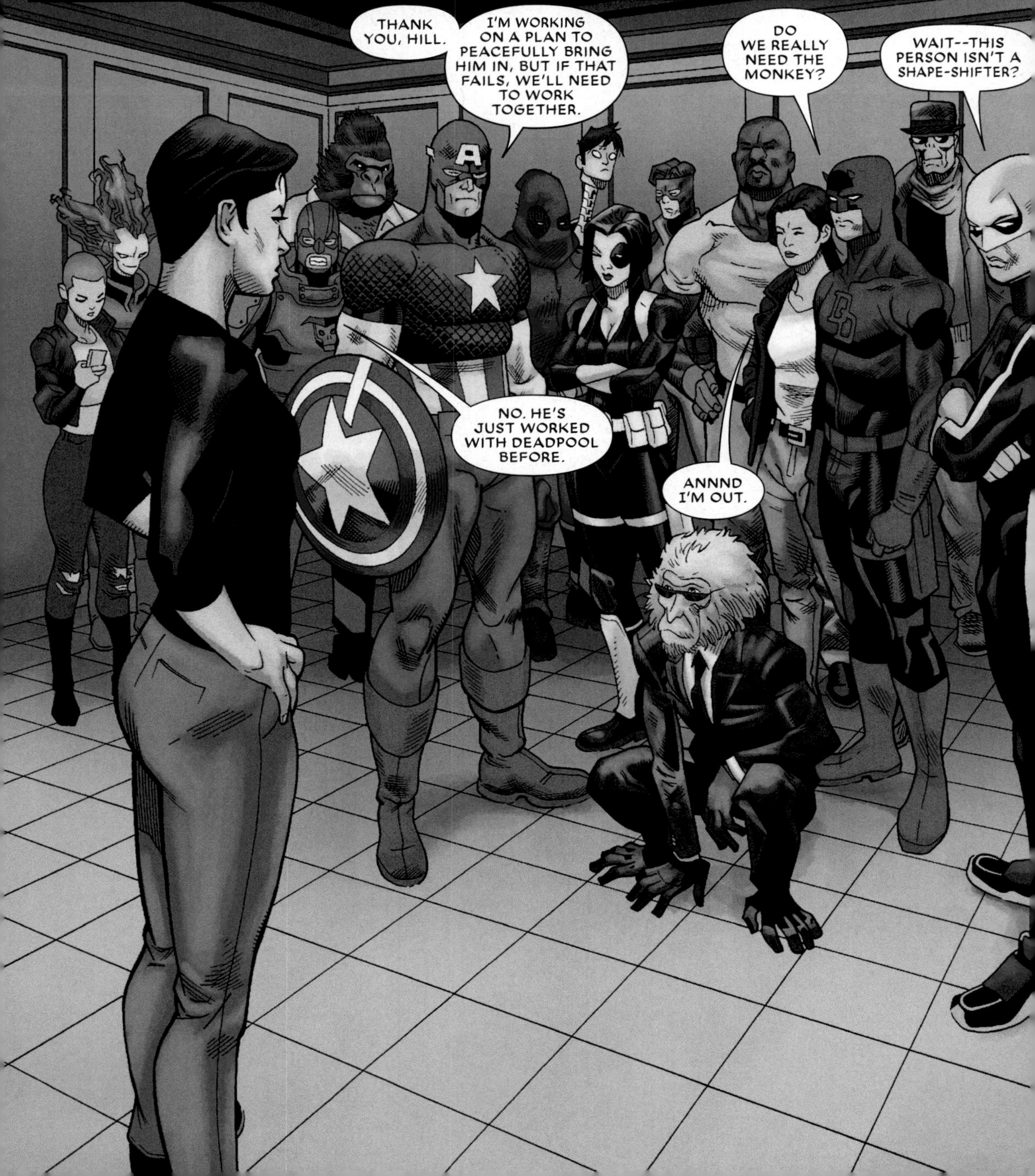
THANK YOU, HILL.
I'M WORKING ON A PLAN TO PEACEFULLY BRING HIM IN, BUT IF THAT FAILS, WE'LL NEED TO WORK TOGETHER.
DO WE REALLY NEED THE MONKEY?
WAIT--THIS PERSON ISN'T A SHAPE-SHIFTER?
NO. HE'S JUST WORKED WITH DEADPOOL BEFORE.
ANNND I'M OUT.

Part Three

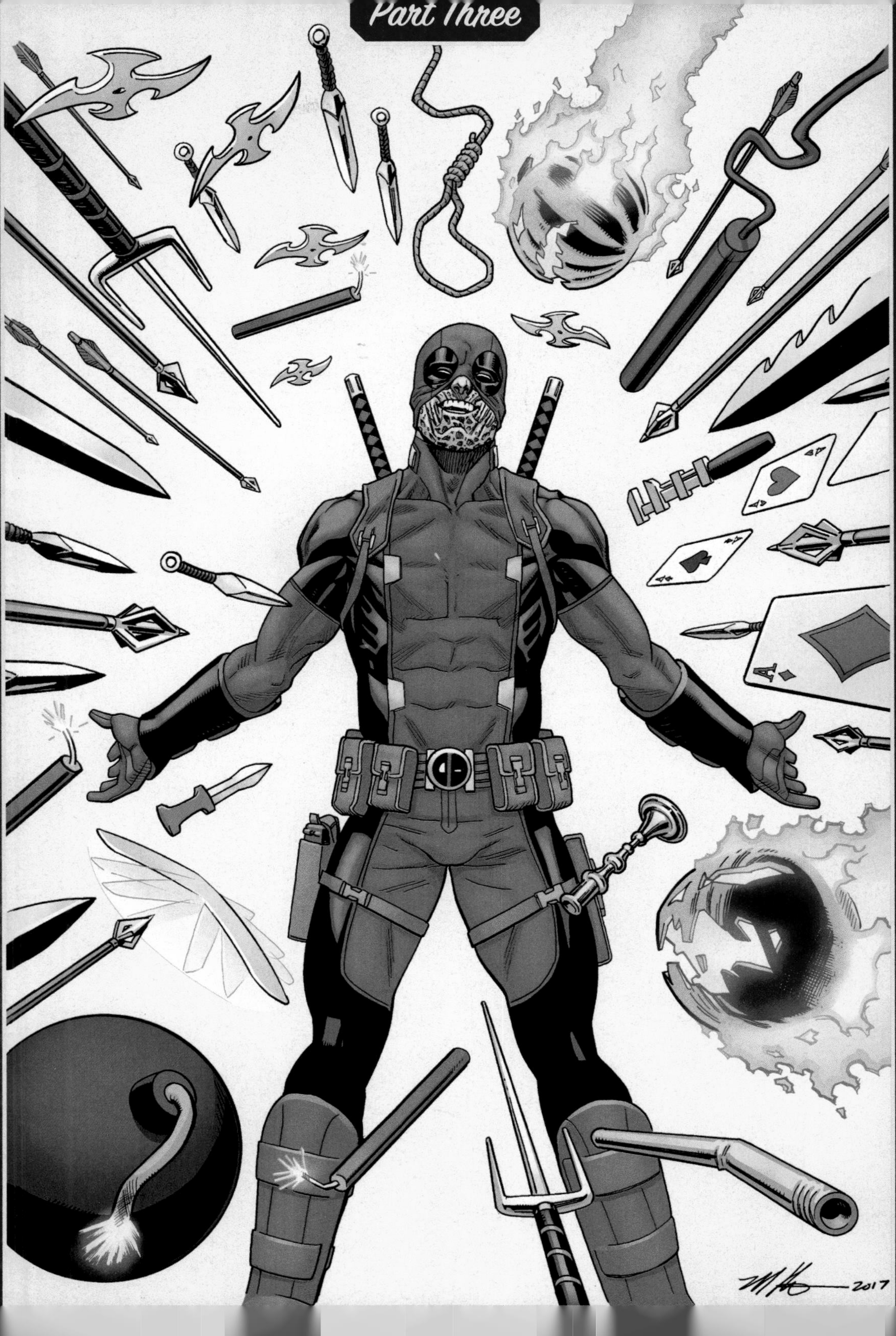

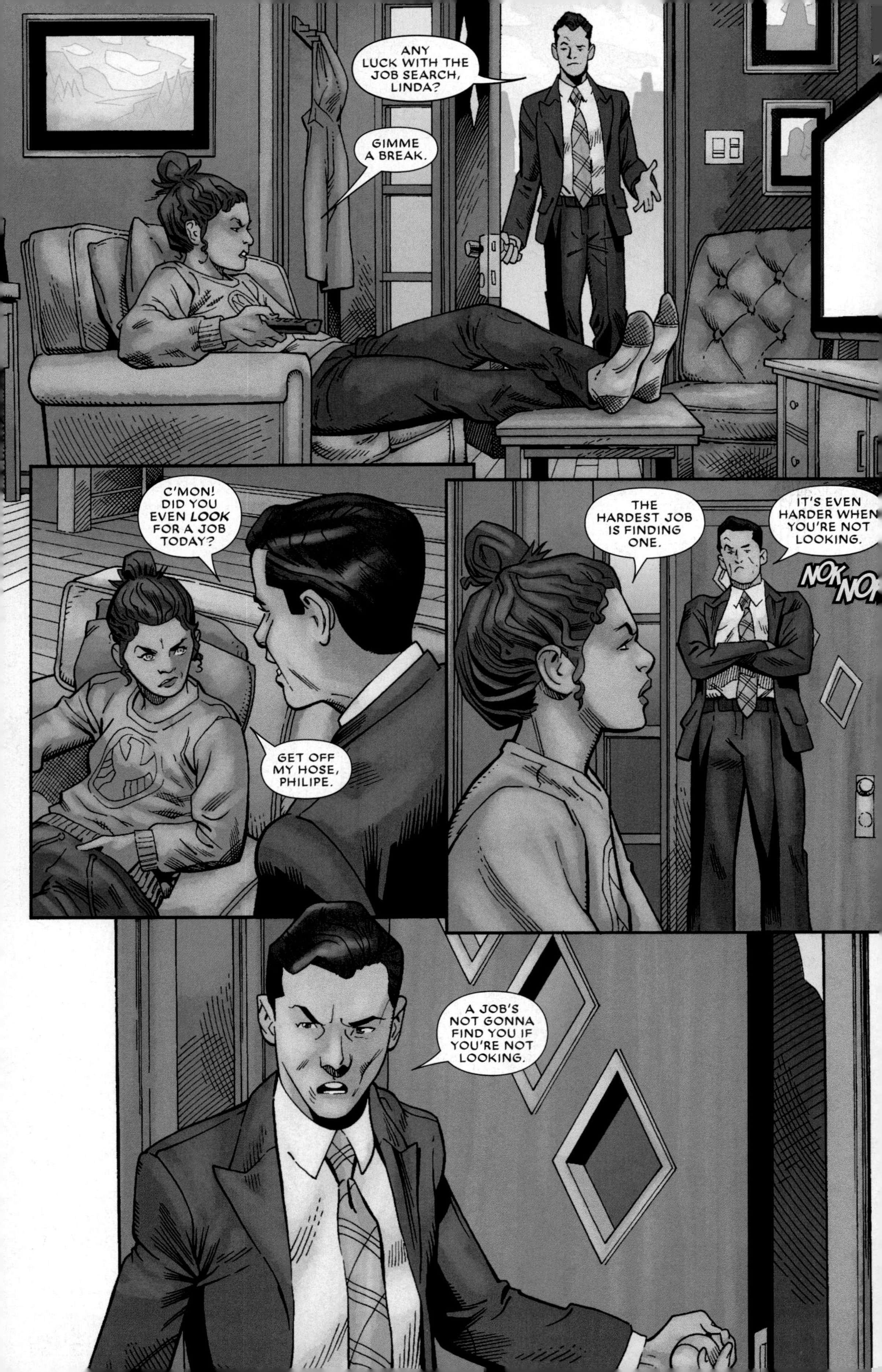
ANY LUCK WITH THE JOB SEARCH, LINDA?
GIMME A BREAK.
C'MON! DID YOU EVEN **LOOK** FOR A JOB TODAY?
GET OFF MY HOSE, PHILIPE.
THE HARDEST JOB IS FINDING ONE.
IT'S EVEN HARDER WHEN YOU'RE NOT LOOKING.
NOK NOK
A JOB'S NOT GONNA FIND YOU IF YOU'RE NOT LOOKING.

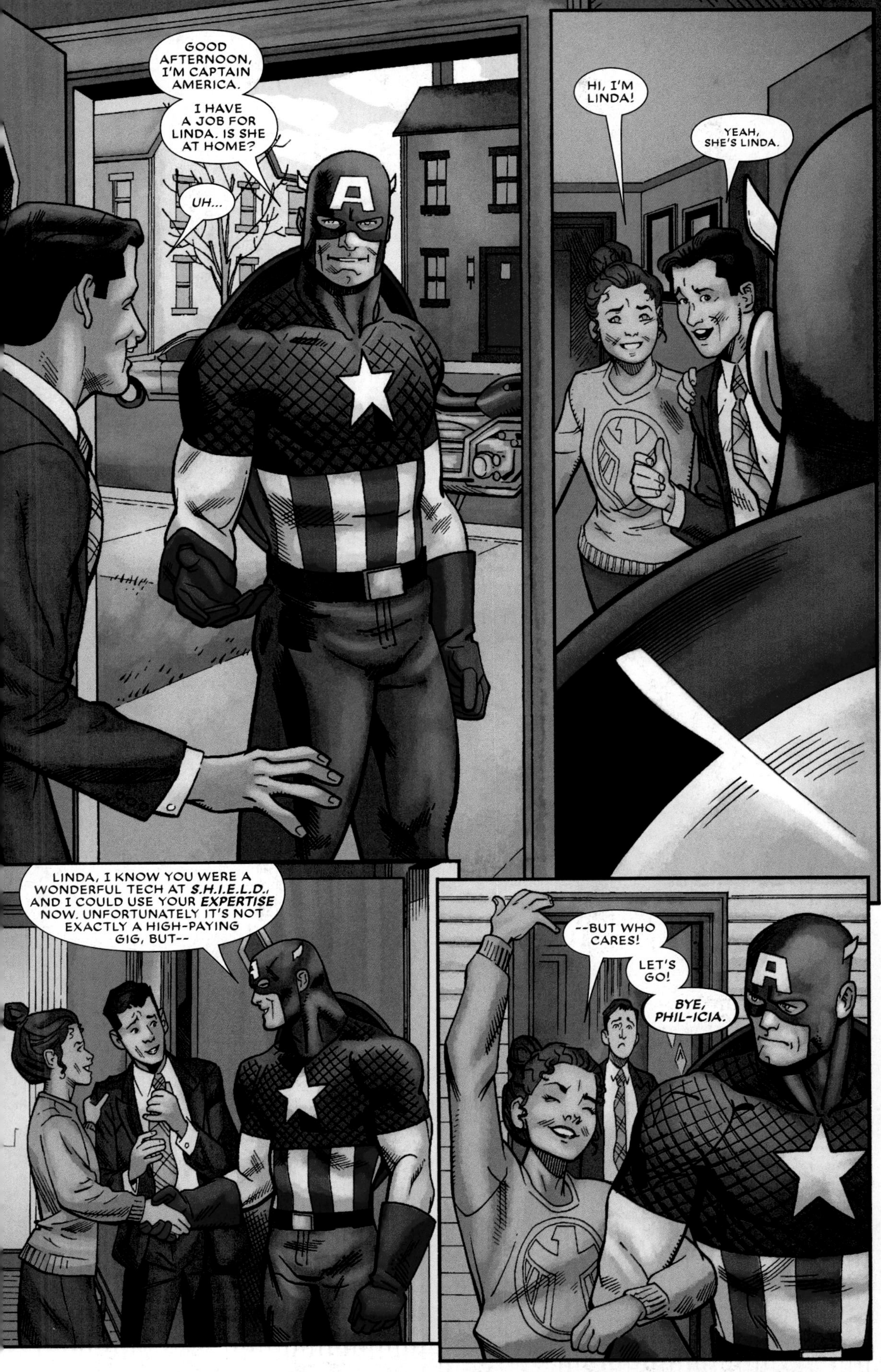
GOOD AFTERNOON, I'M CAPTAIN AMERICA.
I HAVE A JOB FOR LINDA. IS SHE AT HOME?
UH...
HI, I'M LINDA!
YEAH, SHE'S LINDA.
LINDA, I KNOW YOU WERE A WONDERFUL TECH AT S.H.I.E.L.D., AND I COULD USE YOUR EXPERTISE NOW. UNFORTUNATELY IT'S NOT EXACTLY A HIGH-PAYING GIG, BUT--
--BUT WHO CARES!
LET'S GO!
BYE, PHIL-ICIA.

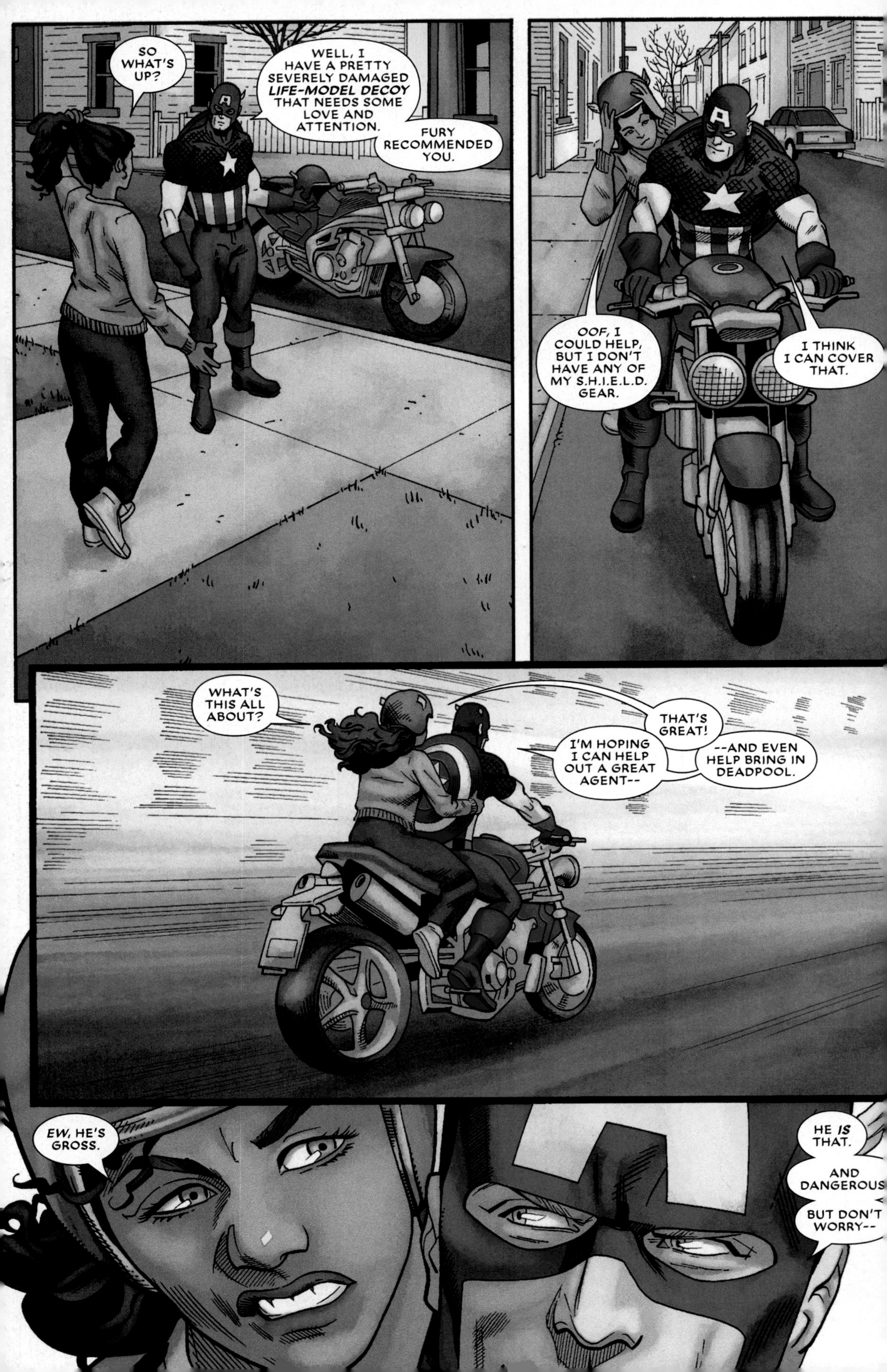
SO WHAT'S UP?
WELL, I HAVE A PRETTY SEVERELY DAMAGED LIFE-MODEL DECOY THAT NEEDS SOME LOVE AND ATTENTION.
FURY RECOMMENDED YOU.
OOF, I COULD HELP, BUT I DON'T HAVE ANY OF MY S.H.I.E.L.D. GEAR.
I THINK I CAN COVER THAT.
WHAT'S THIS ALL ABOUT?
I'M HOPING I CAN HELP OUT A GREAT AGENT--
--AND EVEN HELP BRING IN DEADPOOL.
THAT'S GREAT!
EW, HE'S GROSS.
HE IS THAT.
AND DANGEROUS
BUT DON'T WORRY--

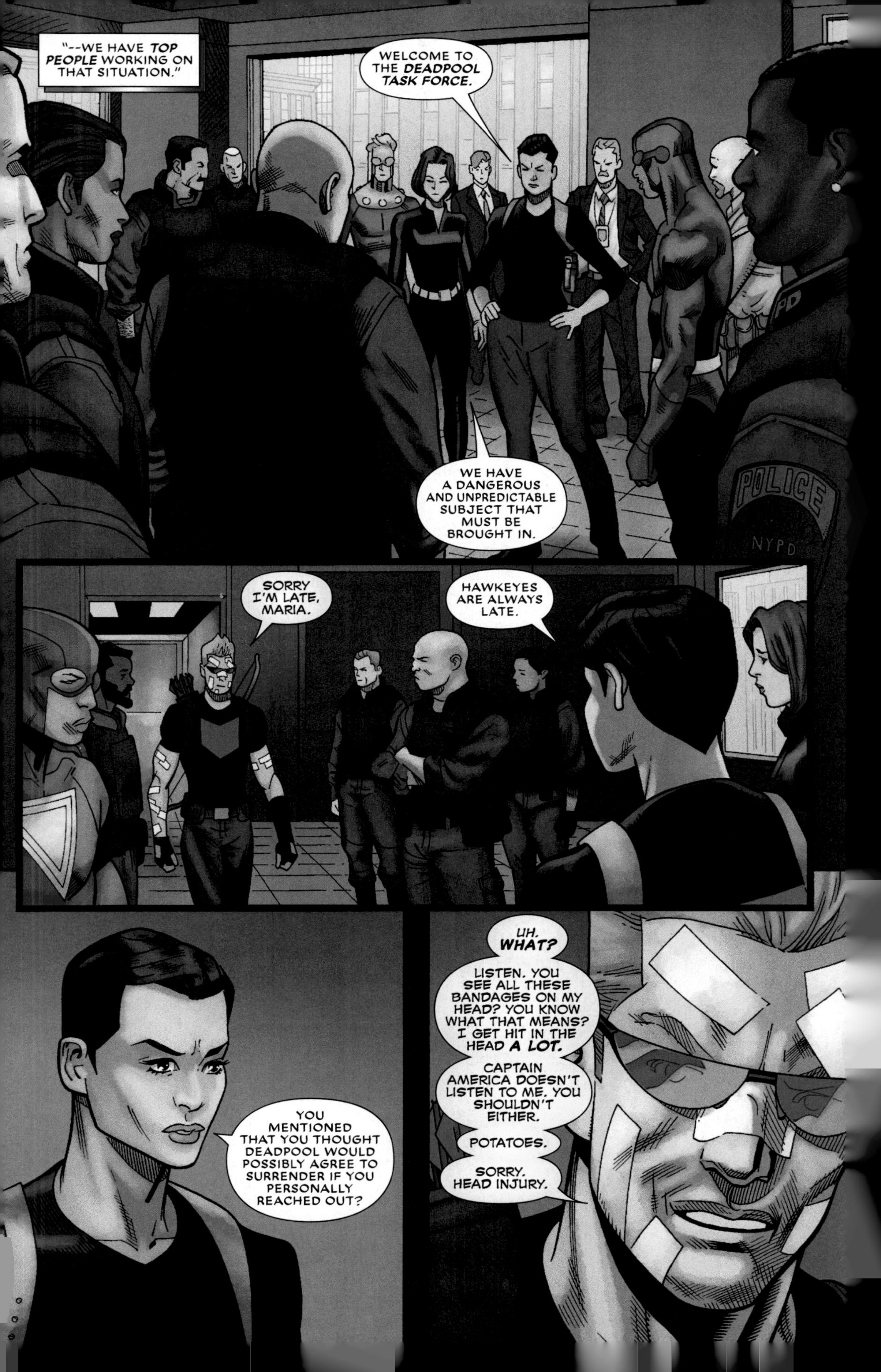
"--WE HAVE TOP PEOPLE WORKING ON THAT SITUATION."
WELCOME TO THE DEADPOOL TASK FORCE.
WE HAVE A DANGEROUS AND UNPREDICTABLE SUBJECT THAT MUST BE BROUGHT IN.
SORRY I'M LATE, MARIA.
HAWKEYES ARE ALWAYS LATE.
POLICE
NYPD
YOU MENTIONED THAT YOU THOUGHT DEADPOOL WOULD POSSIBLY AGREE TO SURRENDER IF YOU PERSONALLY REACHED OUT?
UH. WHAT?
LISTEN. YOU SEE ALL THESE BANDAGES ON MY HEAD? YOU KNOW WHAT THAT MEANS? I GET HIT IN THE HEAD A LOT.
CAPTAIN AMERICA DOESN'T LISTEN TO ME. YOU SHOULDN'T EITHER.
POTATOES.
SORRY. HEAD INJURY.

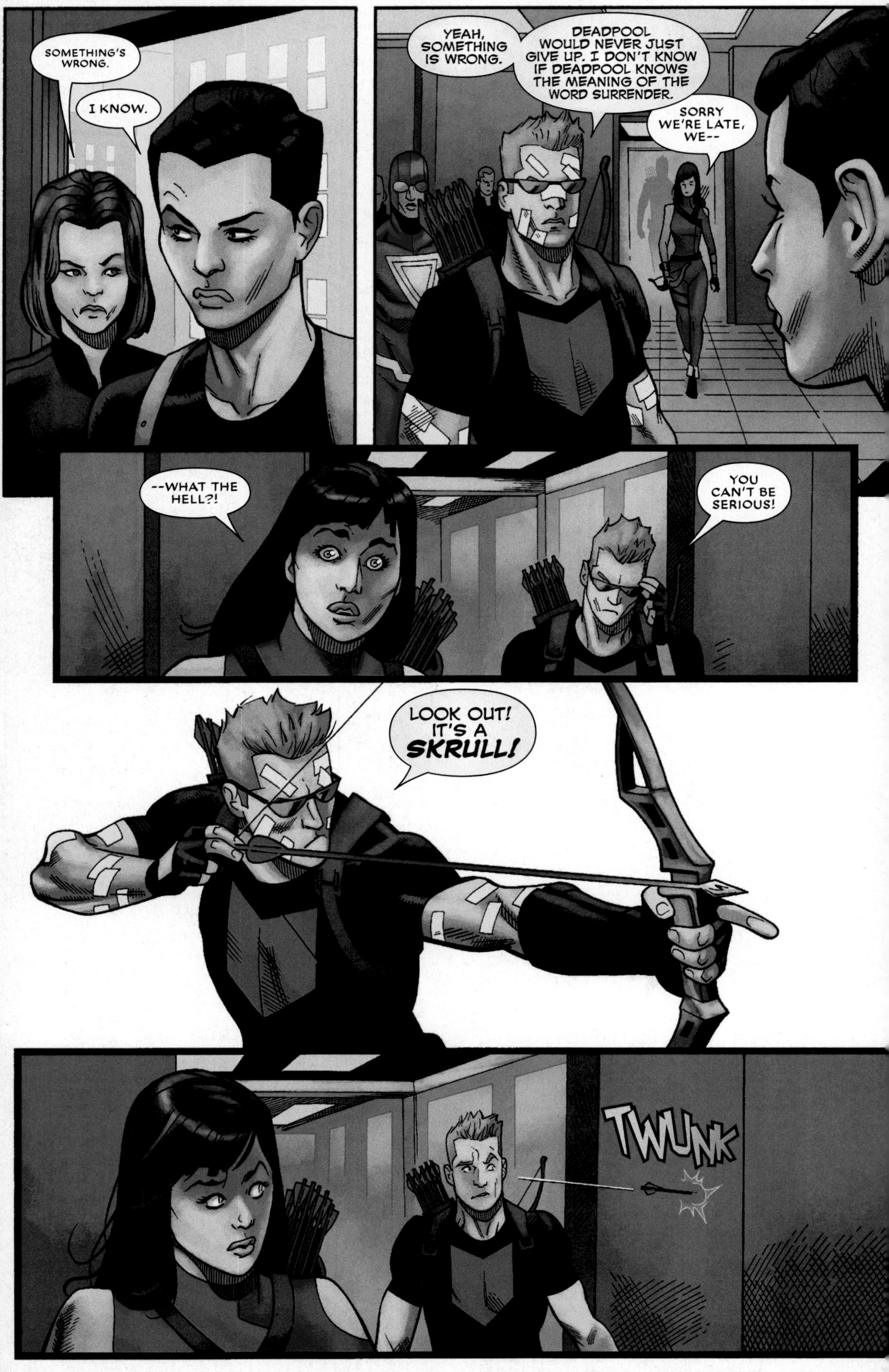
SOMETHING'S WRONG.
I KNOW.
YEAH, SOMETHING IS WRONG.
DEADPOOL WOULD NEVER JUST GIVE UP. I DON'T KNOW IF DEADPOOL KNOWS THE MEANING OF THE WORD SURRENDER.
SORRY WE'RE LATE, WE--
--WHAT THE HELL?!
YOU CAN'T BE SERIOUS!
LOOK OUT! IT'S A SKRULL!
TWUNK

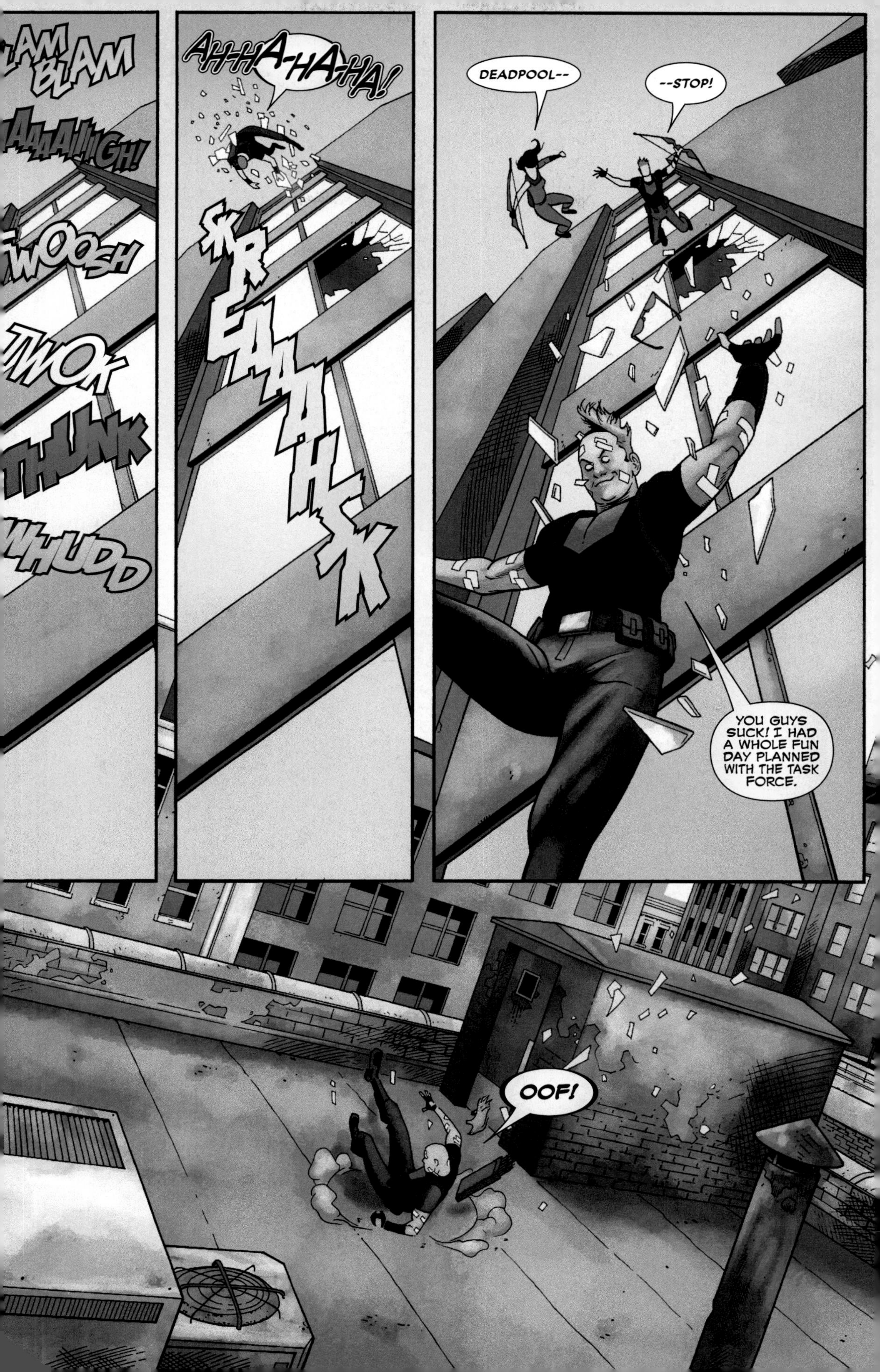

BLAM BLAM
AAAAAIIIGH!
FWOOSH
TWOK
THUNK
WHUDD
AH-HA-HA-HA-HA!
SKREEAAAAHHSK
DEADPOOL--
--STOP!
YOU GUYS SUCK! I HAD A WHOLE FUN DAY PLANNED WITH THE TASK FORCE.
OOF!

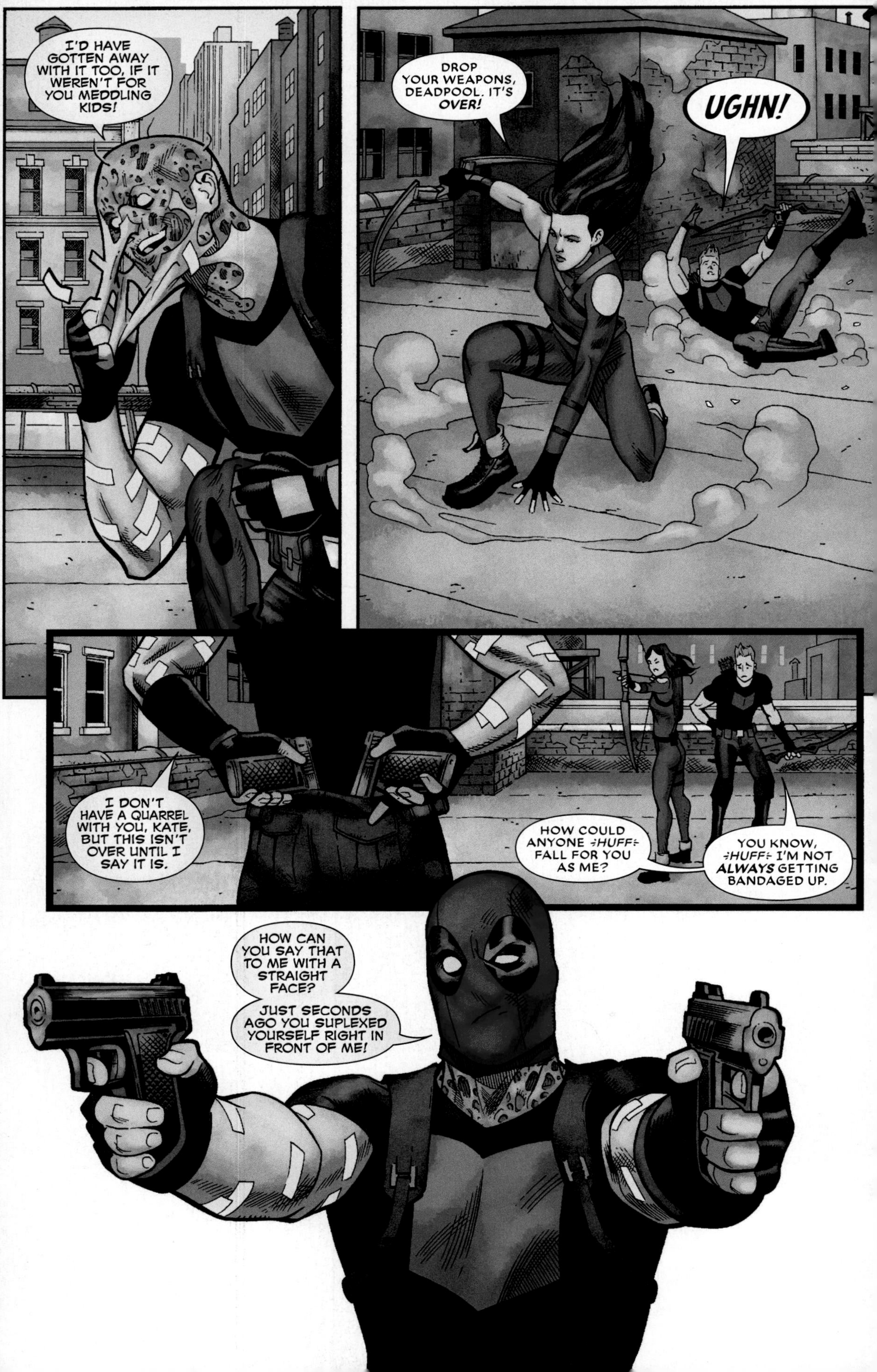
I'D HAVE GOTTEN AWAY WITH IT TOO, IF IT WEREN'T FOR YOU MEDDLING KIDS!
DROP YOUR WEAPONS, DEADPOOL. IT'S OVER!
UGHN!
I DON'T HAVE A QUARREL WITH YOU, KATE, BUT THIS ISN'T OVER UNTIL I SAY IT IS.
HOW COULD ANYONE *HUFF* FALL FOR YOU AS ME?
YOU KNOW, *HUFF* I'M NOT ALWAYS GETTING BANDAGED UP.
HOW CAN YOU SAY THAT TO ME WITH A STRAIGHT FACE?
JUST SECONDS AGO YOU SUPLEXED YOURSELF RIGHT IN FRONT OF ME!

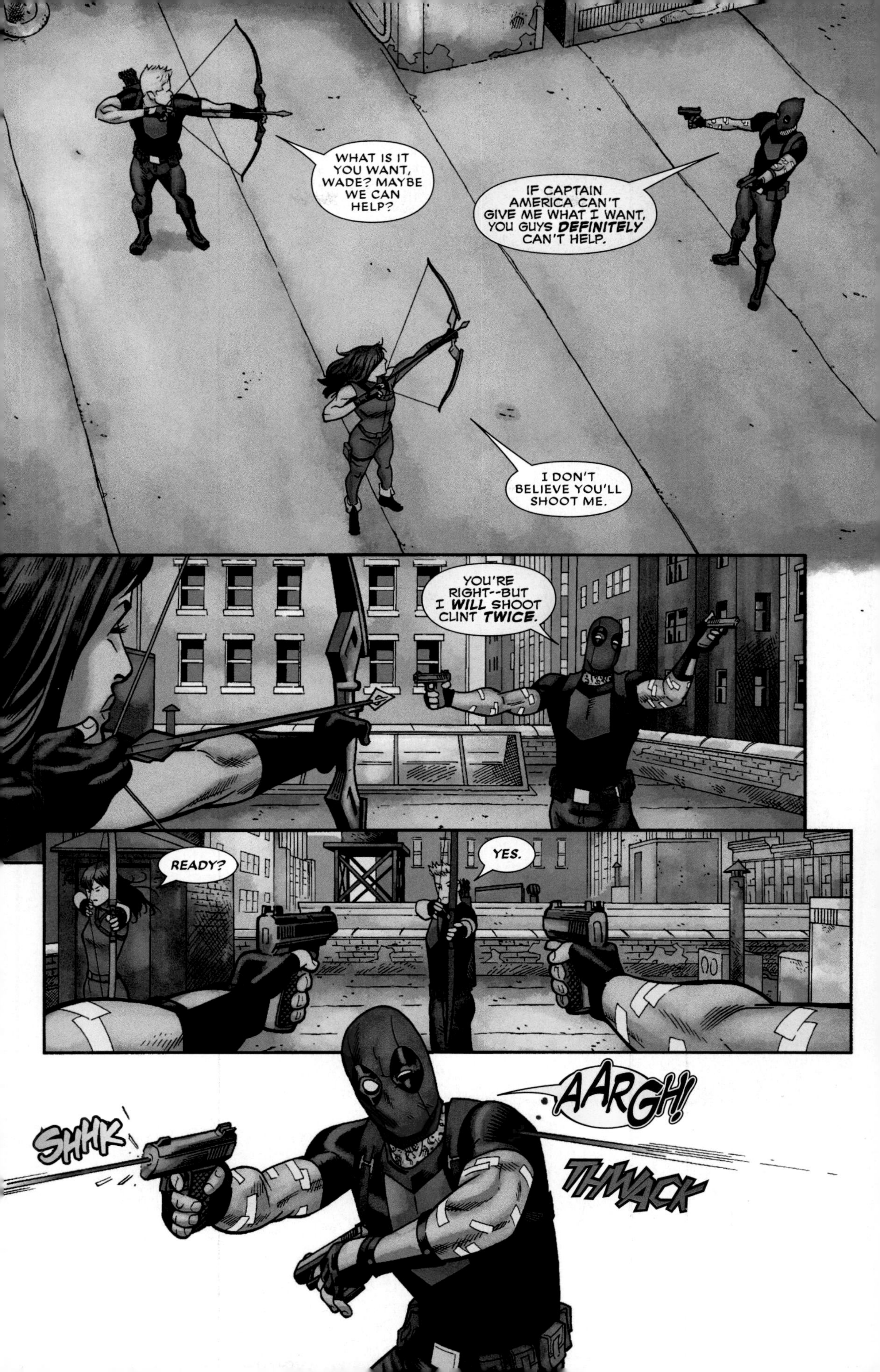

WHAT IS IT YOU WANT, WADE? MAYBE WE CAN HELP?
IF CAPTAIN AMERICA CAN'T GIVE ME WHAT I WANT, YOU GUYS **DEFINITELY** CAN'T HELP.
I DON'T BELIEVE YOU'LL SHOOT ME.
YOU'RE RIGHT--BUT I **WILL** SHOOT CLINT **TWICE**.
READY?
YES.
SHHK
AARGH!
THWACK

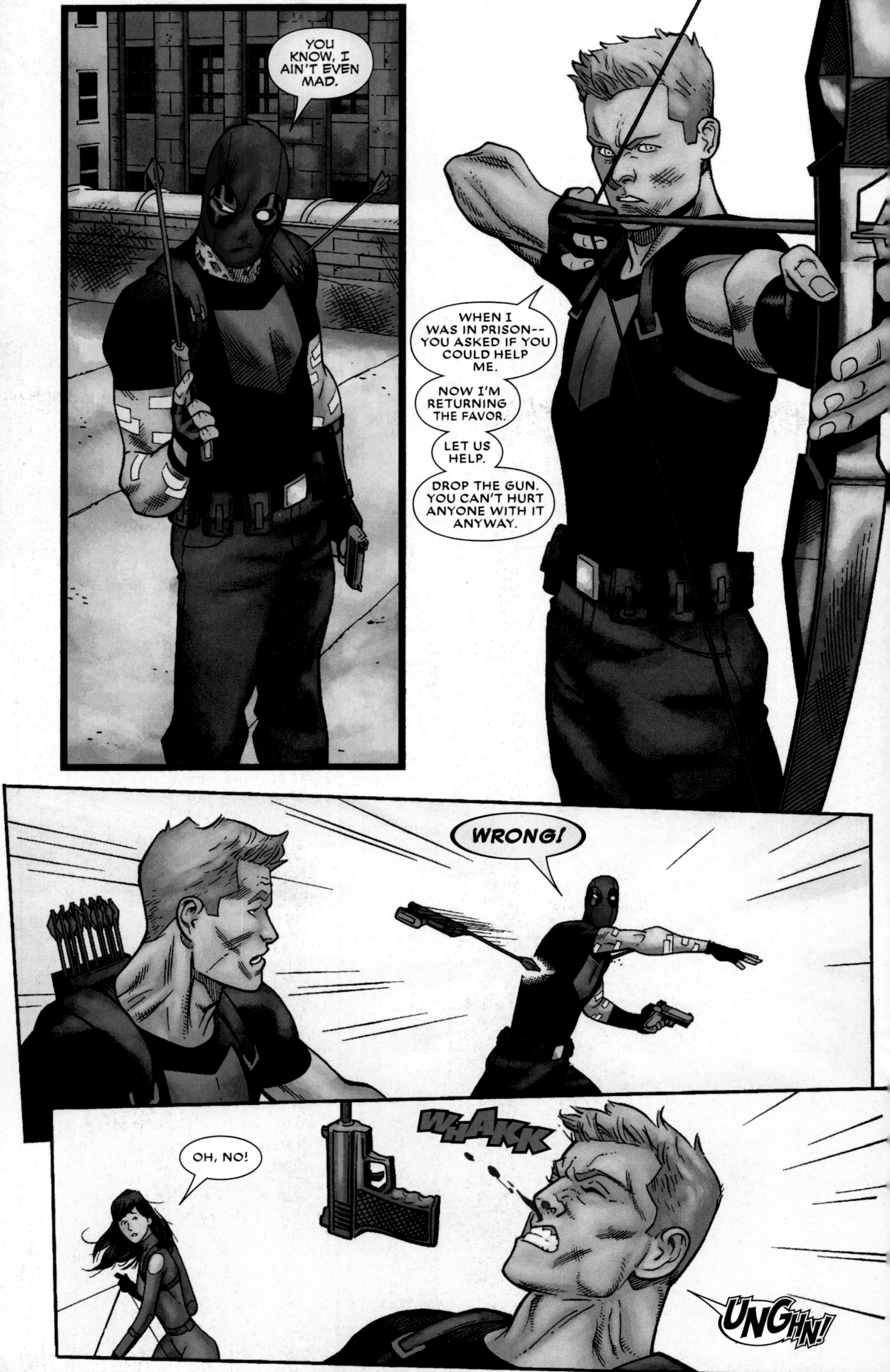

YOU KNOW, I AIN'T EVEN MAD.
WHEN I WAS IN PRISON-- YOU ASKED IF YOU COULD HELP ME.
NOW I'M RETURNING THE FAVOR.
LET US HELP.
DROP THE GUN. YOU CAN'T HURT ANYONE WITH IT ANYWAY.
WRONG!
OH, NO!
WHAKK
UNGHN!

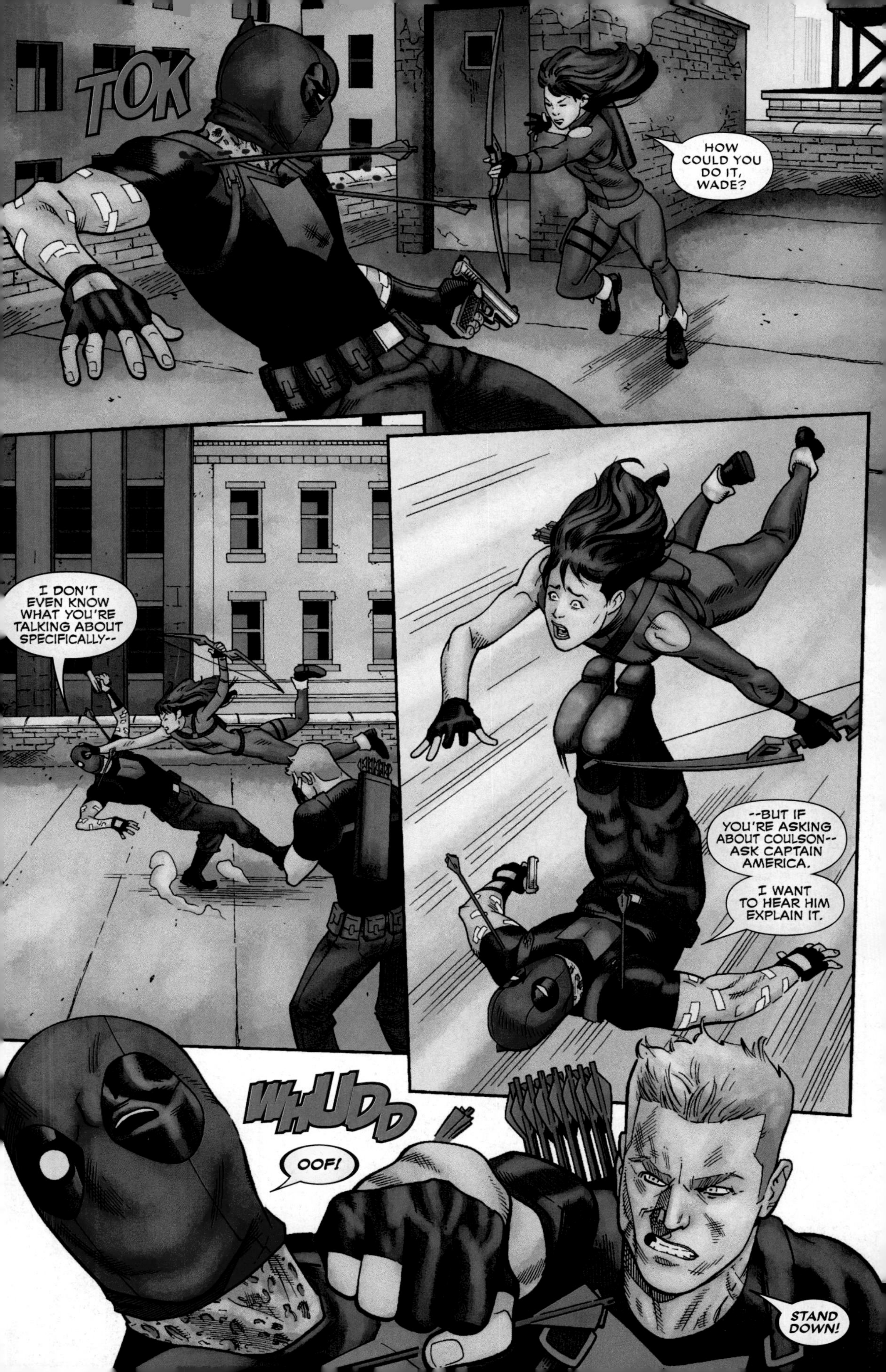
TOK
HOW COULD YOU DO IT, WADE?
I DON'T EVEN KNOW WHAT YOU'RE TALKING ABOUT SPECIFICALLY--
--BUT IF YOU'RE ASKING ABOUT COULSON--ASK CAPTAIN AMERICA.
I WANT TO HEAR HIM EXPLAIN IT.
WHUDD
OOF!
STAND DOWN!

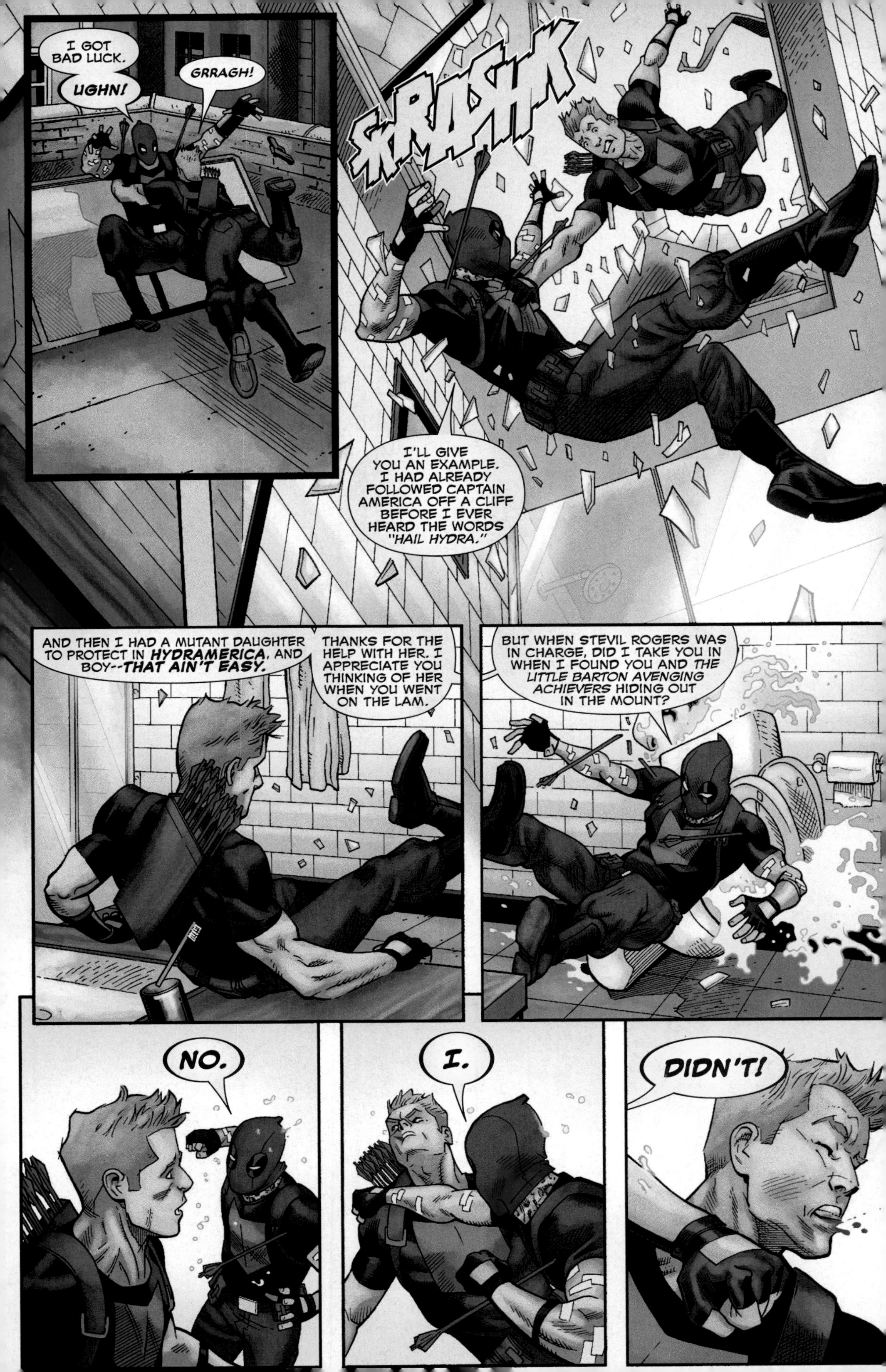
I GOT BAD LUCK.
UGHN!
GRRAGH!
SKRASHK
I'LL GIVE YOU AN EXAMPLE. I HAD ALREADY FOLLOWED CAPTAIN AMERICA OFF A CLIFF BEFORE I EVER HEARD THE WORDS "HAIL HYDRA."
AND THEN I HAD A MUTANT DAUGHTER TO PROTECT IN HYDRAMERICA, AND BOY--THAT AIN'T EASY.
THANKS FOR THE HELP WITH HER. I APPRECIATE YOU THINKING OF HER WHEN YOU WENT ON THE LAM.
BUT WHEN STEVIL ROGERS WAS IN CHARGE, DID I TAKE YOU IN WHEN I FOUND YOU AND THE LITTLE BARTON AVENGING ACHIEVERS HIDING OUT IN THE MOUNT?
NO.
I.
DIDN'T!

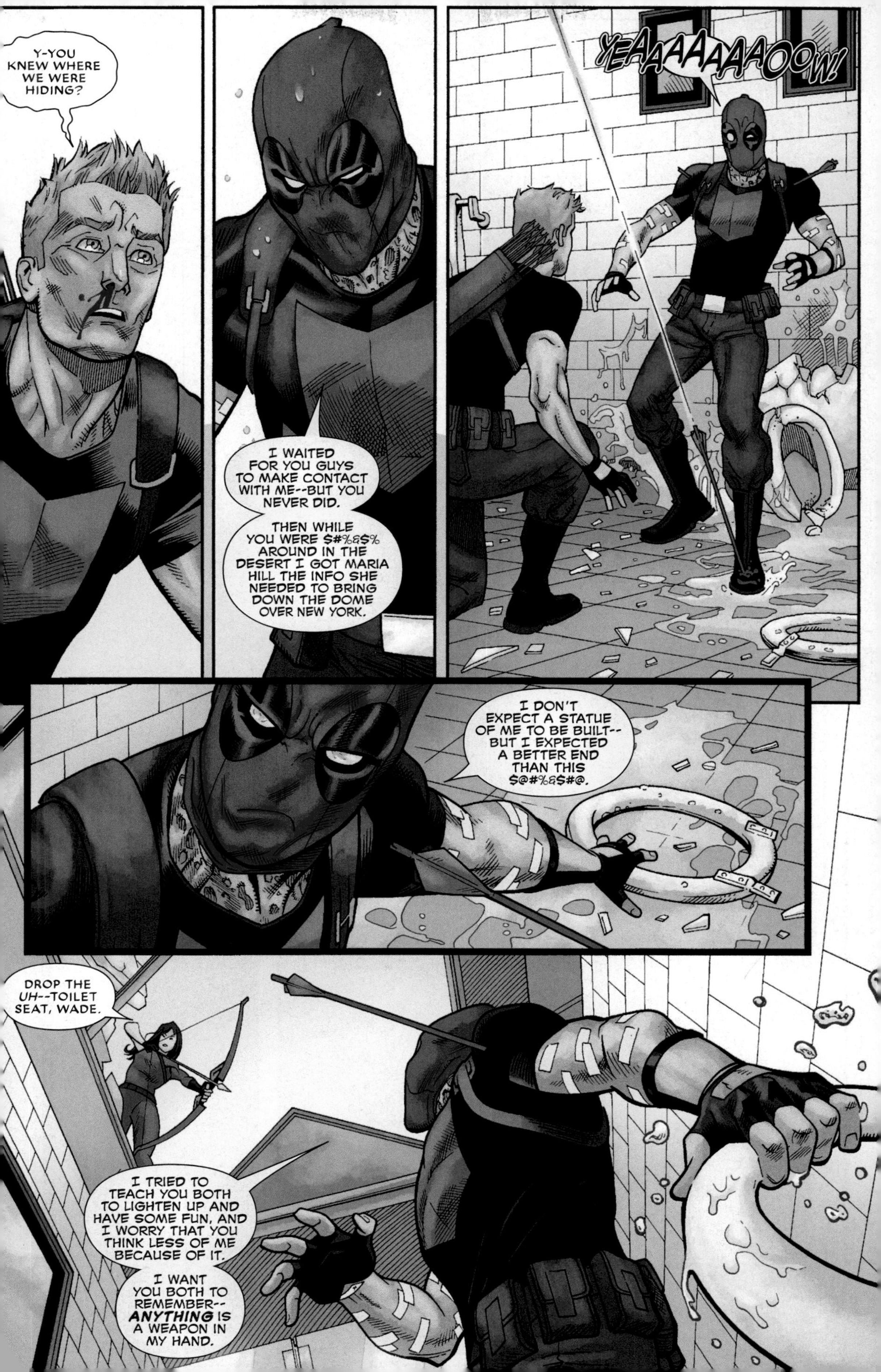

Y-YOU KNEW WHERE WE WERE HIDING?
I WAITED FOR YOU GUYS TO MAKE CONTACT WITH ME--BUT YOU NEVER DID.
THEN WHILE YOU WERE $#%&$% AROUND IN THE DESERT I GOT MARIA HILL THE INFO SHE NEEDED TO BRING DOWN THE DOME OVER NEW YORK.
YEAAAAAAAOOW!
I DON'T EXPECT A STATUE OF ME TO BE BUILT--BUT I EXPECTED A BETTER END THAN THIS $@#%&$#@.
DROP THE *UH*--TOILET SEAT, WADE.
I TRIED TO TEACH YOU BOTH TO LIGHTEN UP AND HAVE SOME FUN, AND I WORRY THAT YOU THINK LESS OF ME BECAUSE OF IT.
I WANT YOU BOTH TO REMEMBER-- ***ANYTHING*** IS A WEAPON IN MY HAND.

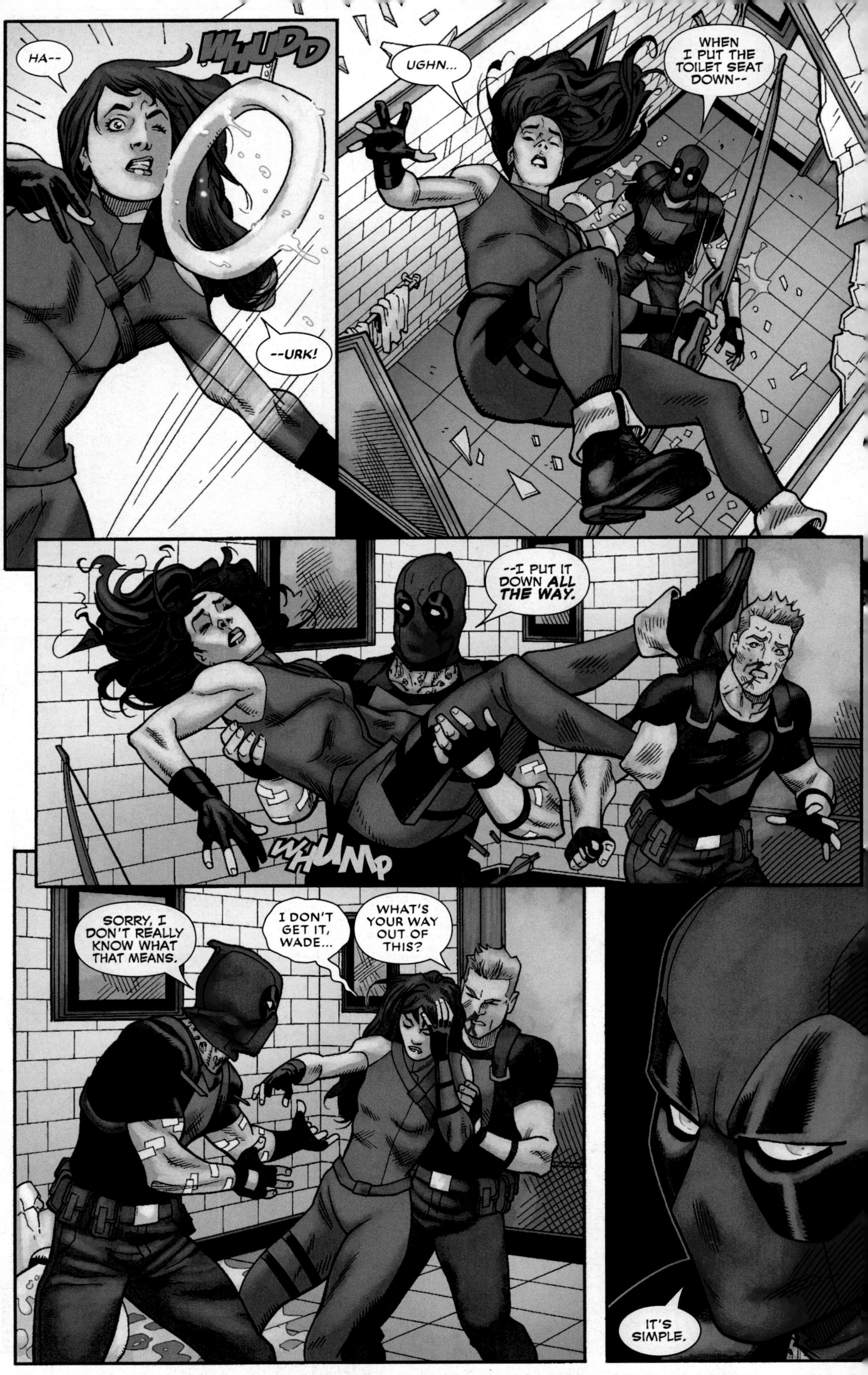
HA--
WHUDD
--URK!
UGHN...
WHEN I PUT THE TOILET SEAT DOWN--
--I PUT IT DOWN ALL THE WAY.
WHUMP
SORRY, I DON'T REALLY KNOW WHAT THAT MEANS.
I DON'T GET IT, WADE...
WHAT'S YOUR WAY OUT OF THIS?
IT'S SIMPLE.

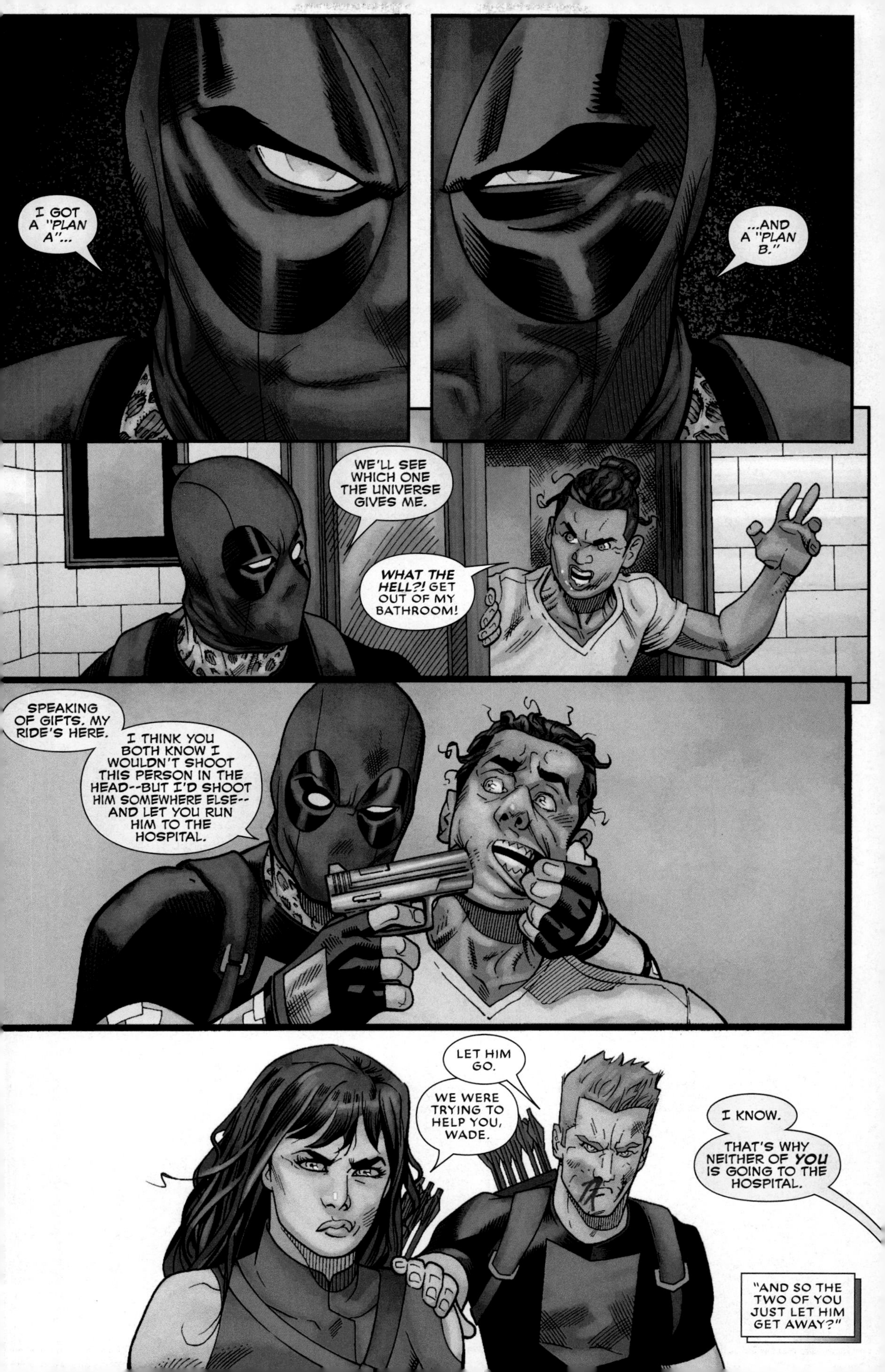

I GOT A "PLAN A"...
...AND A "PLAN B."
WE'LL SEE WHICH ONE THE UNIVERSE GIVES ME.
WHAT THE HELL?! GET OUT OF MY BATHROOM!
SPEAKING OF GIFTS, MY RIDE'S HERE.
I THINK YOU BOTH KNOW I WOULDN'T SHOOT THIS PERSON IN THE HEAD--BUT I'D SHOOT HIM SOMEWHERE ELSE--AND LET YOU RUN HIM TO THE HOSPITAL.
LET HIM GO.
WE WERE TRYING TO HELP YOU, WADE.
I KNOW.
THAT'S WHY NEITHER OF YOU IS GOING TO THE HOSPITAL.
"AND SO THE TWO OF YOU JUST LET HIM GET AWAY?"

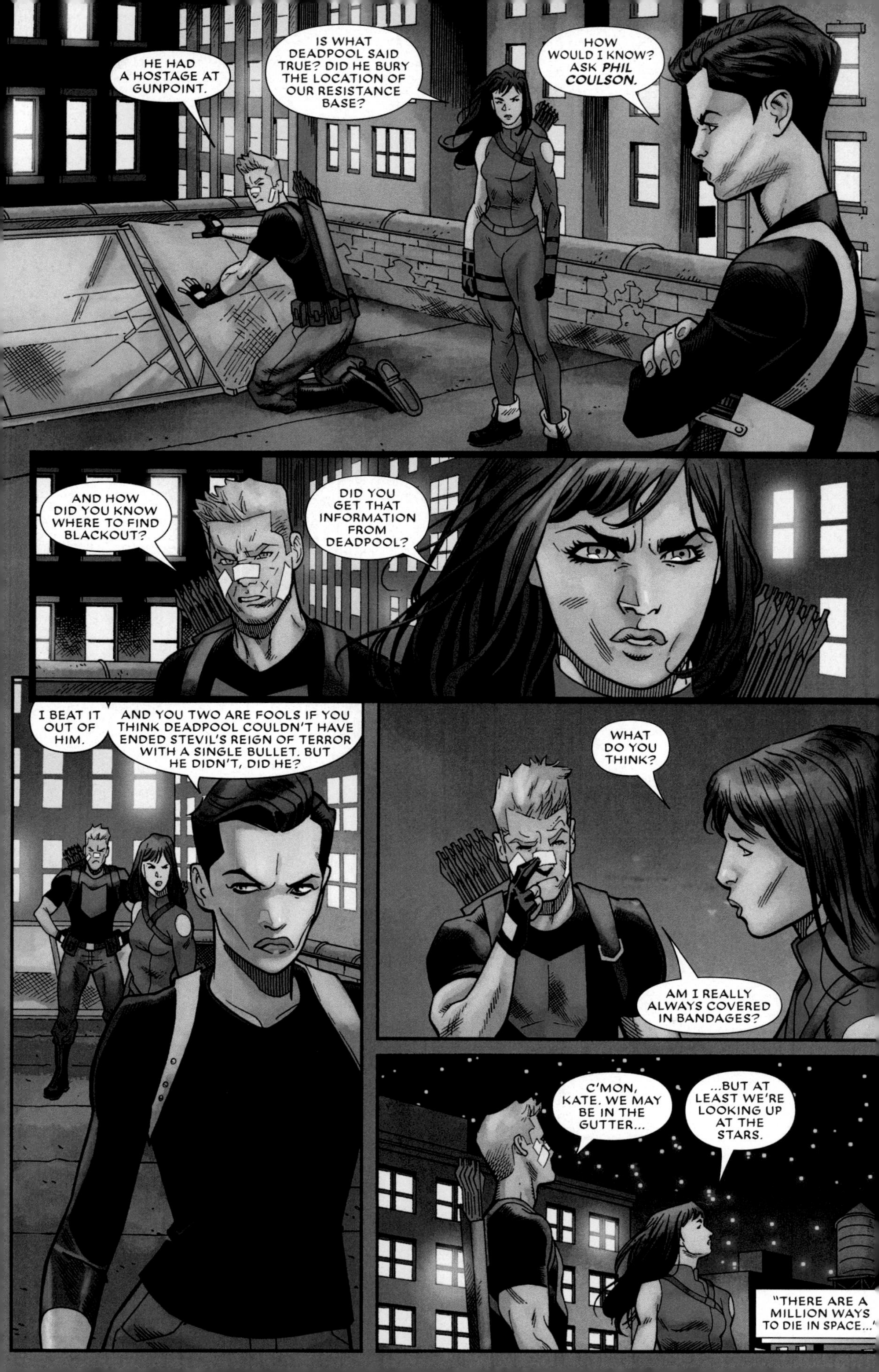
HE HAD A HOSTAGE AT GUNPOINT.
IS WHAT DEADPOOL SAID TRUE? DID HE BURY THE LOCATION OF OUR RESISTANCE BASE?
HOW WOULD I KNOW? ASK PHIL COULSON.
AND HOW DID YOU KNOW WHERE TO FIND BLACKOUT?
DID YOU GET THAT INFORMATION FROM DEADPOOL?
I BEAT IT OUT OF HIM.
AND YOU TWO ARE FOOLS IF YOU THINK DEADPOOL COULDN'T HAVE ENDED STEVIL'S REIGN OF TERROR WITH A SINGLE BULLET. BUT HE DIDN'T, DID HE?
WHAT DO YOU THINK?
AM I REALLY ALWAYS COVERED IN BANDAGES?
C'MON, KATE. WE MAY BE IN THE GUTTER...
...BUT AT LEAST WE'RE LOOKING UP AT THE STARS.
"THERE ARE A MILLION WAYS TO DIE IN SPACE..."

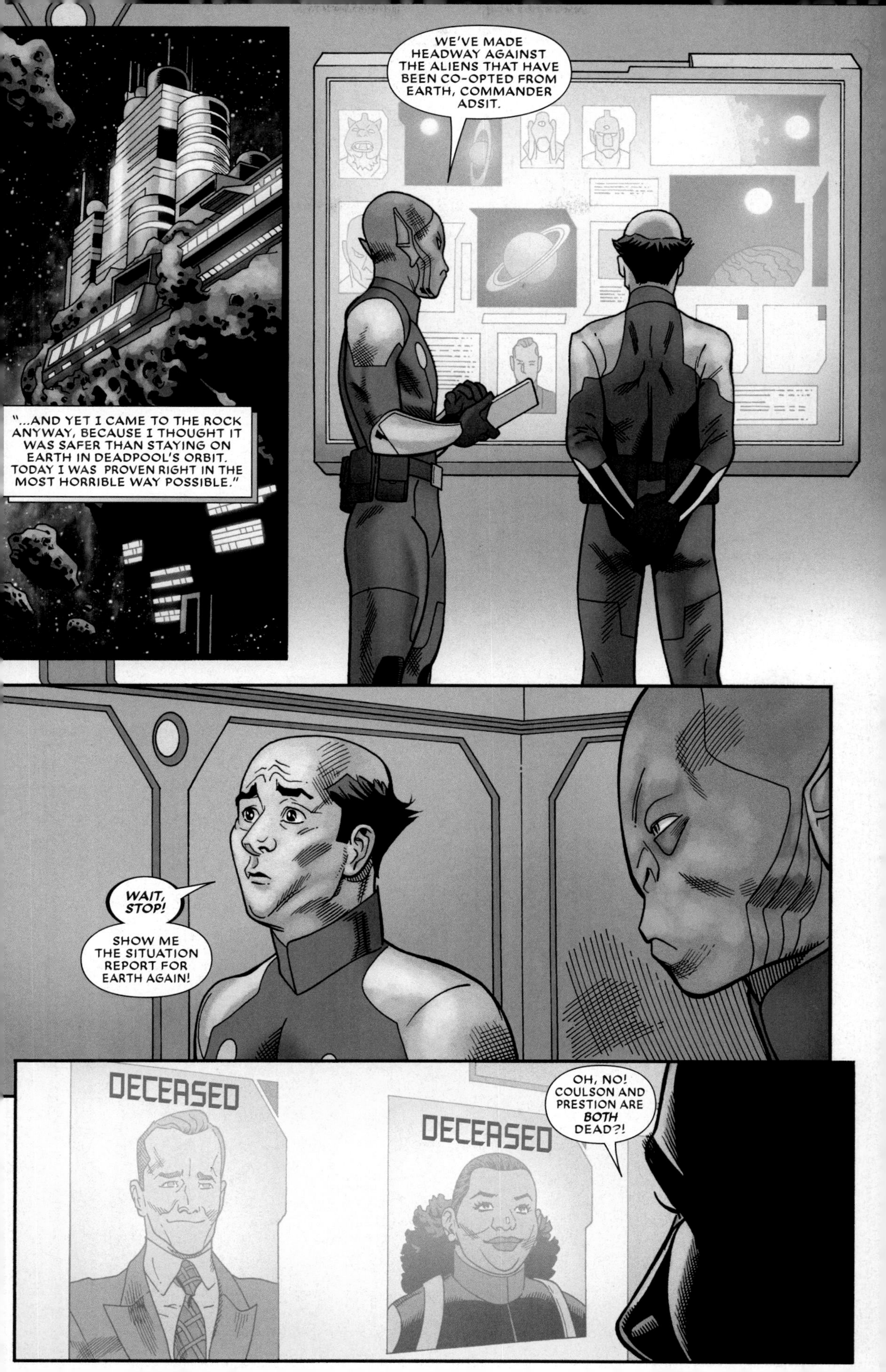
"...AND YET I CAME TO THE ROCK ANYWAY, BECAUSE I THOUGHT IT WAS SAFER THAN STAYING ON EARTH IN DEADPOOL'S ORBIT. TODAY I WAS PROVEN RIGHT IN THE MOST HORRIBLE WAY POSSIBLE."
WE'VE MADE HEADWAY AGAINST THE ALIENS THAT HAVE BEEN CO-OPTED FROM EARTH, COMMANDER ADSIT.
WAIT, STOP!
SHOW ME THE SITUATION REPORT FOR EARTH AGAIN!
DECEASED
DECEASED
OH, NO! COULSON AND PRESTION ARE BOTH DEAD?!

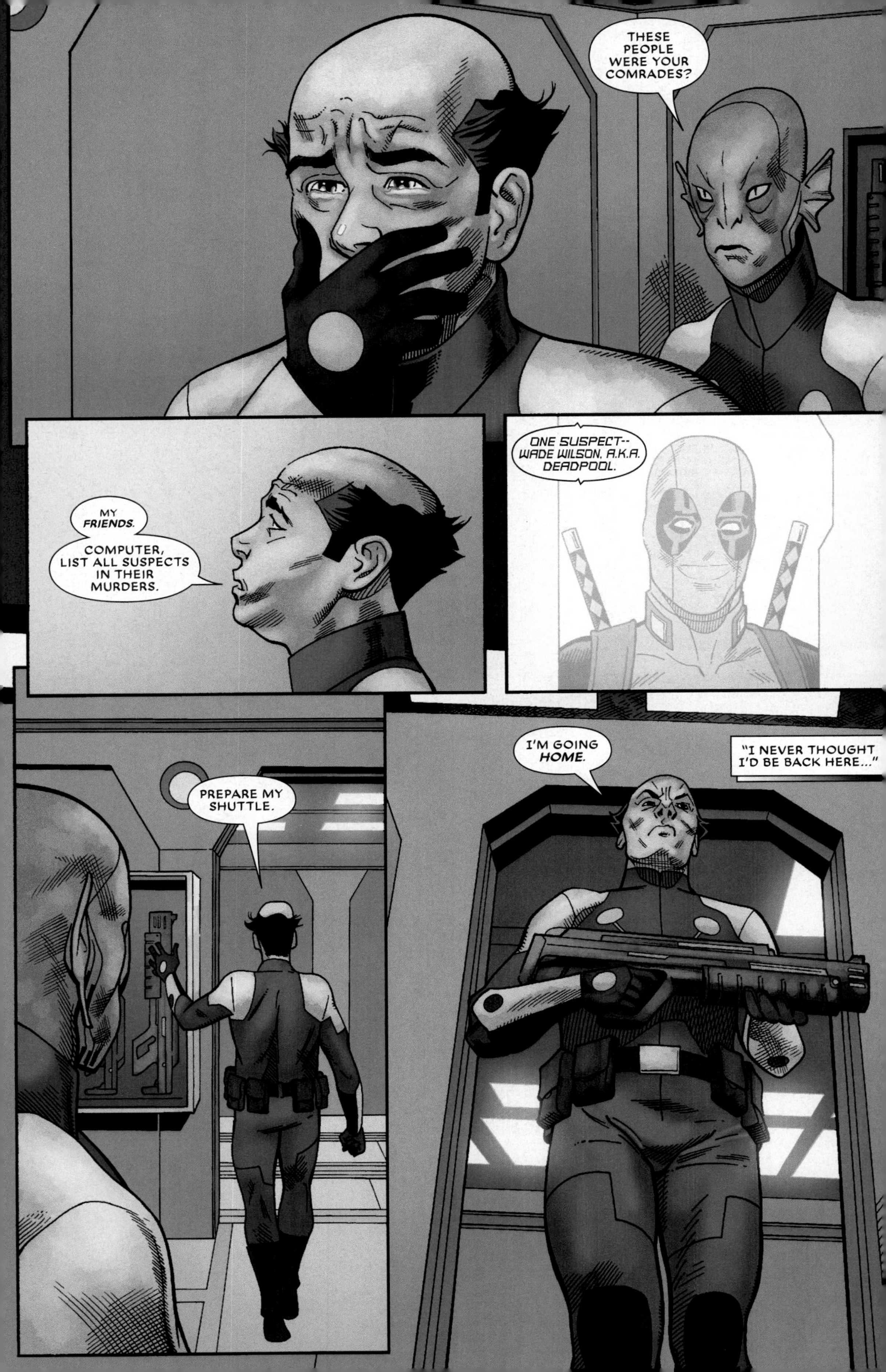
THESE PEOPLE WERE YOUR COMRADES?
MY *FRIENDS.*
COMPUTER, LIST ALL SUSPECTS IN THEIR MURDERS.
ONE SUSPECT-- WADE WILSON, A.K.A. DEADPOOL.
PREPARE MY SHUTTLE.
I'M GOING *HOME*.
"I NEVER THOUGHT I'D BE BACK HERE..."

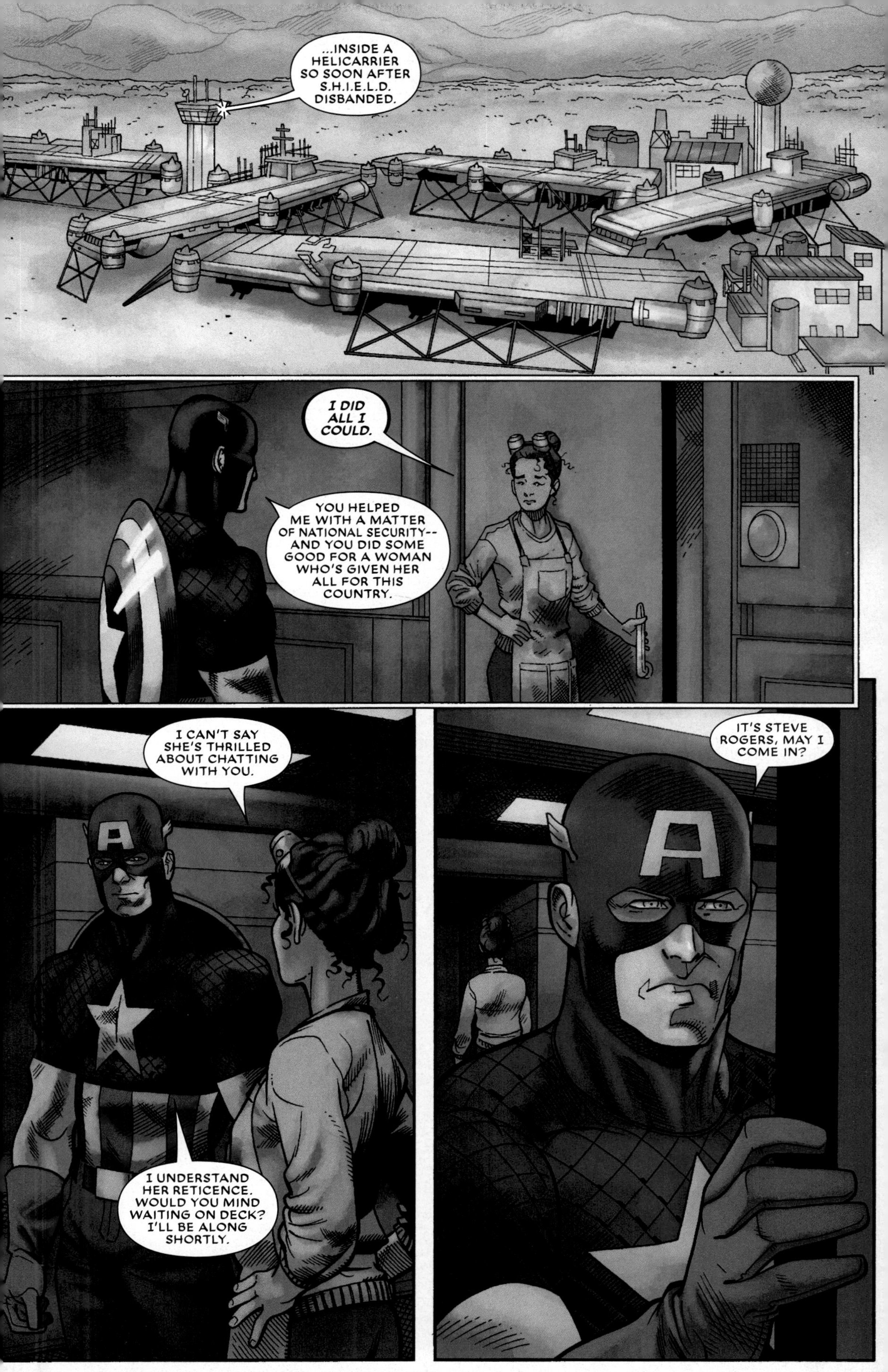
...INSIDE A HELICARRIER SO SOON AFTER S.H.I.E.L.D. DISBANDED.
I DID ALL I COULD.
YOU HELPED ME WITH A MATTER OF NATIONAL SECURITY-- AND YOU DID SOME GOOD FOR A WOMAN WHO'S GIVEN HER ALL FOR THIS COUNTRY.
I CAN'T SAY SHE'S THRILLED ABOUT CHATTING WITH YOU.
I UNDERSTAND HER RETICENCE. WOULD YOU MIND WAITING ON DECK? I'LL BE ALONG SHORTLY.
IT'S STEVE ROGERS, MAY I COME IN?

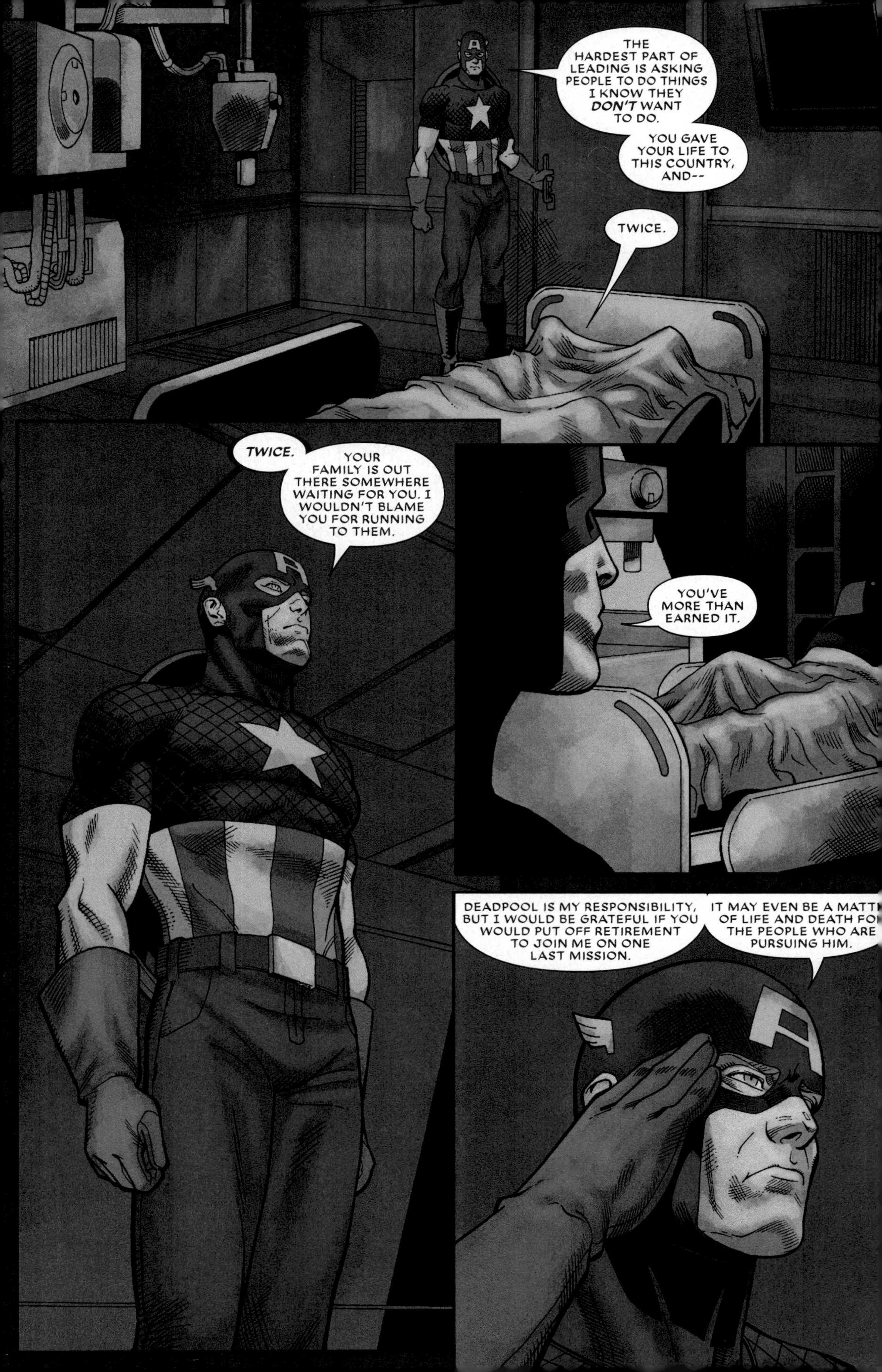
THE HARDEST PART OF LEADING IS ASKING PEOPLE TO DO THINGS I KNOW THEY *DON'T* WANT TO DO.
YOU GAVE YOUR LIFE TO THIS COUNTRY, AND--
TWICE.
TWICE.
YOUR FAMILY IS OUT THERE SOMEWHERE WAITING FOR YOU. I WOULDN'T BLAME YOU FOR RUNNING TO THEM.
YOU'VE MORE THAN EARNED IT.
DEADPOOL IS MY RESPONSIBILITY, BUT I WOULD BE GRATEFUL IF YOU WOULD PUT OFF RETIREMENT TO JOIN ME ON ONE LAST MISSION.
IT MAY EVEN BE A MATT OF LIFE AND DEATH FO THE PEOPLE WHO ARE PURSUING HIM.

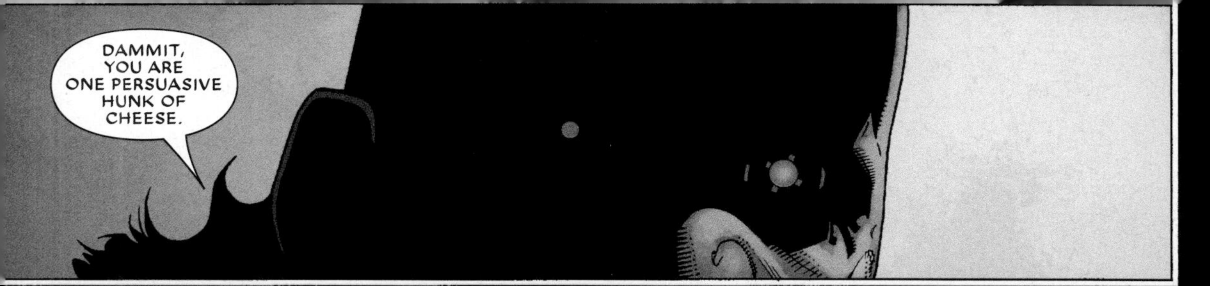
DAMMIT, YOU ARE ONE PERSUASIVE HUNK OF CHEESE.

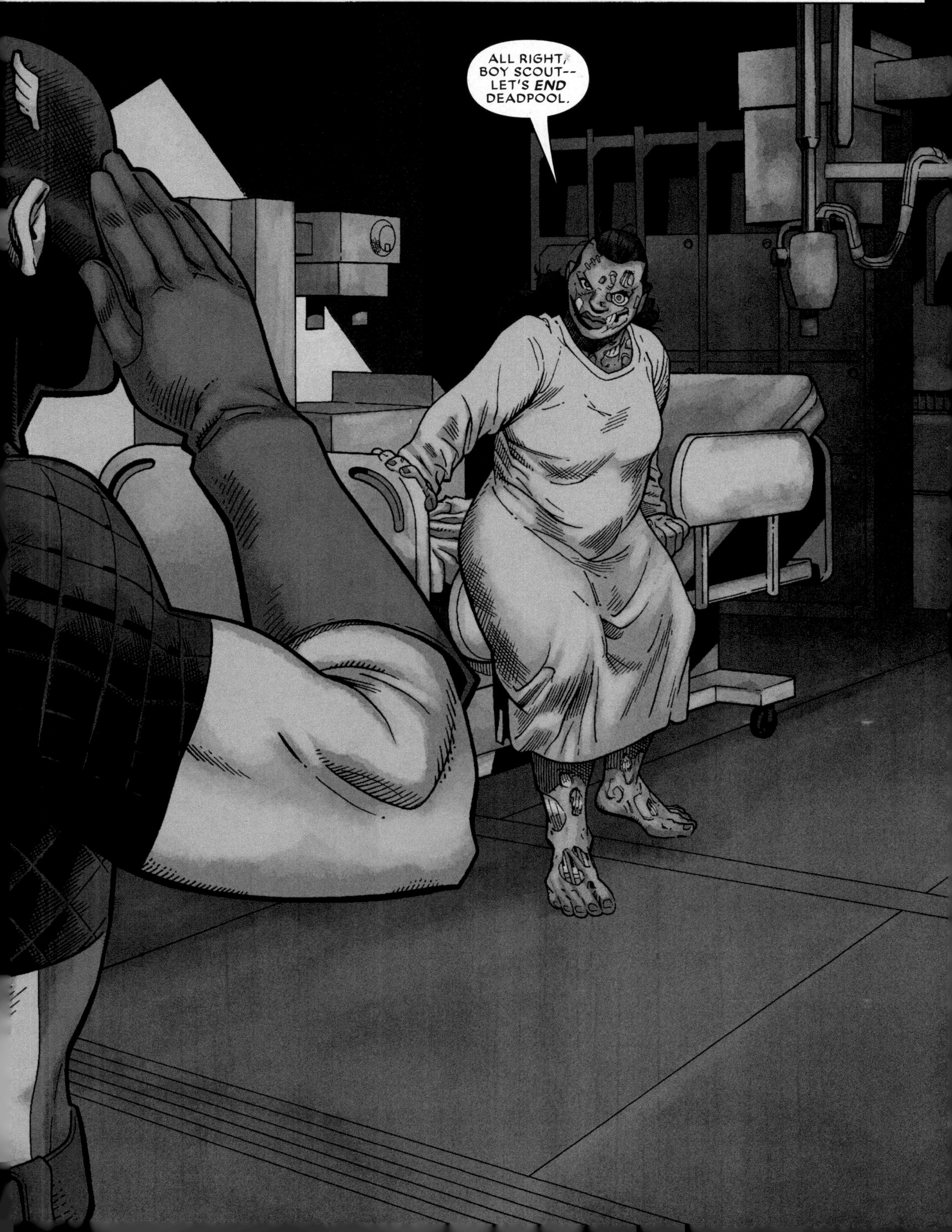
ALL RIGHT, BOY SCOUT-- LET'S END DEADPOOL.

300
"The Marvel Universe Kills Deadpool"
Part Four

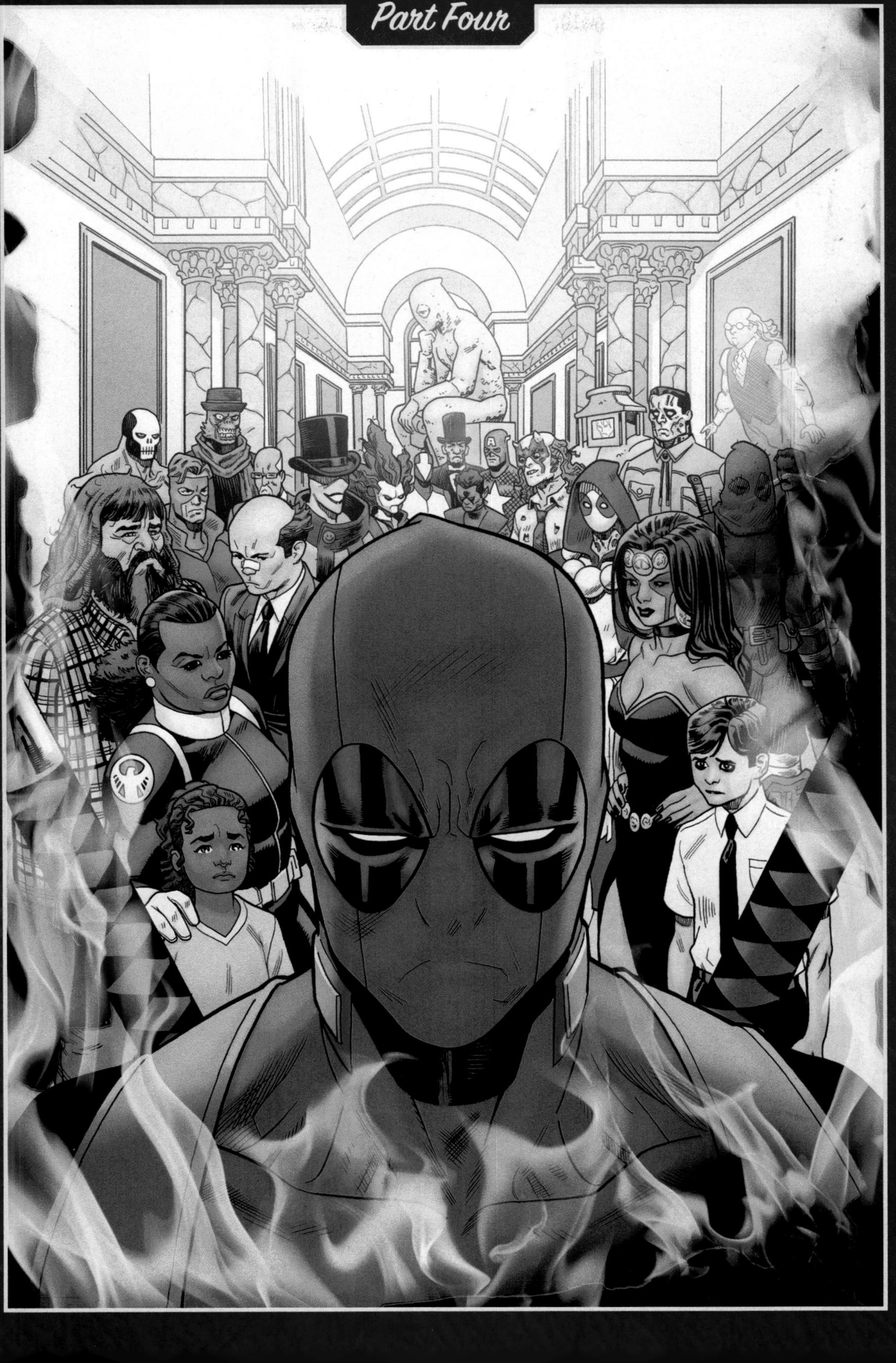

A lot has
happened.

Deadpool was
a nobody.

Then he was
somebody.

Now...
he's not.

It's all
gone.

The
money.

The
friends.

The
family.

The
Avengers.

He followed an evil
version of Steve Rogers
into the abyss and now
he has to pay the price.

He's wanted
for murder.

And he's
guilty.

The Marvel Universe is
out to kill Deadpool,
but there's only one
man up to the job...

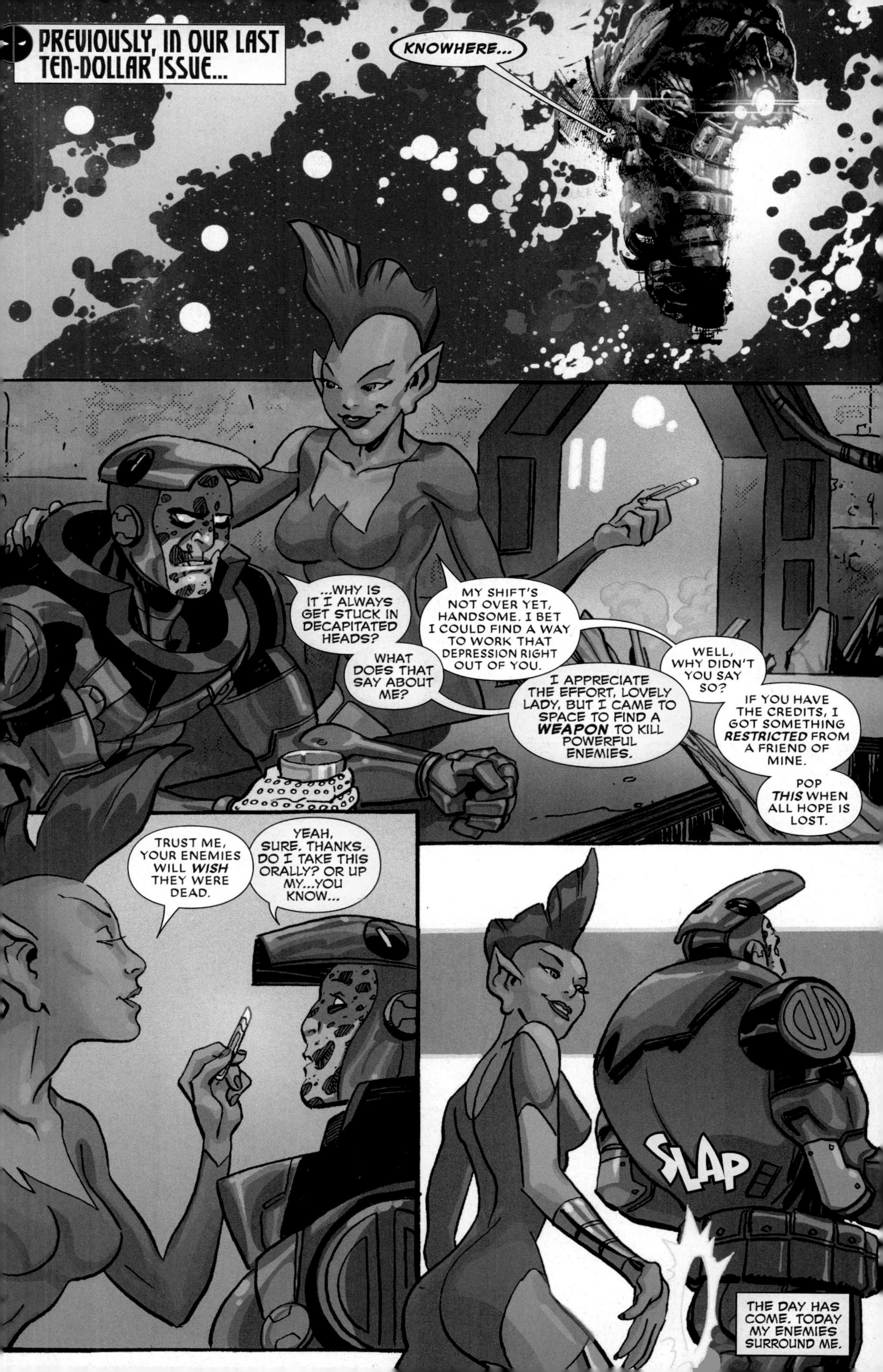
PREVIOUSLY, IN OUR LAST TEN-DOLLAR ISSUE...
KNOWHERE...
...WHY IS IT I ALWAYS GET STUCK IN DECAPITATED HEADS?
WHAT DOES THAT SAY ABOUT ME?
MY SHIFT'S NOT OVER YET, HANDSOME. I BET I COULD FIND A WAY TO WORK THAT DEPRESSION RIGHT OUT OF YOU.
I APPRECIATE THE EFFORT, LOVELY LADY, BUT I CAME TO SPACE TO FIND A WEAPON TO KILL POWERFUL ENEMIES.
WELL, WHY DIDN'T YOU SAY SO?
IF YOU HAVE THE CREDITS, I GOT SOMETHING RESTRICTED FROM A FRIEND OF MINE.
POP THIS WHEN ALL HOPE IS LOST.
TRUST ME, YOUR ENEMIES WILL WISH THEY WERE DEAD.
YEAH, SURE. THANKS. DO I TAKE THIS ORALLY? OR UP MY...YOU KNOW...
SLAP
THE DAY HAS COME. TODAY MY ENEMIES SURROUND ME.

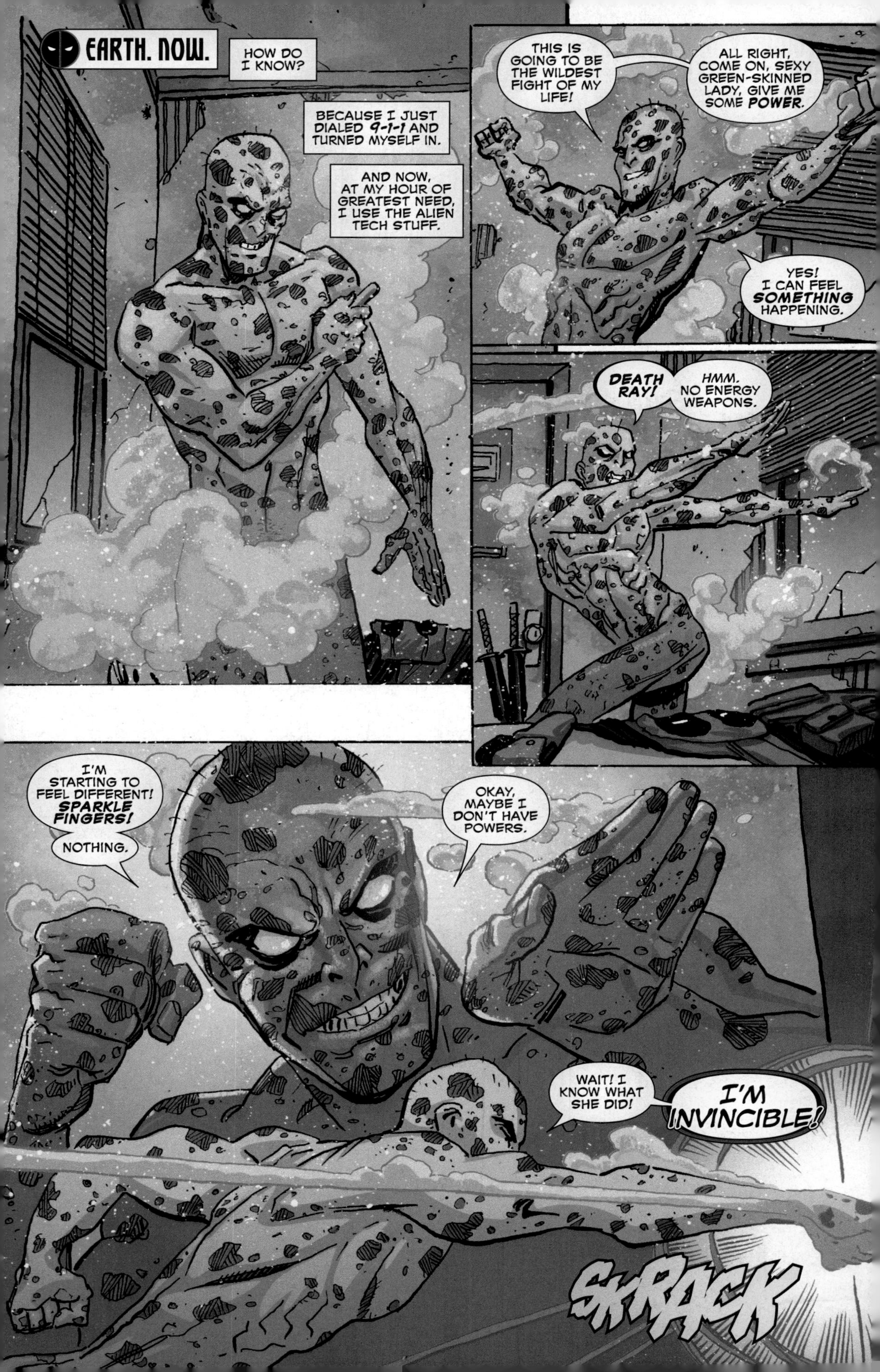
EARTH. NOW.
HOW DO I KNOW?
BECAUSE I JUST DIALED 9-1-1 AND TURNED MYSELF IN.
AND NOW, AT MY HOUR OF GREATEST NEED, I USE THE ALIEN TECH STUFF.
THIS IS GOING TO BE THE WILDEST FIGHT OF MY LIFE!
ALL RIGHT, COME ON, SEXY GREEN-SKINNED LADY, GIVE ME SOME POWER.
YES! I CAN FEEL SOMETHING HAPPENING.
DEATH RAY!
HMM. NO ENERGY WEAPONS.
I'M STARTING TO FEEL DIFFERENT! SPARKLE FINGERS!
NOTHING.
OKAY, MAYBE I DON'T HAVE POWERS.
WAIT! I KNOW WHAT SHE DID!
I'M INVINCIBLE!
SKRACK

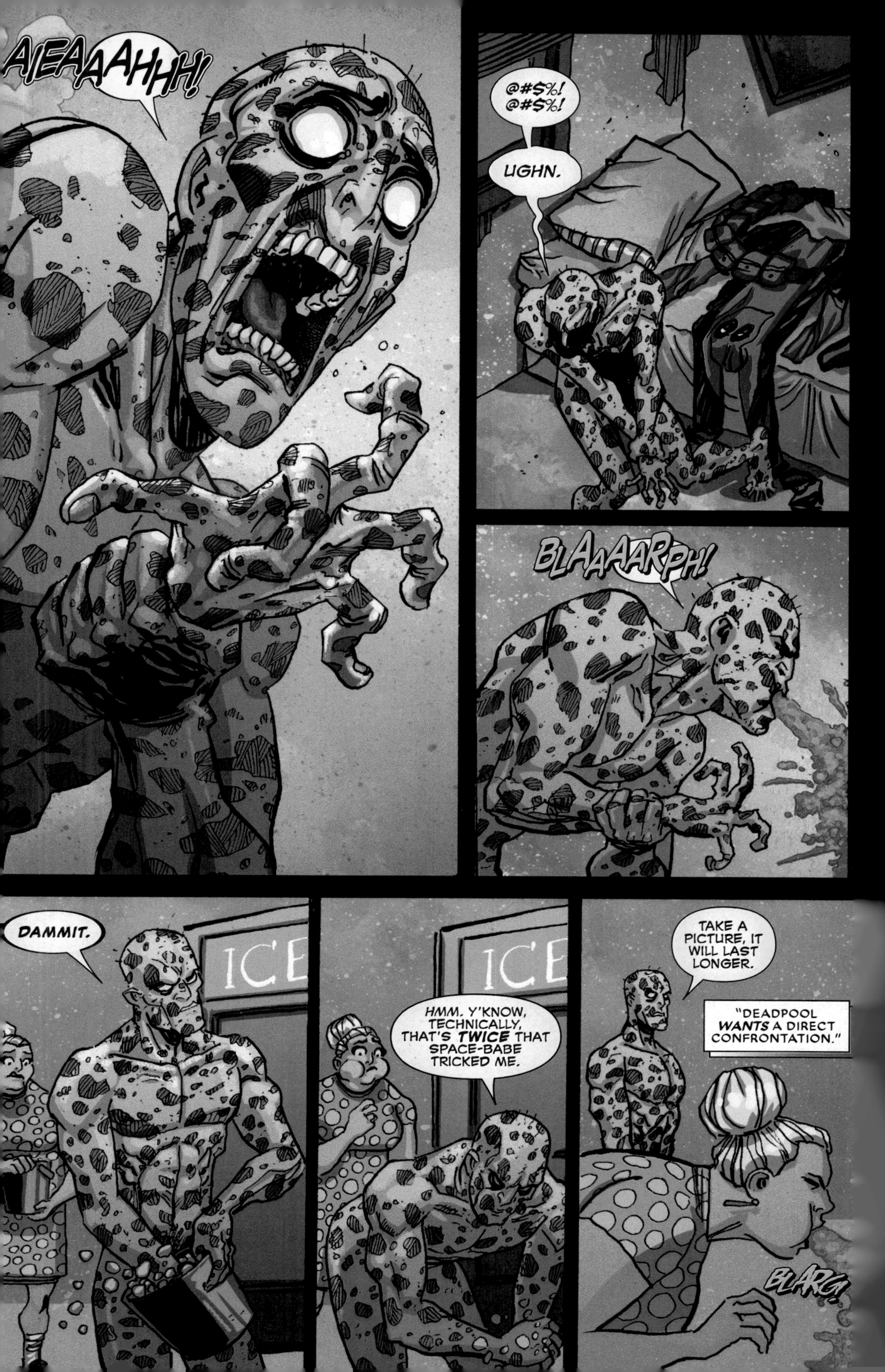
AIEAAAHHH!
@#$%! @#$%!
UGHN.
BLAAAARPH!
DAMMIT.
HMM. Y'KNOW, TECHNICALLY, THAT'S TWICE THAT SPACE-BABE TRICKED ME.
ICE
TAKE A PICTURE, IT WILL LAST LONGER.
"DEADPOOL WANTS A DIRECT CONFRONTATION."
BLARG!

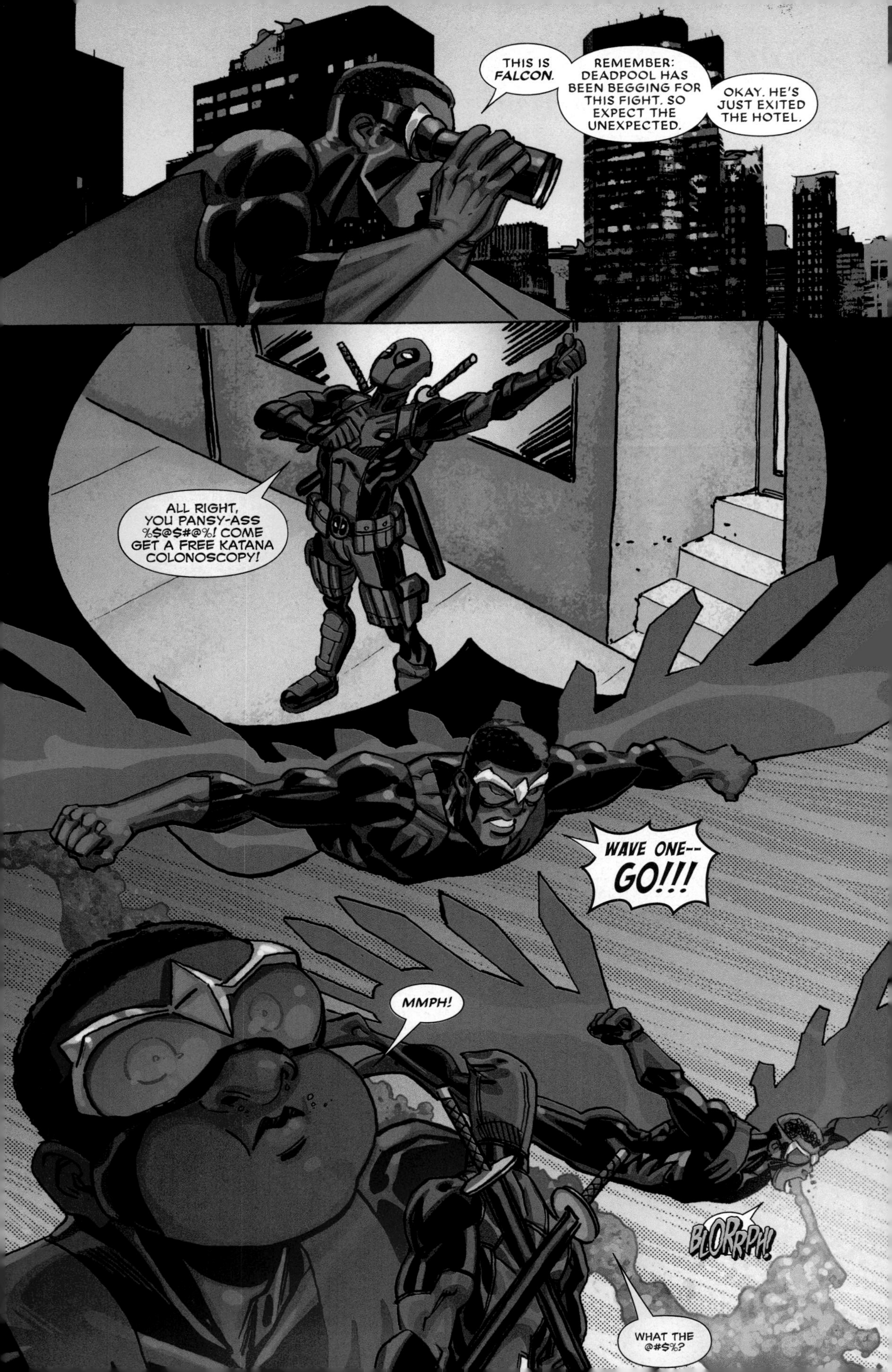
THIS IS *FALCON.*
REMEMBER: DEADPOOL HAS BEEN BEGGING FOR THIS FIGHT. SO EXPECT THE UNEXPECTED.
OKAY. HE'S JUST EXITED THE HOTEL.
ALL RIGHT, YOU PANSY-ASS %$@$#@%! COME GET A FREE KATANA COLONOSCOPY!
WAVE ONE-- GO!!!
MMPH!
BLORRPH!
WHAT THE @#$%?

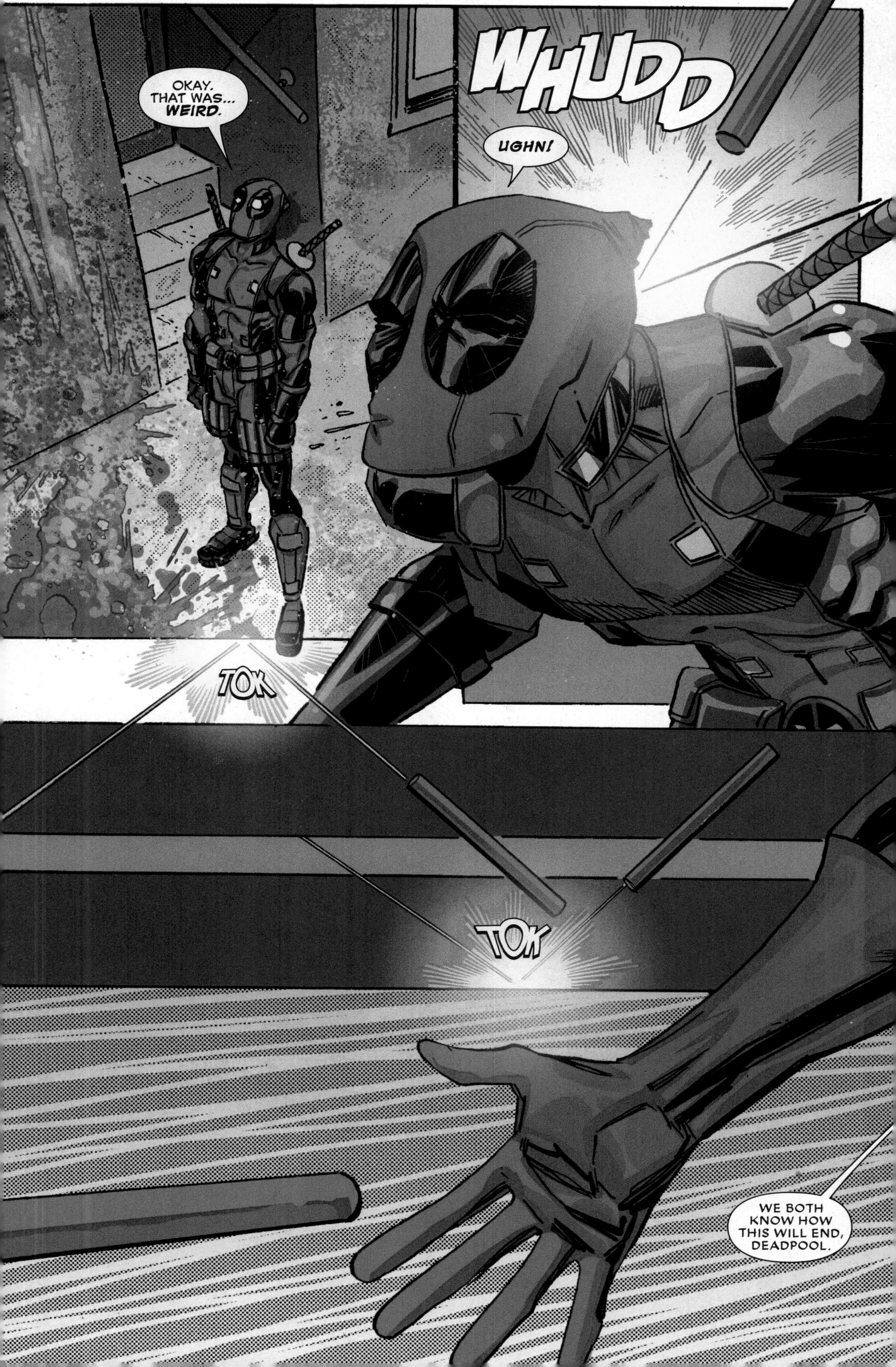
OKAY. THAT WAS... WEIRD.
WHUDD
UGHN!
TOK
TOK
WE BOTH KNOW HOW THIS WILL END, DEADPOOL.

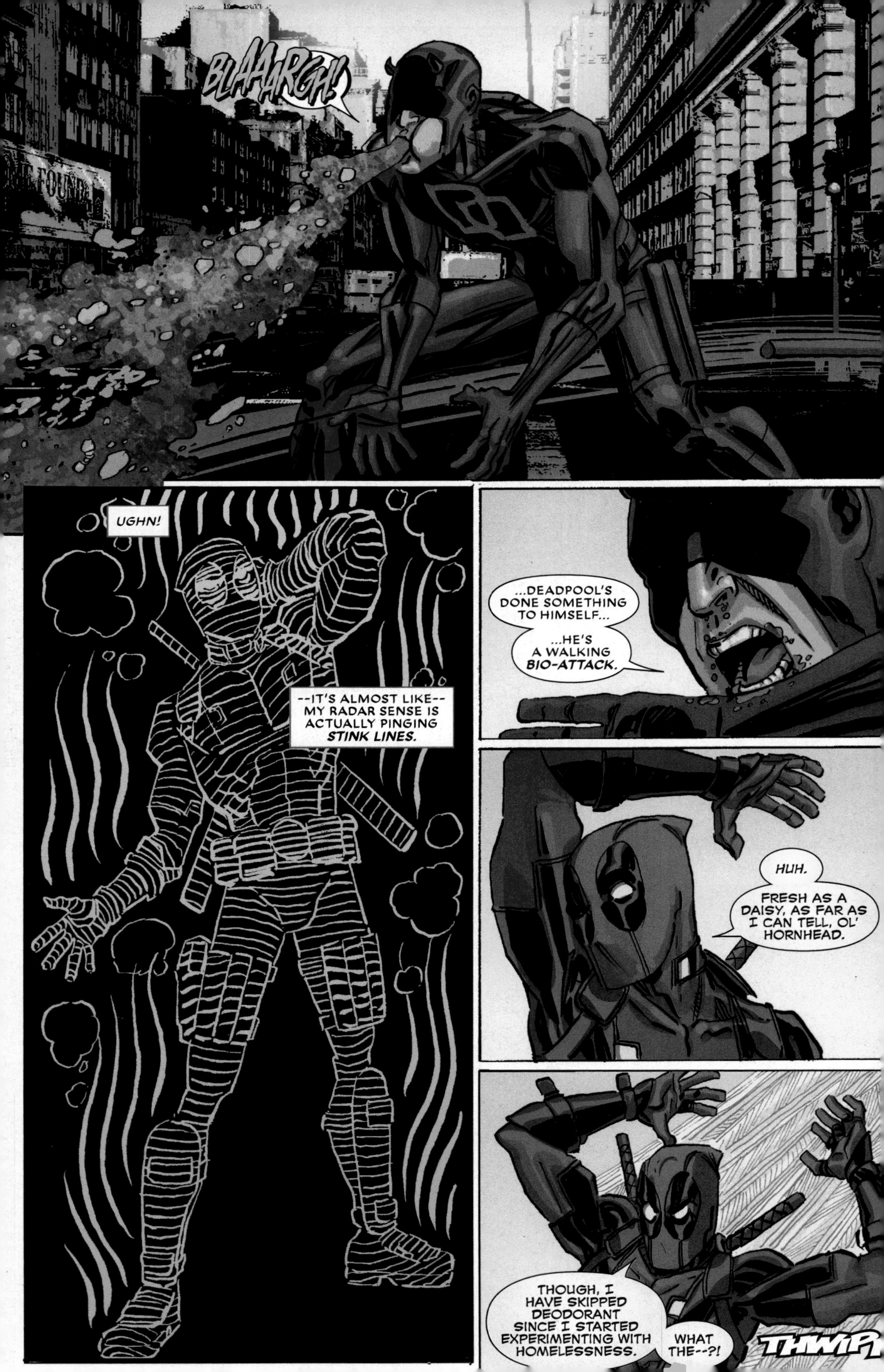
BLAAARGH!
UGHN!
--IT'S ALMOST LIKE--
MY RADAR SENSE IS
ACTUALLY PINGING
STINK LINES.
...DEADPOOL'S DONE SOMETHING TO HIMSELF...
...HE'S A WALKING BIO-ATTACK.
HUH.
FRESH AS A DAISY, AS FAR AS I CAN TELL, OL' HORNHEAD.
THOUGH, I HAVE SKIPPED DEODORANT SINCE I STARTED EXPERIMENTING WITH HOMELESSNESS.
WHAT THE--?!
THWIP

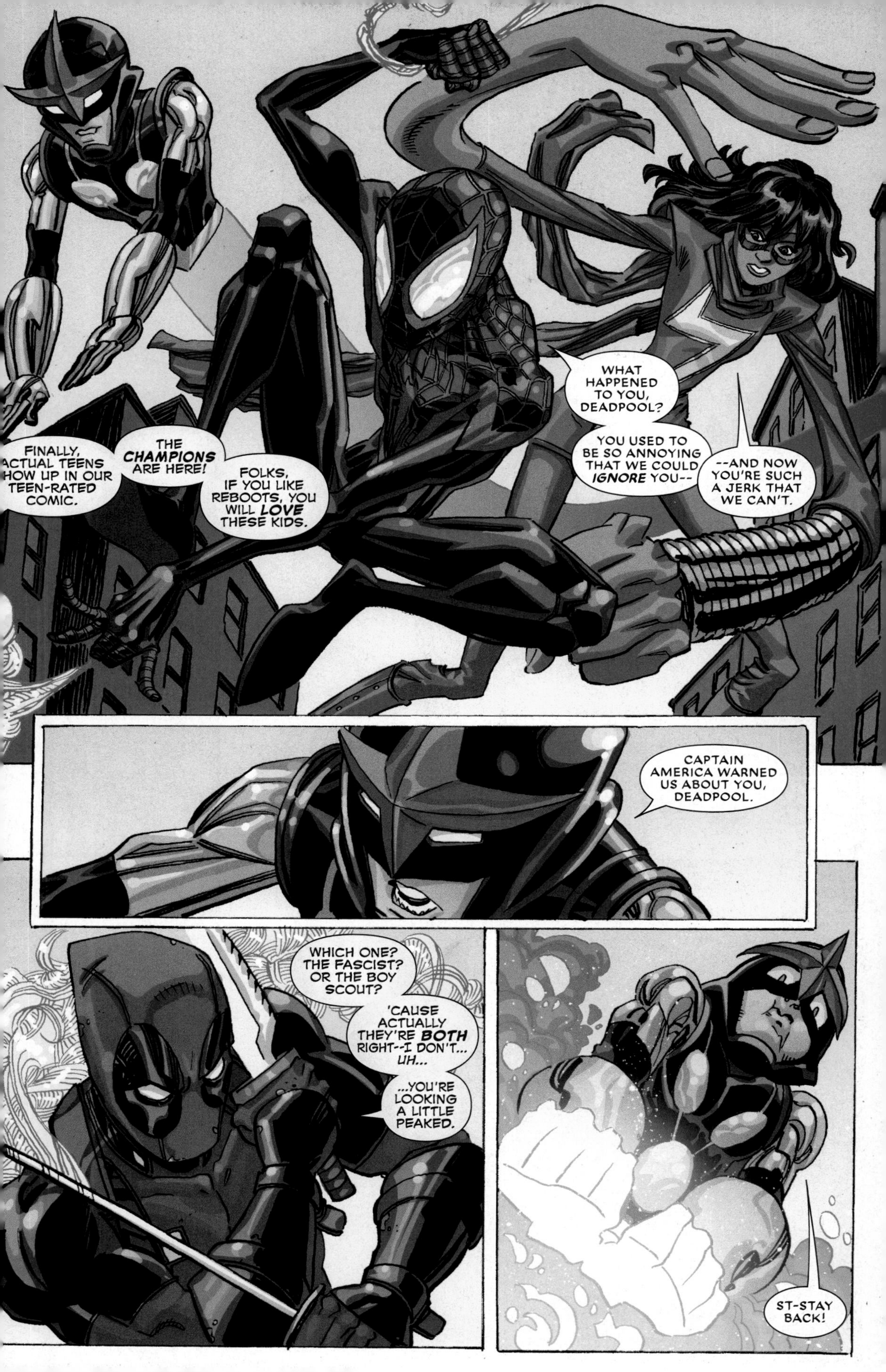
FINALLY, ACTUAL TEENS HOW UP IN OUR TEEN-RATED COMIC.
THE CHAMPIONS ARE HERE!
FOLKS, IF YOU LIKE REBOOTS, YOU WILL LOVE THESE KIDS.
WHAT HAPPENED TO YOU, DEADPOOL?
YOU USED TO BE SO ANNOYING THAT WE COULD IGNORE YOU--
--AND NOW YOU'RE SUCH A JERK THAT WE CAN'T.
CAPTAIN AMERICA WARNED US ABOUT YOU, DEADPOOL.
WHICH ONE? THE FASCIST? OR THE BOY SCOUT?
'CAUSE ACTUALLY THEY'RE BOTH RIGHT--I DON'T... UH...
...YOU'RE LOOKING A LITTLE PEAKED.
ST-STAY BACK!

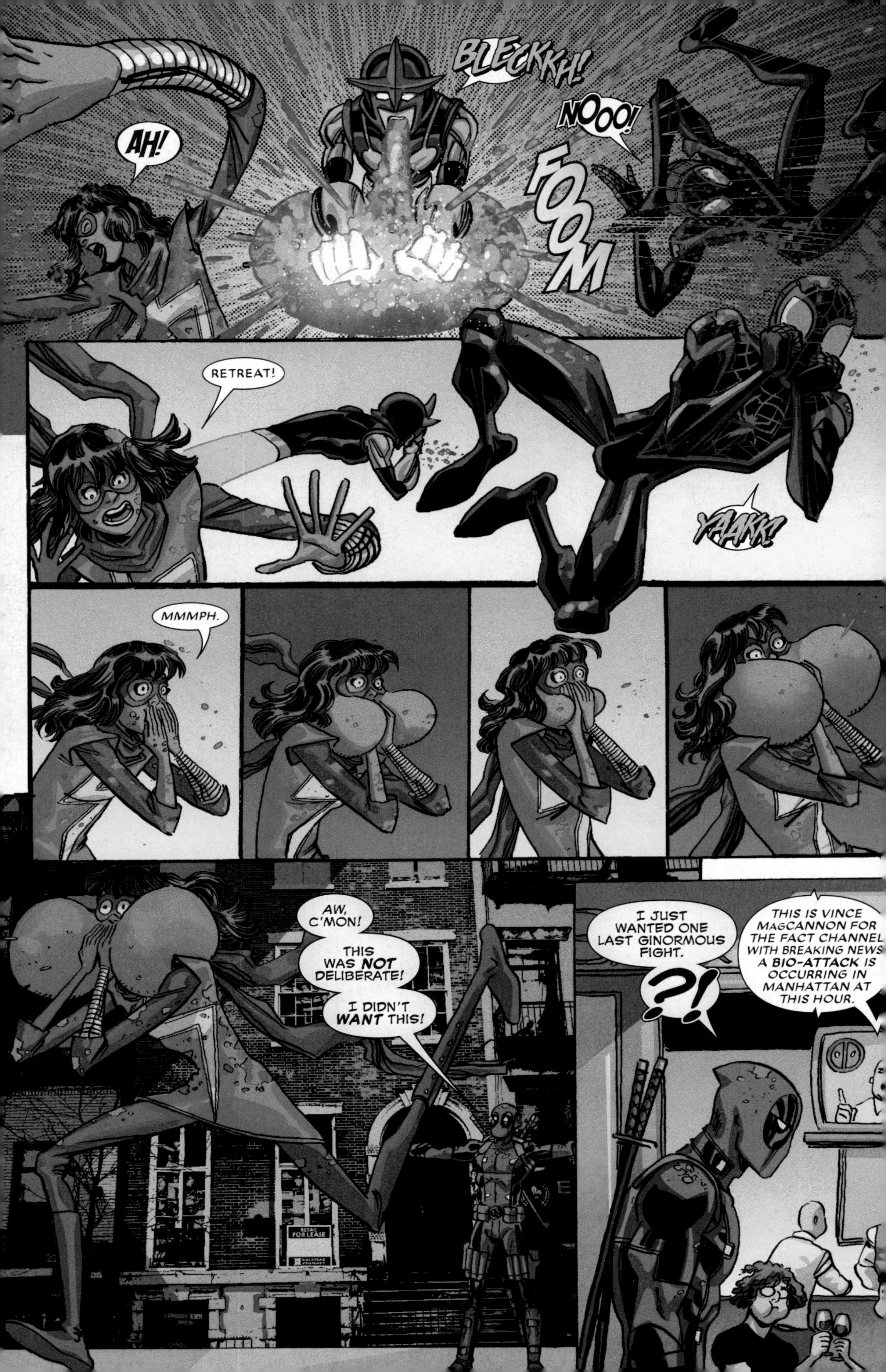
AH!
BLECKKH!
NOOO!
FOOM
RETREAT!
YAAKK!
MMMPH.
AW, C'MON!
THIS WAS NOT DELIBERATE!
I DIDN'T WANT THIS!
I JUST WANTED ONE LAST GINORMOUS FIGHT.
?!
THIS IS VINCE MAGCANNON FOR THE FACT CHANNEL WITH BREAKING NEWS. A BIO-ATTACK IS OCCURRING IN MANHATTAN AT THIS HOUR.
RETAIL FOR LEASE

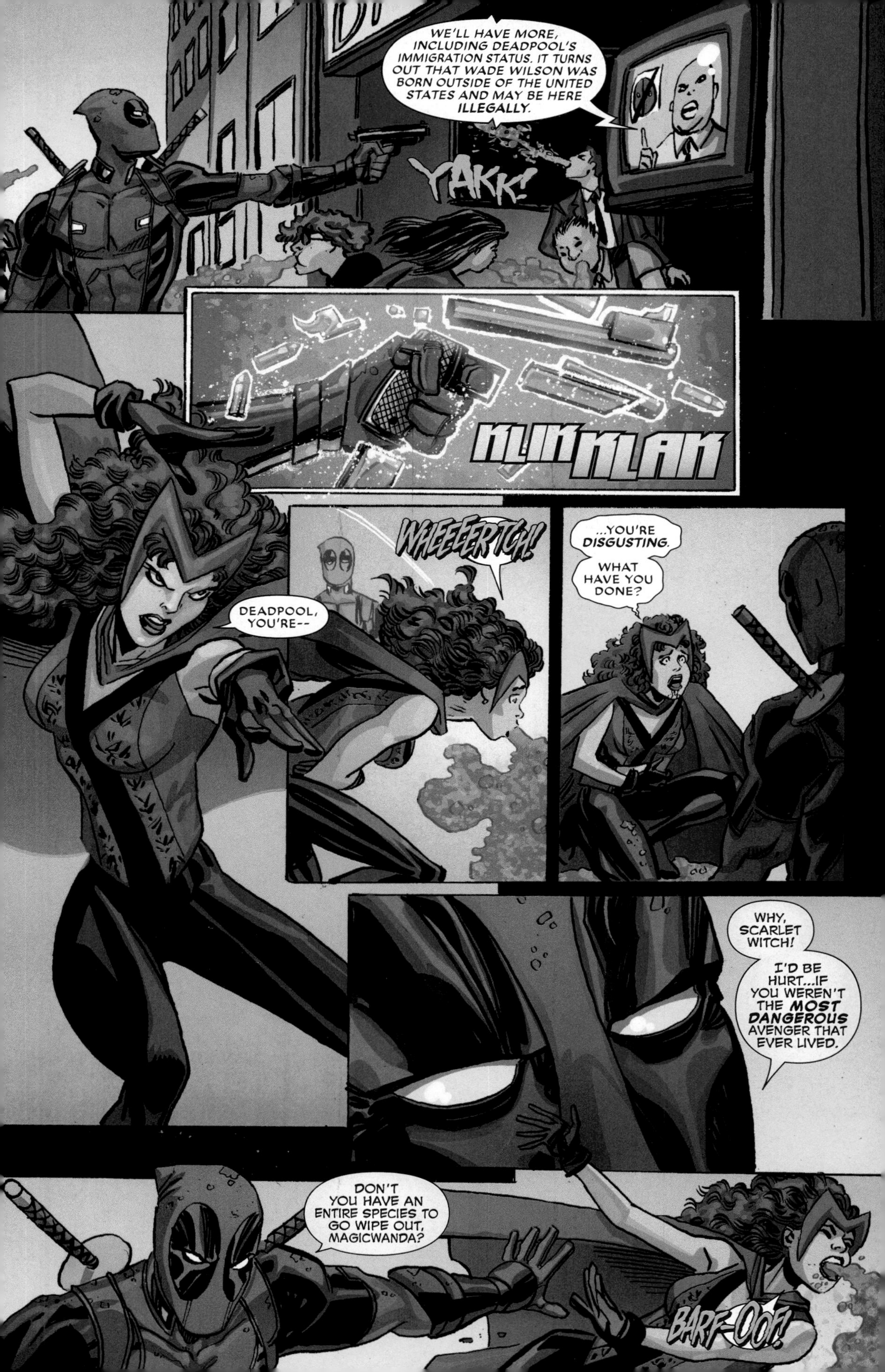

WE'LL HAVE MORE, INCLUDING DEADPOOL'S IMMIGRATION STATUS. IT TURNS OUT THAT WADE WILSON WAS BORN OUTSIDE OF THE UNITED STATES AND MAY BE HERE ILLEGALLY.
YAKK!
KLIK KLAK
DEADPOOL, YOU'RE--
WHEEEERTCH!
...YOU'RE DISGUSTING.
WHAT HAVE YOU DONE?
WHY, SCARLET WITCH!
I'D BE HURT...IF YOU WEREN'T THE MOST DANGEROUS AVENGER THAT EVER LIVED.
DON'T YOU HAVE AN ENTIRE SPECIES TO GO WIPE OUT, MAGICWANDA?
BARF-OOF!

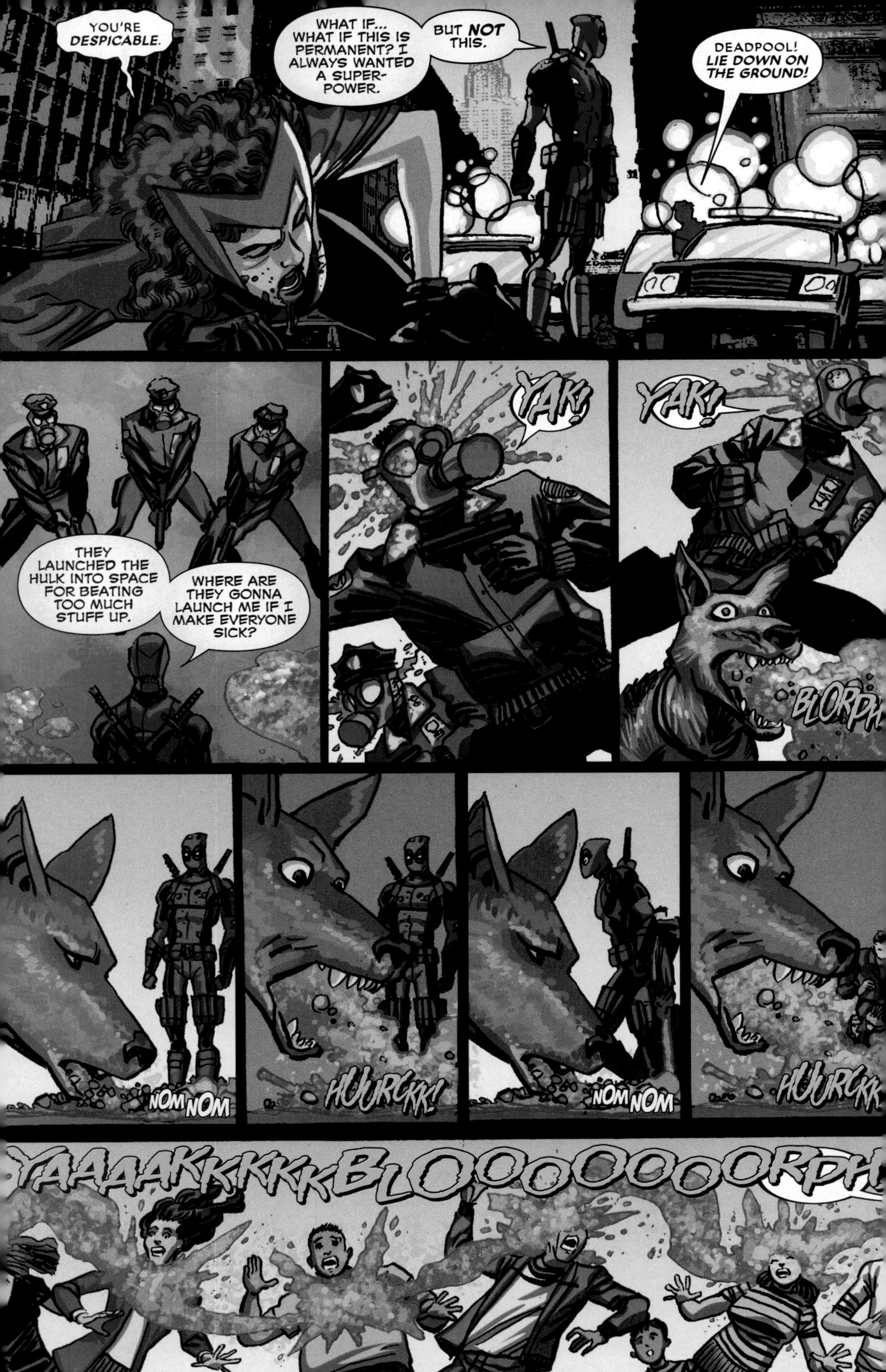
YOU'RE DESPICABLE.
WHAT IF... WHAT IF THIS IS PERMANENT? I ALWAYS WANTED A SUPER-POWER.
BUT NOT THIS.
DEADPOOL! LIE DOWN ON THE GROUND!
THEY LAUNCHED THE HULK INTO SPACE FOR BEATING TOO MUCH STUFF UP.
WHERE ARE THEY GONNA LAUNCH ME IF I MAKE EVERYONE SICK?
YAK!
YAK!
BLORPH
NOM NOM
HUURGKK!
NOM NOM
HUURGKK
YAAAAKKKKKBLOOOOOOOORPH!

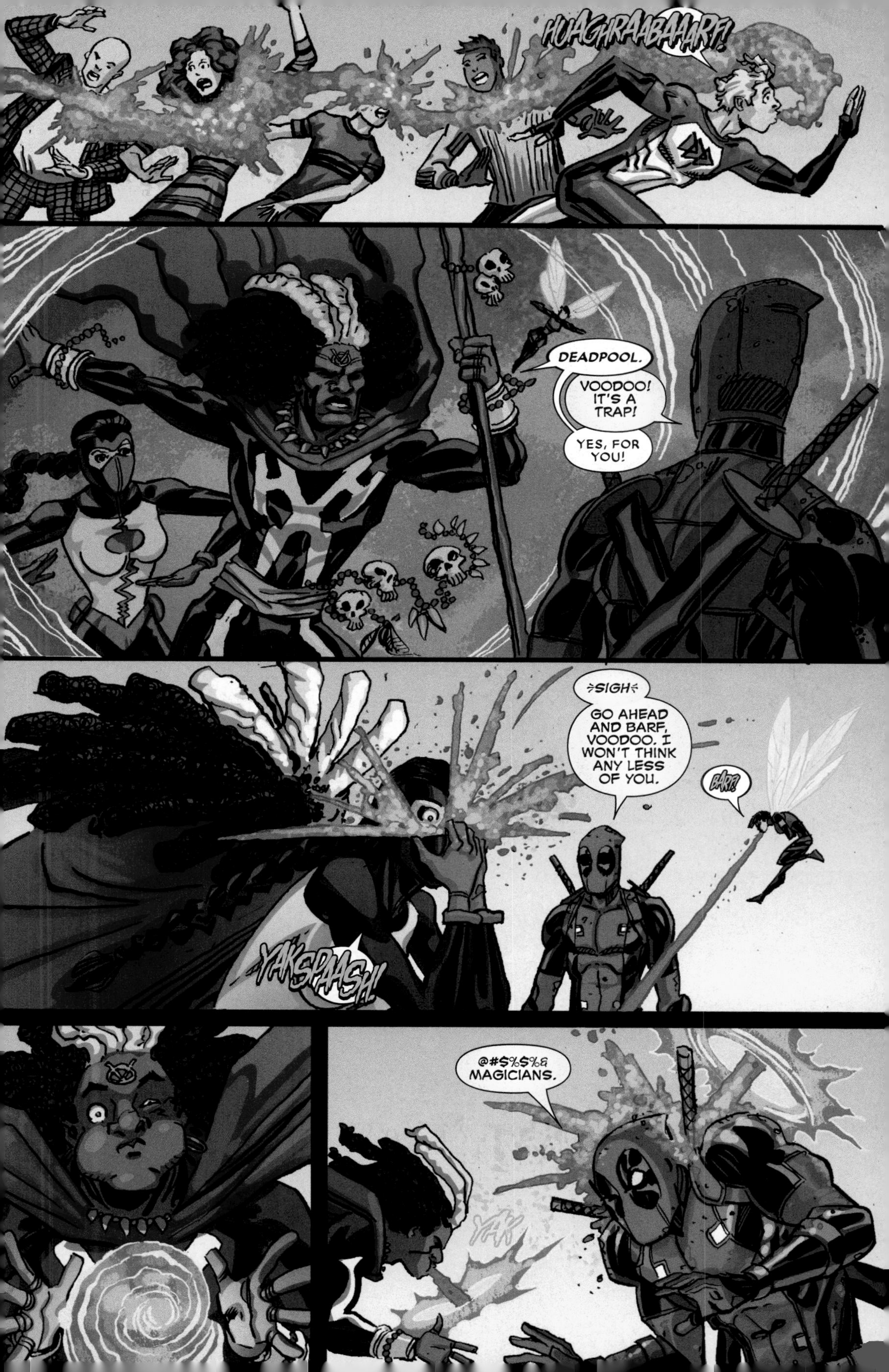
HUAGHRAABAAARF!
DEADPOOL.
VOODOO! IT'S A TRAP!
YES, FOR YOU!
SIGH
GO AHEAD AND BARF, VOODOO. I WON'T THINK ANY LESS OF YOU.
BARF!
YAKSPAASH!
@#$%$%& MAGICIANS.
YAK

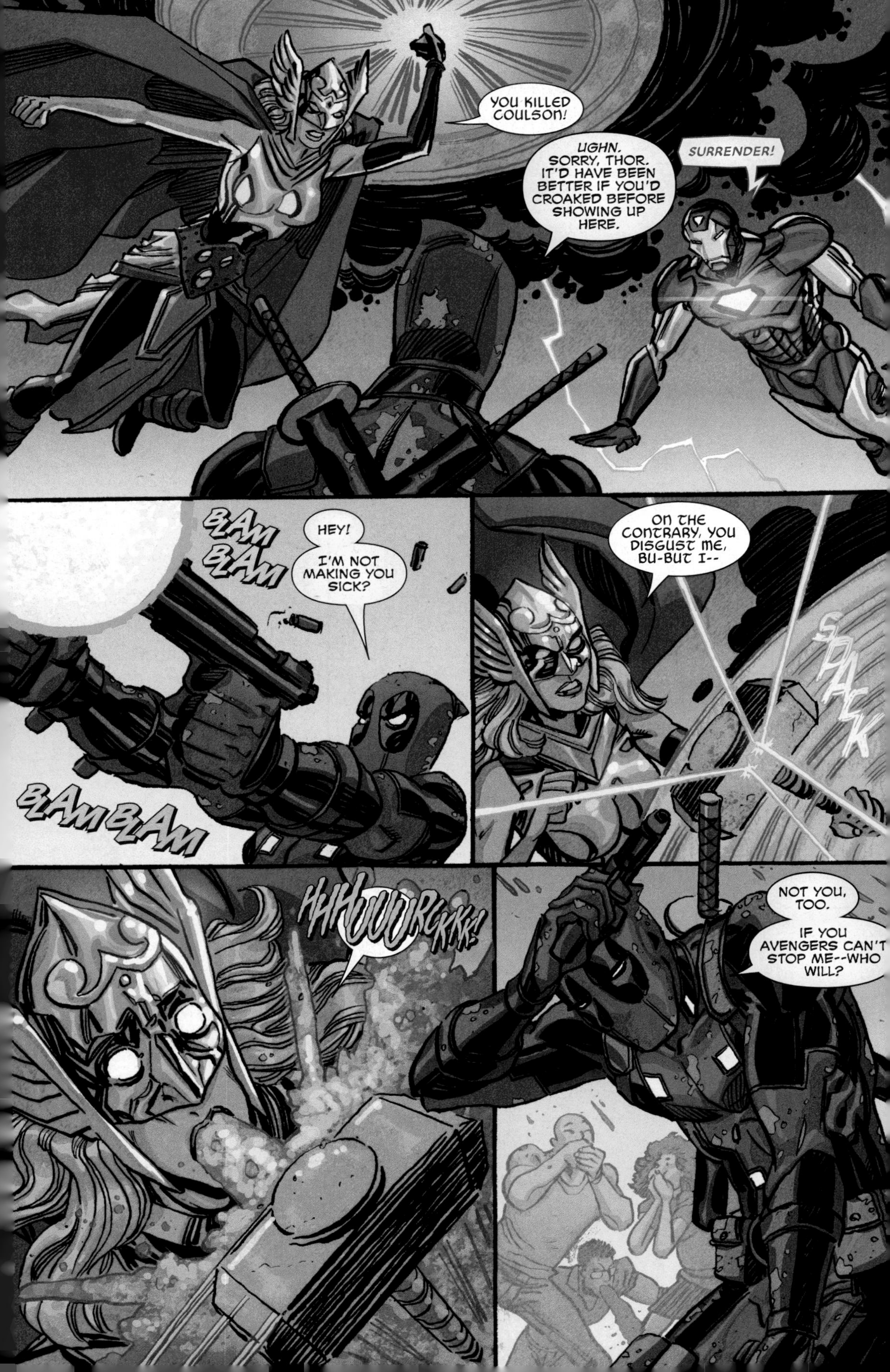
YOU KILLED COULSON!
UGHN. SORRY, THOR. IT'D HAVE BEEN BETTER IF YOU'D CROAKED BEFORE SHOWING UP HERE.
SURRENDER!
BLAM BLAM
HEY!
I'M NOT MAKING YOU SICK?
BLAM BLAM
ON THE CONTRARY, YOU DISGUST ME, BU-BUT I--
SPAK
HHHUUURCKKK!
NOT YOU, TOO.
IF YOU AVENGERS CAN'T STOP ME--WHO WILL?

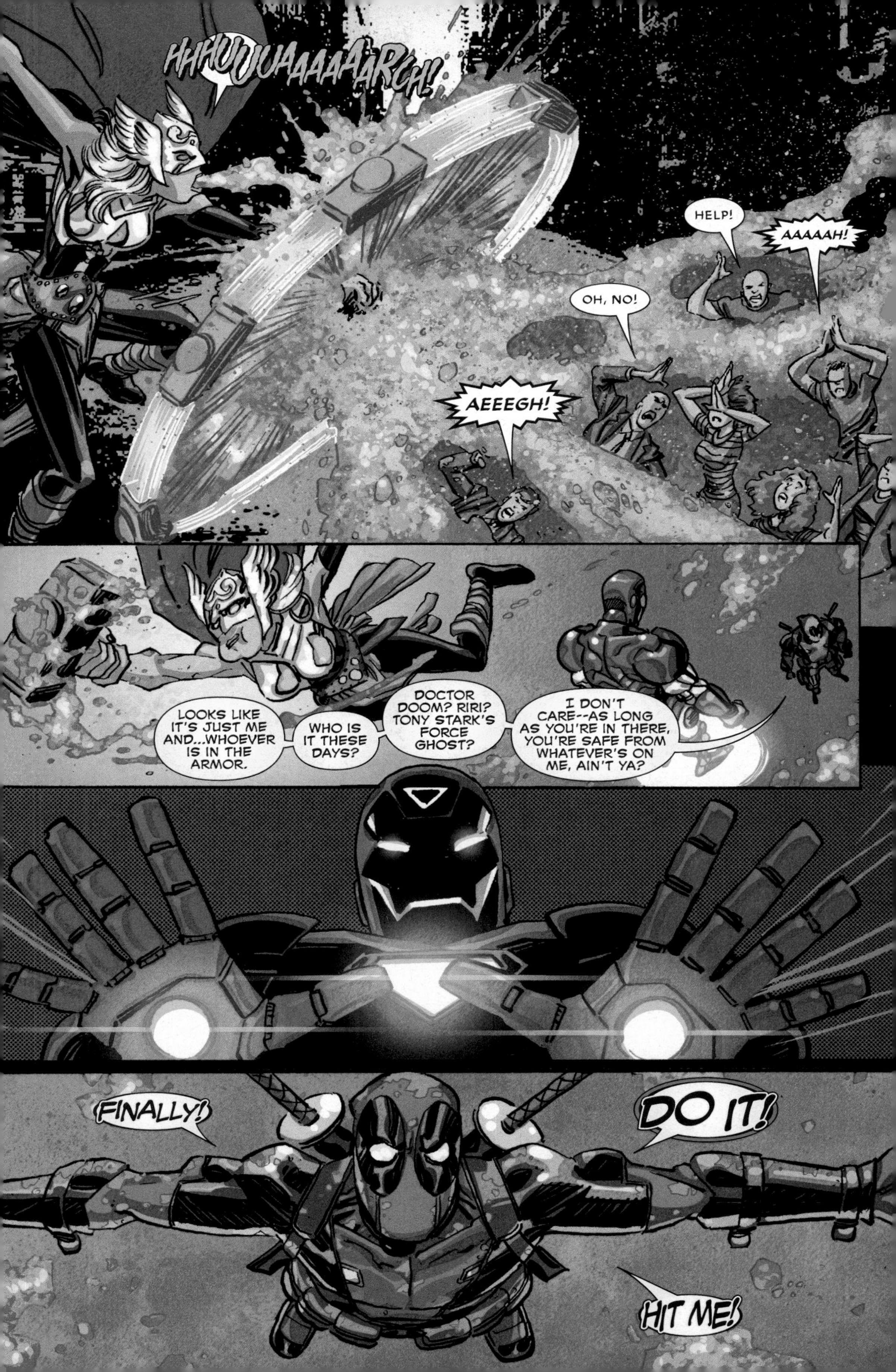
HHHUUUUAAAAAARCH!
HELP!
AAAAAH!
OH, NO!
AEEEGH!
LOOKS LIKE IT'S JUST ME AND...WHOEVER IS IN THE ARMOR.
WHO IS IT THESE DAYS?
DOCTOR DOOM? RIRI? TONY STARK'S FORCE GHOST?
I DON'T CARE--AS LONG AS YOU'RE IN THERE, YOU'RE SAFE FROM WHATEVER'S ON ME, AIN'T YA?
FINALLY!
DO IT!
HIT ME!

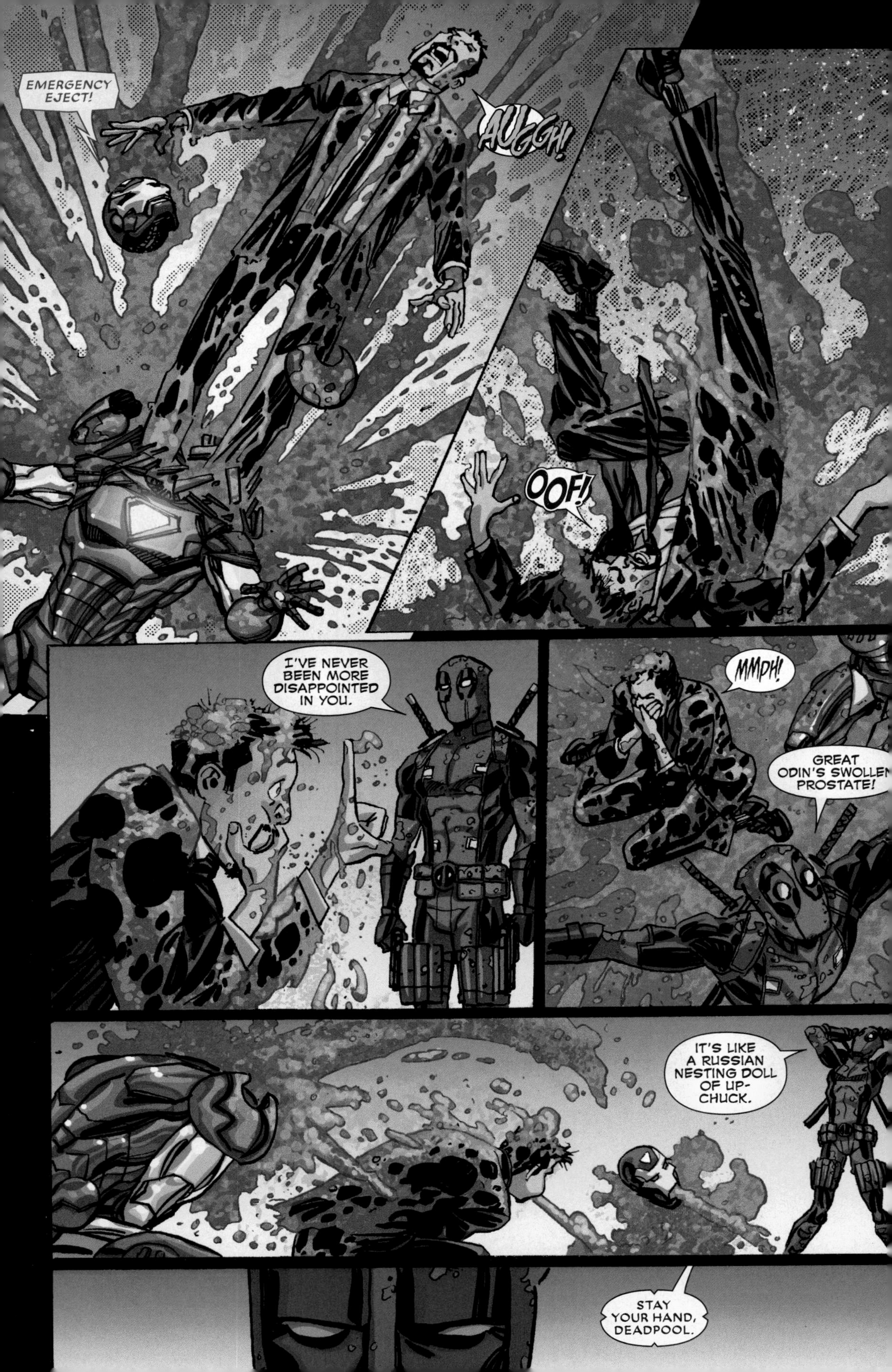
EMERGENCY EJECT!
AUGGH!
OOF!
I'VE NEVER BEEN MORE DISAPPOINTED IN YOU.
MMPH!
GREAT ODIN'S SWOLLEN PROSTATE!
IT'S LIKE A RUSSIAN NESTING DOLL OF UP-CHUCK.
STAY YOUR HAND, DEADPOOL.

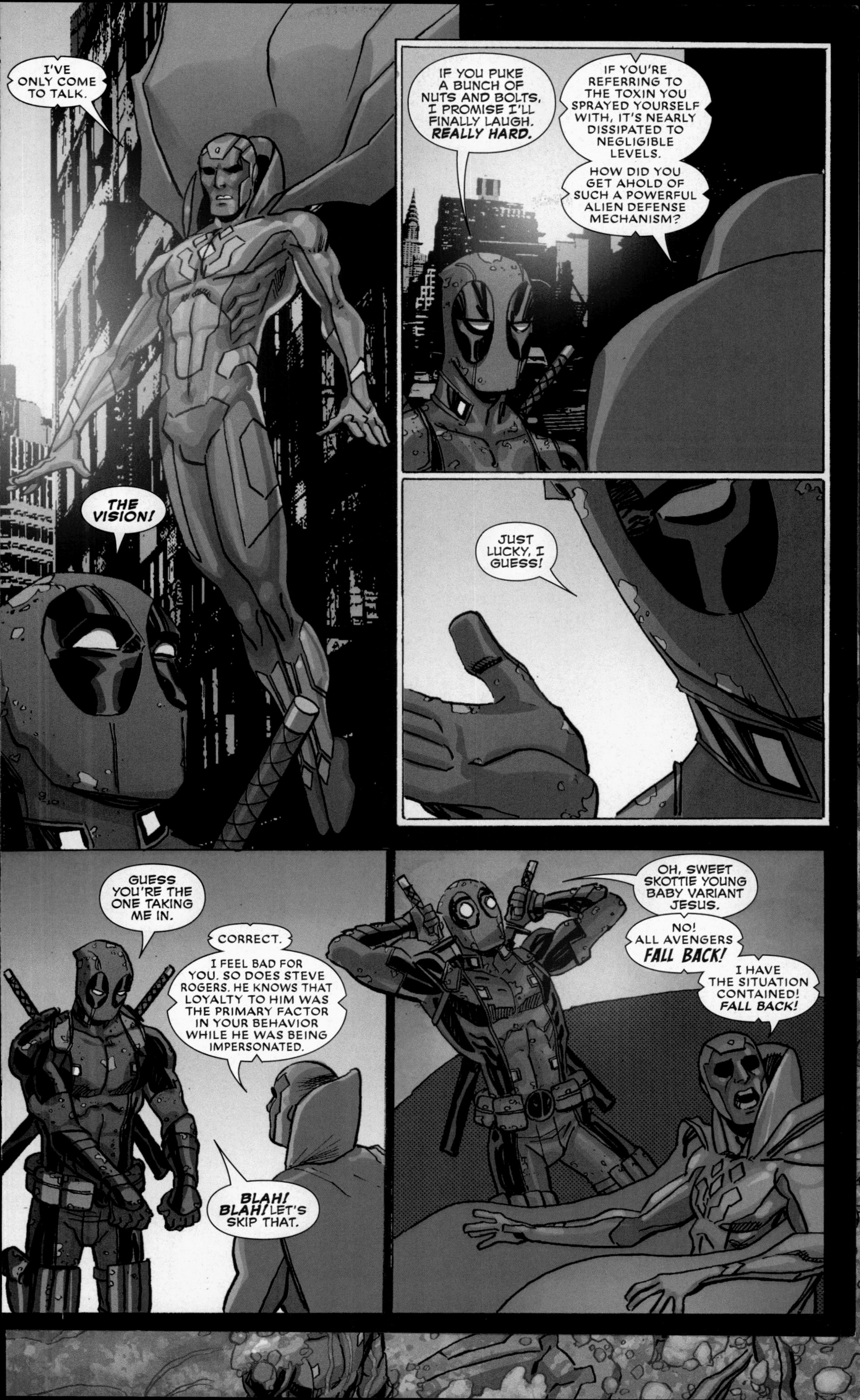
I'VE ONLY COME TO TALK.
THE VISION!
IF YOU PUKE A BUNCH OF NUTS AND BOLTS, I PROMISE I'LL FINALLY LAUGH. REALLY HARD.
IF YOU'RE REFERRING TO THE TOXIN YOU SPRAYED YOURSELF WITH, IT'S NEARLY DISSIPATED TO NEGLIGIBLE LEVELS.
HOW DID YOU GET AHOLD OF SUCH A POWERFUL ALIEN DEFENSE MECHANISM?
JUST LUCKY, I GUESS!
GUESS YOU'RE THE ONE TAKING ME IN.
CORRECT.
I FEEL BAD FOR YOU. SO DOES STEVE ROGERS. HE KNOWS THAT LOYALTY TO HIM WAS THE PRIMARY FACTOR IN YOUR BEHAVIOR WHILE HE WAS BEING IMPERSONATED.
BLAH! BLAH! LET'S SKIP THAT.
OH, SWEET SKOTTIE YOUNG BABY VARIANT JESUS.
NO! ALL AVENGERS FALL BACK!
I HAVE THE SITUATION CONTAINED! FALL BACK!

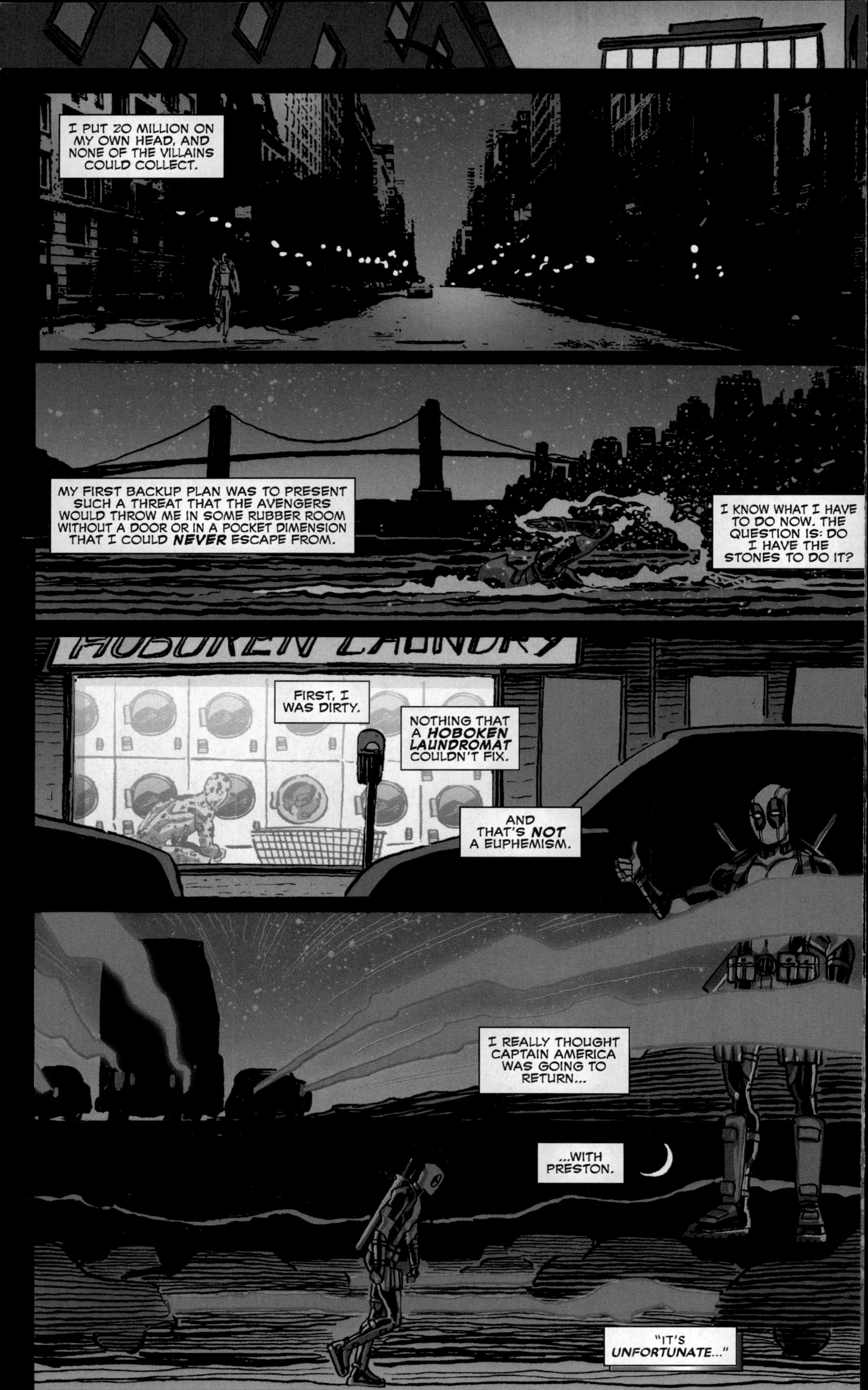
I PUT 20 MILLION ON MY OWN HEAD, AND NONE OF THE VILLAINS COULD COLLECT.
MY FIRST BACKUP PLAN WAS TO PRESENT SUCH A THREAT THAT THE AVENGERS WOULD THROW ME IN SOME RUBBER ROOM WITHOUT A DOOR OR IN A POCKET DIMENSION THAT I COULD NEVER ESCAPE FROM.
I KNOW WHAT I HAVE TO DO NOW. THE QUESTION IS: DO I HAVE THE STONES TO DO IT?
HOBOKEN LAUNDRY
FIRST, I WAS DIRTY.
NOTHING THAT A HOBOKEN LAUNDROMAT COULDN'T FIX.
AND THAT'S NOT A EUPHEMISM.
I REALLY THOUGHT CAPTAIN AMERICA WAS GOING TO RETURN...
...WITH PRESTON.
"IT'S UNFORTUNATE..."

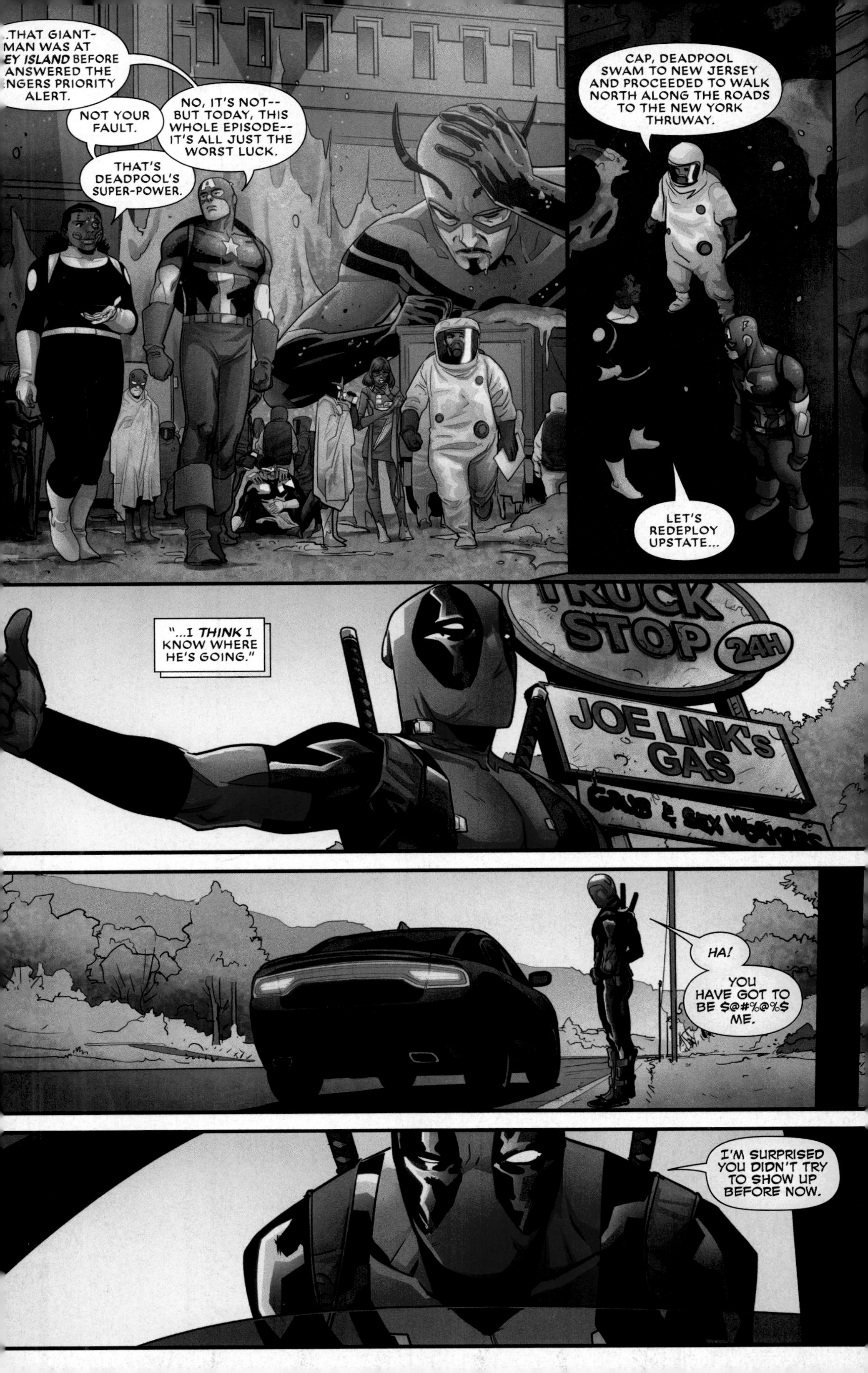
..THAT GIANT-MAN WAS AT EY ISLAND BEFORE ANSWERED THE ENGERS PRIORITY ALERT.
NOT YOUR FAULT.
NO, IT'S NOT-- BUT TODAY, THIS WHOLE EPISODE-- IT'S ALL JUST THE WORST LUCK.
THAT'S DEADPOOL'S SUPER-POWER.
CAP, DEADPOOL SWAM TO NEW JERSEY AND PROCEEDED TO WALK NORTH ALONG THE ROADS TO THE NEW YORK THRUWAY.
LET'S REDEPLOY UPSTATE...
"...I THINK I KNOW WHERE HE'S GOING."
TRUCK STOP 24H
JOE LINK's GAS
GRUB & SEX WORKERS
HA!
YOU HAVE GOT TO BE $@#%@%$ ME.
I'M SURPRISED YOU DIDN'T TRY TO SHOW UP BEFORE NOW.

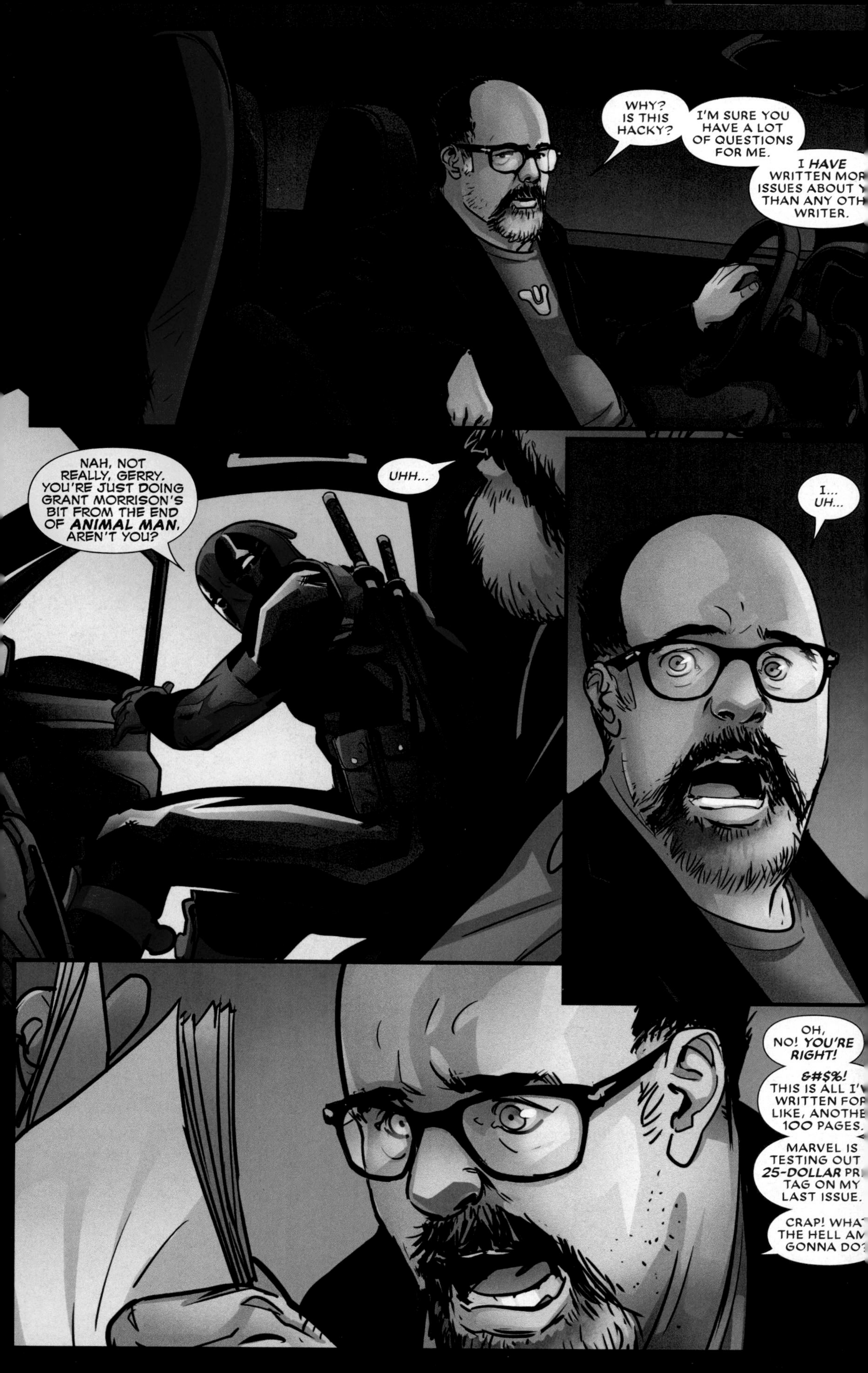

WHY? IS THIS HACKY?
I'M SURE YOU HAVE A LOT OF QUESTIONS FOR ME.
I HAVE WRITTEN MOR ISSUES ABOUT Y THAN ANY OTH WRITER.
NAH, NOT REALLY, GERRY. YOU'RE JUST DOING GRANT MORRISON'S BIT FROM THE END OF ANIMAL MAN, AREN'T YOU?
UHH...
I... UH...
OH, NO! YOU'RE RIGHT!
&#$%! THIS IS ALL I' WRITTEN FOR LIKE, ANOTHE 100 PAGES.
MARVEL IS TESTING OUT 25-DOLLAR PR TAG ON MY LAST ISSUE.
CRAP! WHA THE HELL AM GONNA DO

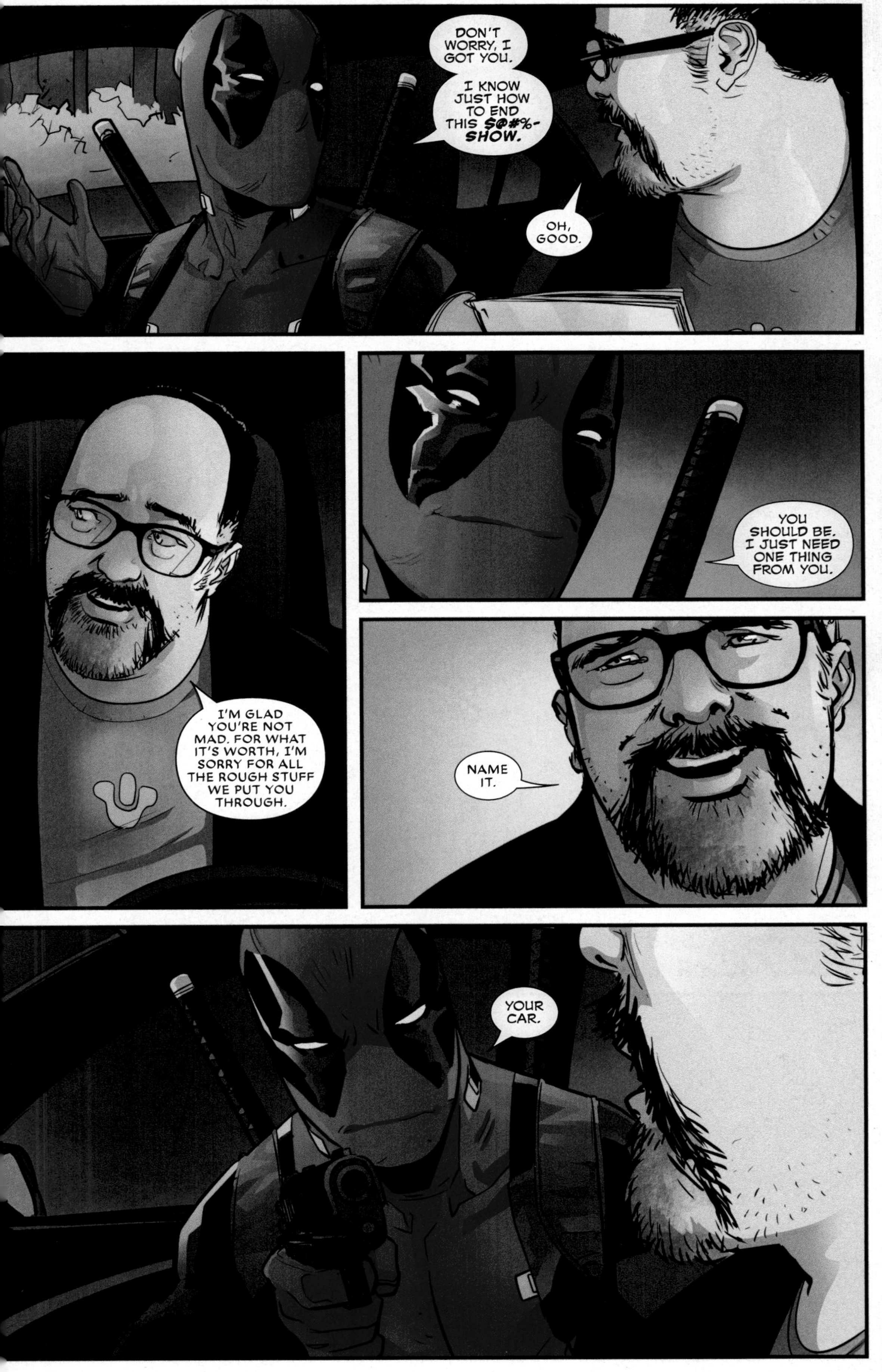

DON'T WORRY, I GOT YOU.
I KNOW JUST HOW TO END THIS $@#%-SHOW.
OH, GOOD.
I'M GLAD YOU'RE NOT MAD. FOR WHAT IT'S WORTH, I'M SORRY FOR ALL THE ROUGH STUFF WE PUT YOU THROUGH.
YOU SHOULD BE. I JUST NEED ONE THING FROM YOU.
NAME IT.
YOUR CAR.

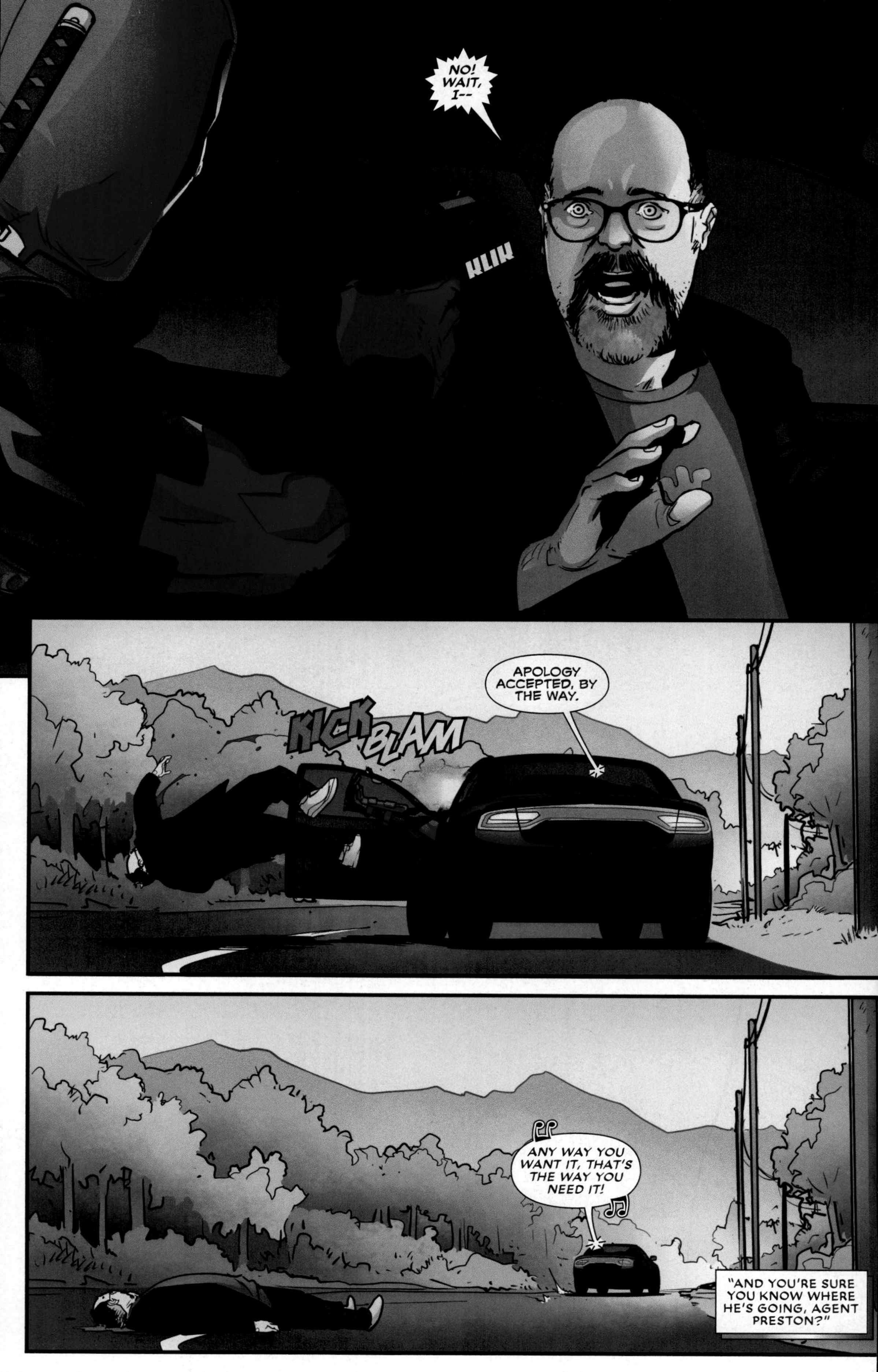
NO! WAIT, I--
KLIK
APOLOGY ACCEPTED, BY THE WAY.
KICK
BLAM
ANY WAY YOU WANT IT, THAT'S THE WAY YOU NEED IT!
"AND YOU'RE SURE YOU KNOW WHERE HE'S GOING, AGENT PRESTON?"

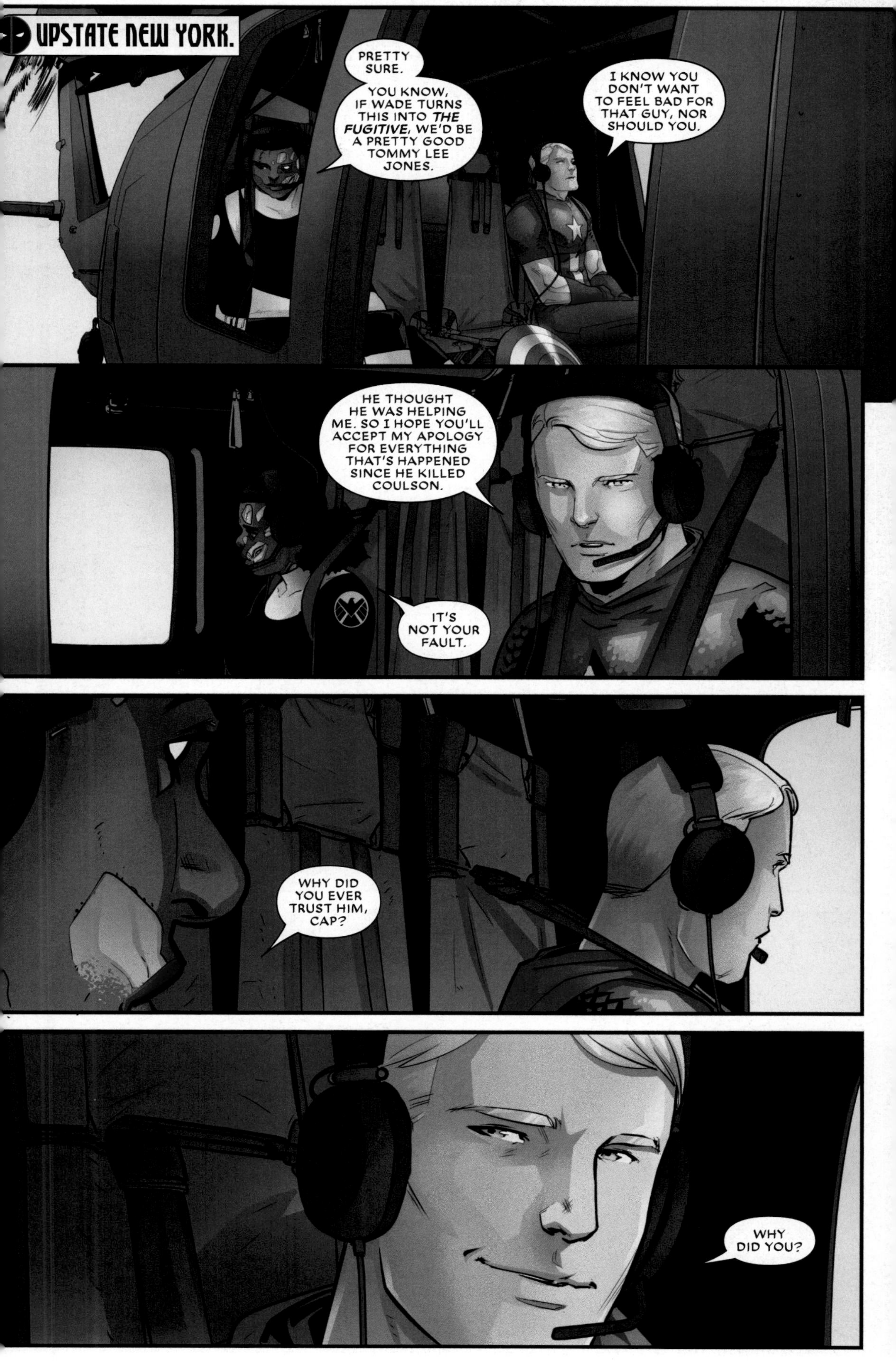
UPSTATE NEW YORK.
PRETTY SURE.
YOU KNOW, IF WADE TURNS THIS INTO *THE FUGITIVE*, WE'D BE A PRETTY GOOD TOMMY LEE JONES.
I KNOW YOU DON'T WANT TO FEEL BAD FOR THAT GUY, NOR SHOULD YOU.
HE THOUGHT HE WAS HELPING ME. SO I HOPE YOU'LL ACCEPT MY APOLOGY FOR EVERYTHING THAT'S HAPPENED SINCE HE KILLED COULSON.
IT'S NOT YOUR FAULT.
WHY DID YOU EVER TRUST HIM, CAP?
WHY DID YOU?

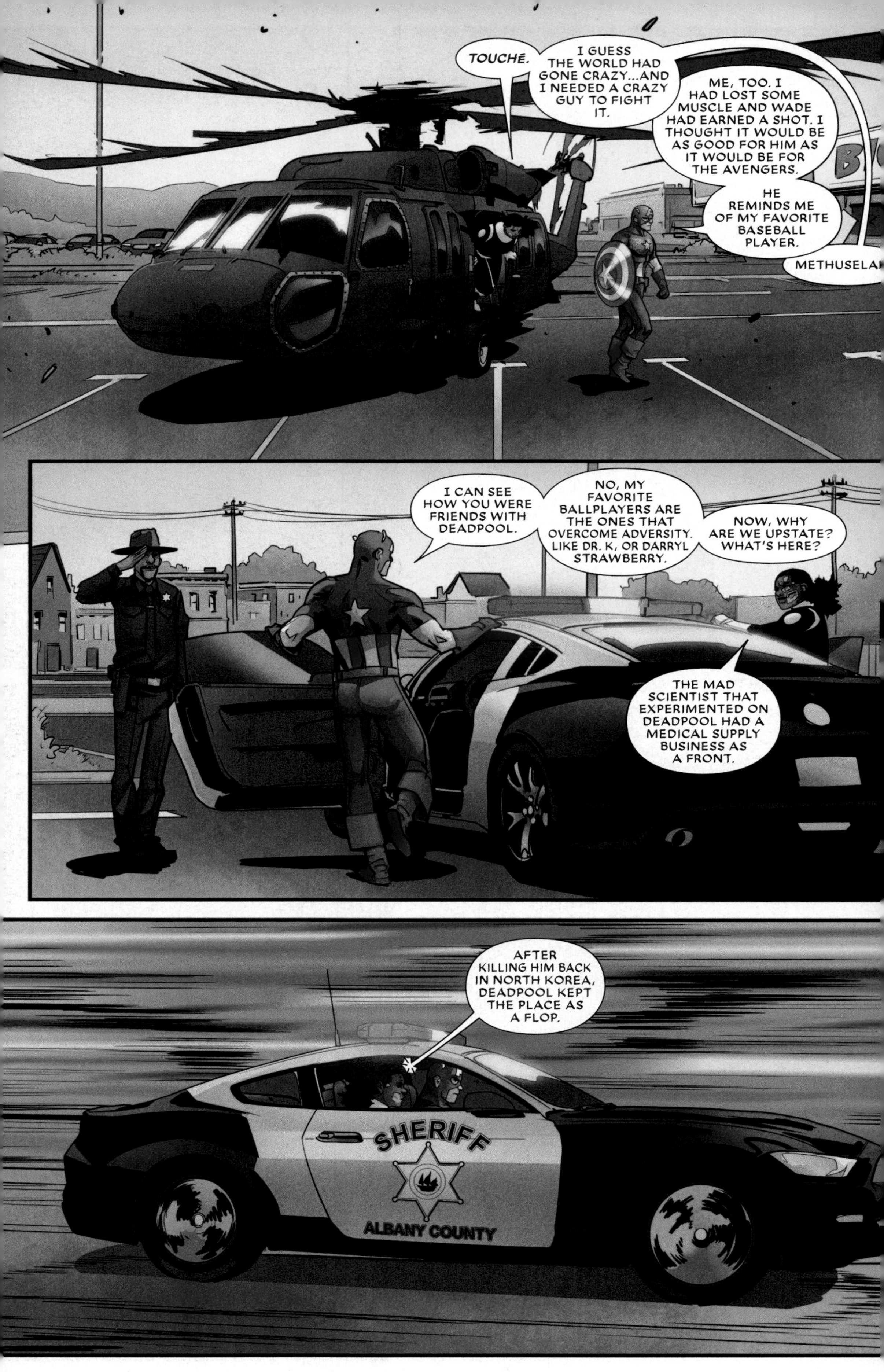
TOUCHÉ.
I GUESS THE WORLD HAD GONE CRAZY...AND I NEEDED A CRAZY GUY TO FIGHT IT.
ME, TOO. I HAD LOST SOME MUSCLE AND WADE HAD EARNED A SHOT. I THOUGHT IT WOULD BE AS GOOD FOR HIM AS IT WOULD BE FOR THE AVENGERS.
HE REMINDS ME OF MY FAVORITE BASEBALL PLAYER.
METHUSELA
I CAN SEE HOW YOU WERE FRIENDS WITH DEADPOOL.
NO, MY FAVORITE BALLPLAYERS ARE THE ONES THAT OVERCOME ADVERSITY. LIKE DR. K, OR DARRYL STRAWBERRY.
NOW, WHY ARE WE UPSTATE? WHAT'S HERE?
THE MAD SCIENTIST THAT EXPERIMENTED ON DEADPOOL HAD A MEDICAL SUPPLY BUSINESS AS A FRONT.
AFTER KILLING HIM BACK IN NORTH KOREA, DEADPOOL KEPT THE PLACE AS A FLOP.
SHERIFF
ALBANY COUNTY

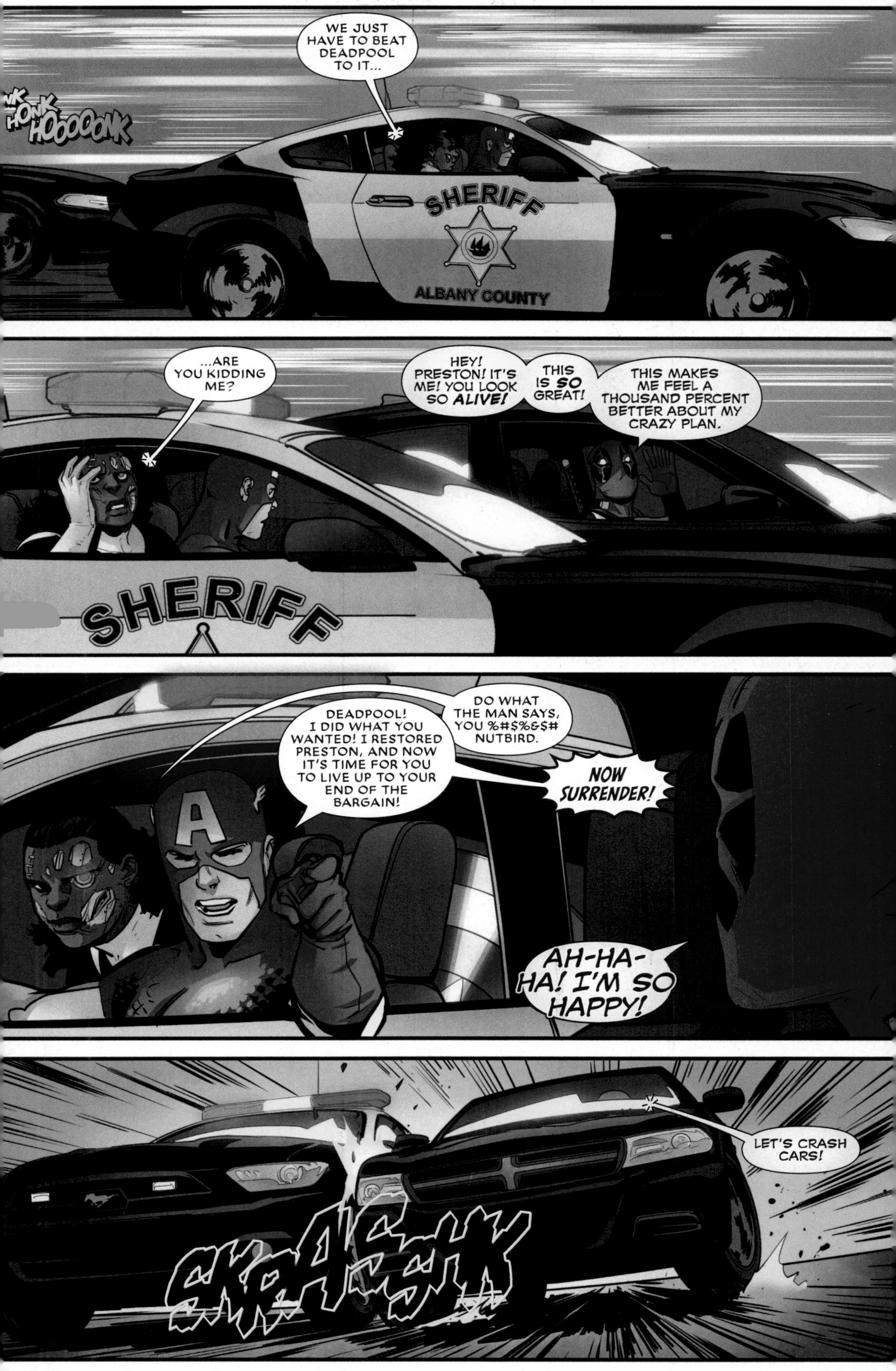
WE JUST HAVE TO BEAT DEADPOOL TO IT...
NK HONK HOOOOONK
SHERIFF
ALBANY COUNTY
...ARE YOU KIDDING ME?
HEY! PRESTON! IT'S ME! YOU LOOK SO ALIVE!
THIS IS SO GREAT!
THIS MAKES ME FEEL A THOUSAND PERCENT BETTER ABOUT MY CRAZY PLAN.
SHERIFF
DEADPOOL! I DID WHAT YOU WANTED! I RESTORED PRESTON, AND NOW IT'S TIME FOR YOU TO LIVE UP TO YOUR END OF THE BARGAIN!
DO WHAT THE MAN SAYS, YOU %#$%&$# NUTBIRD.
NOW SURRENDER!
AH-HA-HA! I'M SO HAPPY!
LET'S CRASH CARS!
SKRASSHK

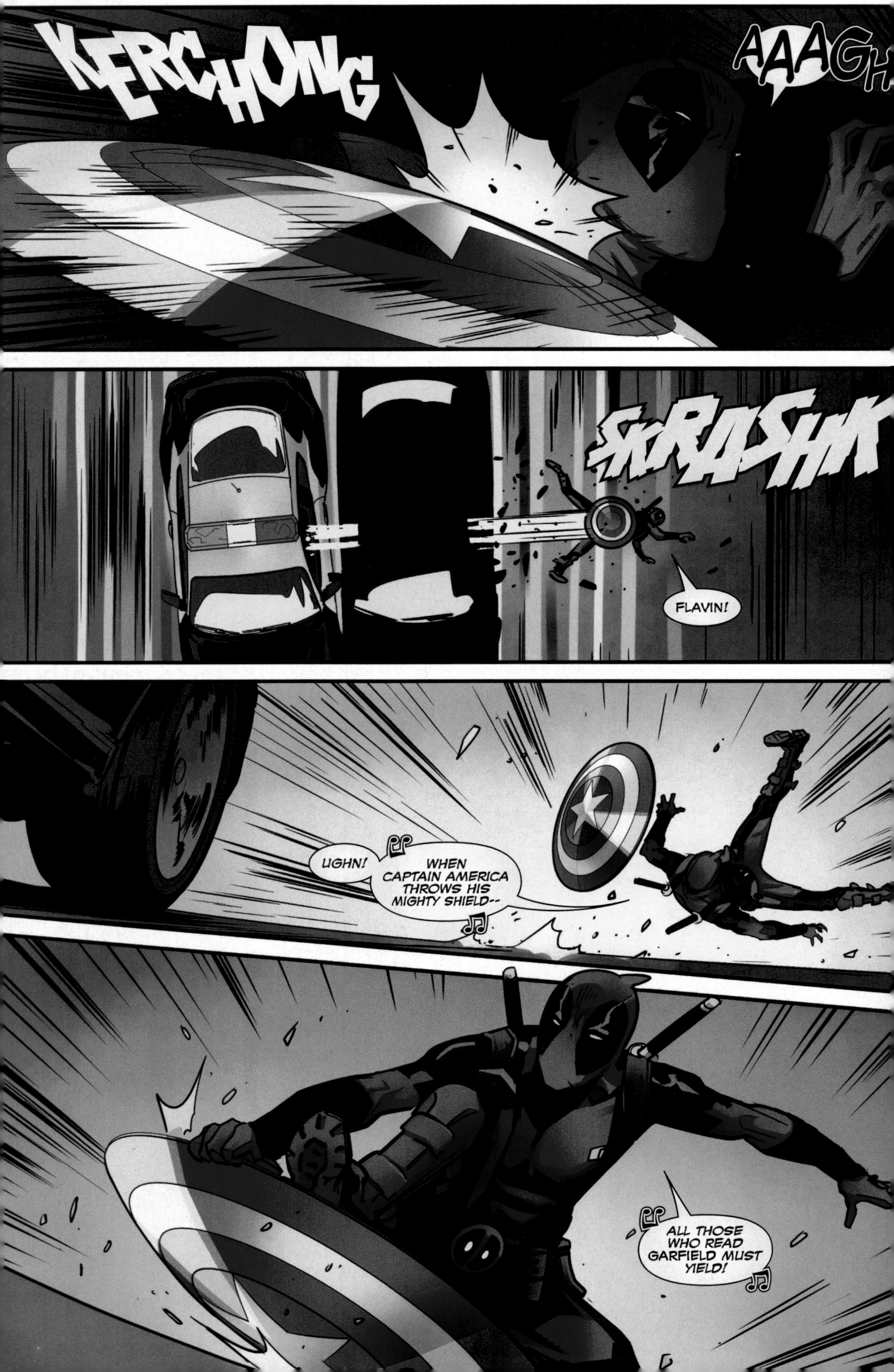
KERCHONG
AAAGH
SKRASHK
FLAVIN!
UGHN!
WHEN CAPTAIN AMERICA THROWS HIS MIGHTY SHIELD--
ALL THOSE WHO READ GARFIELD MUST YIELD!

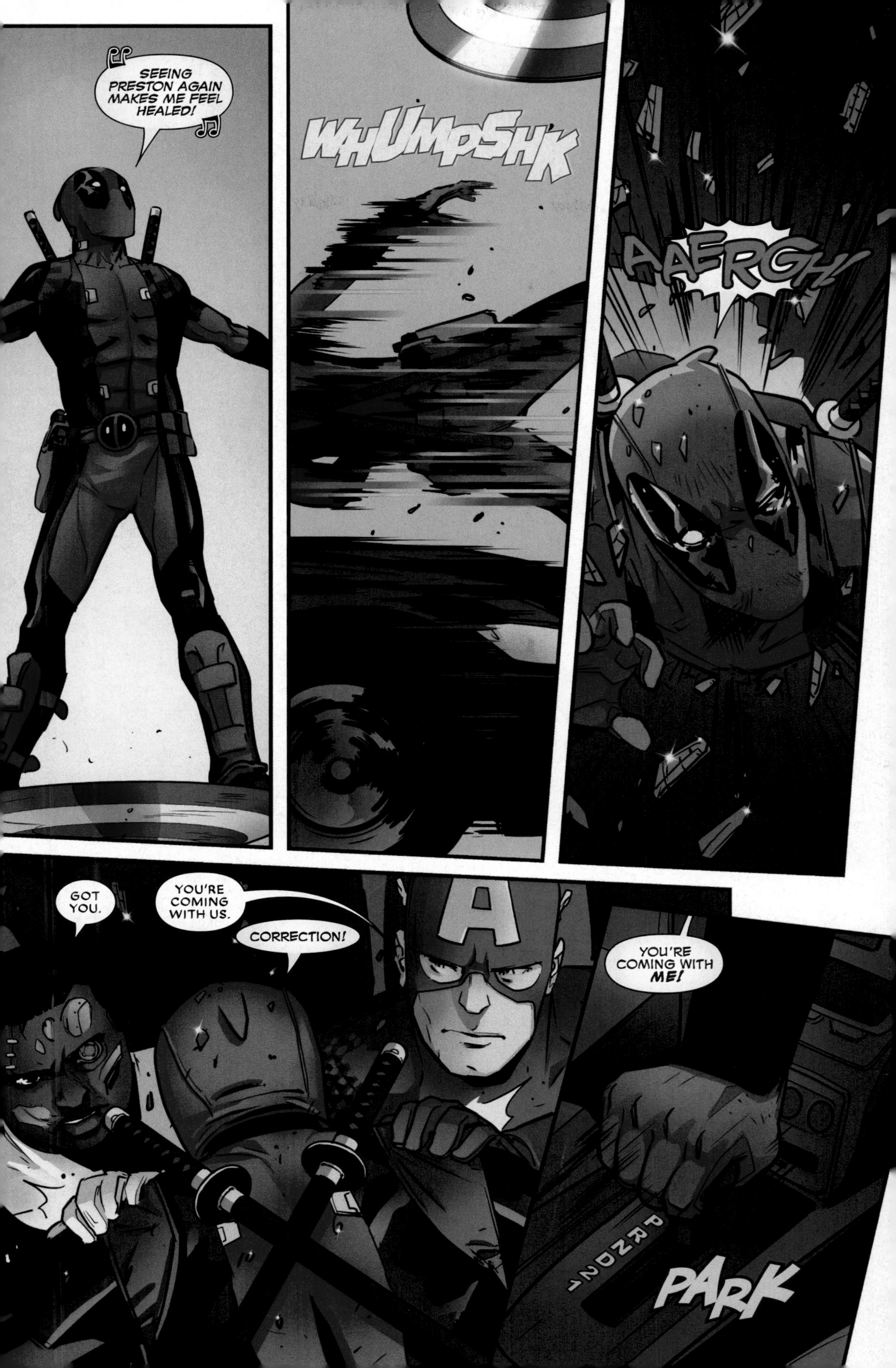
SEEING PRESTON AGAIN MAKES ME FEEL HEALED!
WHUMPSHK
AAERGH!
GOT YOU.
YOU'RE COMING WITH US.
CORRECTION!
YOU'RE COMING WITH ME!
PRNDL
PARK

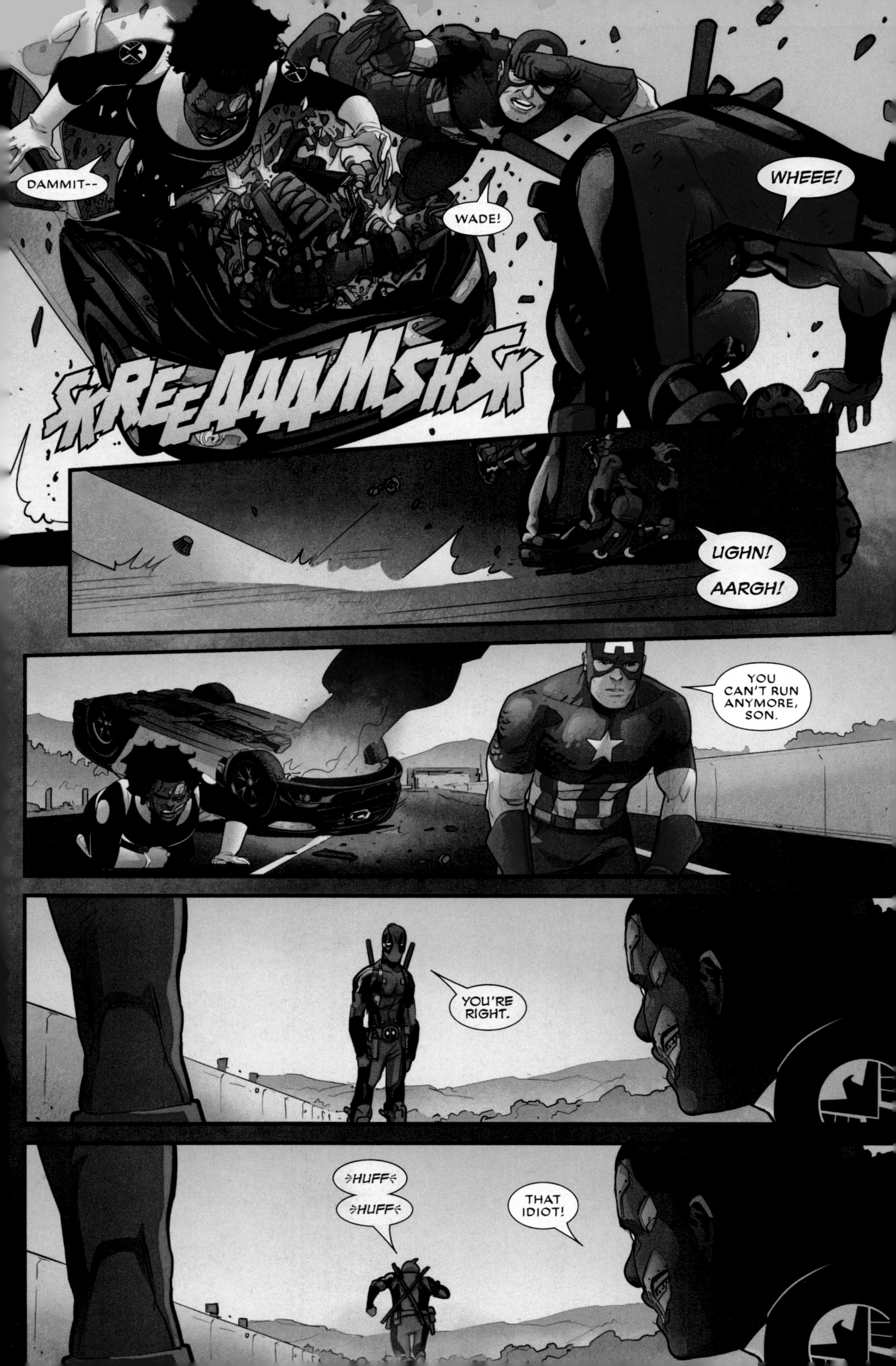
DAMMIT--
WADE!
WHEEE!
SKREEAAAMSHSK
UGHN!
AARGH!
YOU CAN'T RUN ANYMORE, SON.
YOU'RE RIGHT.
HUFF
HUFF
THAT IDIOT!

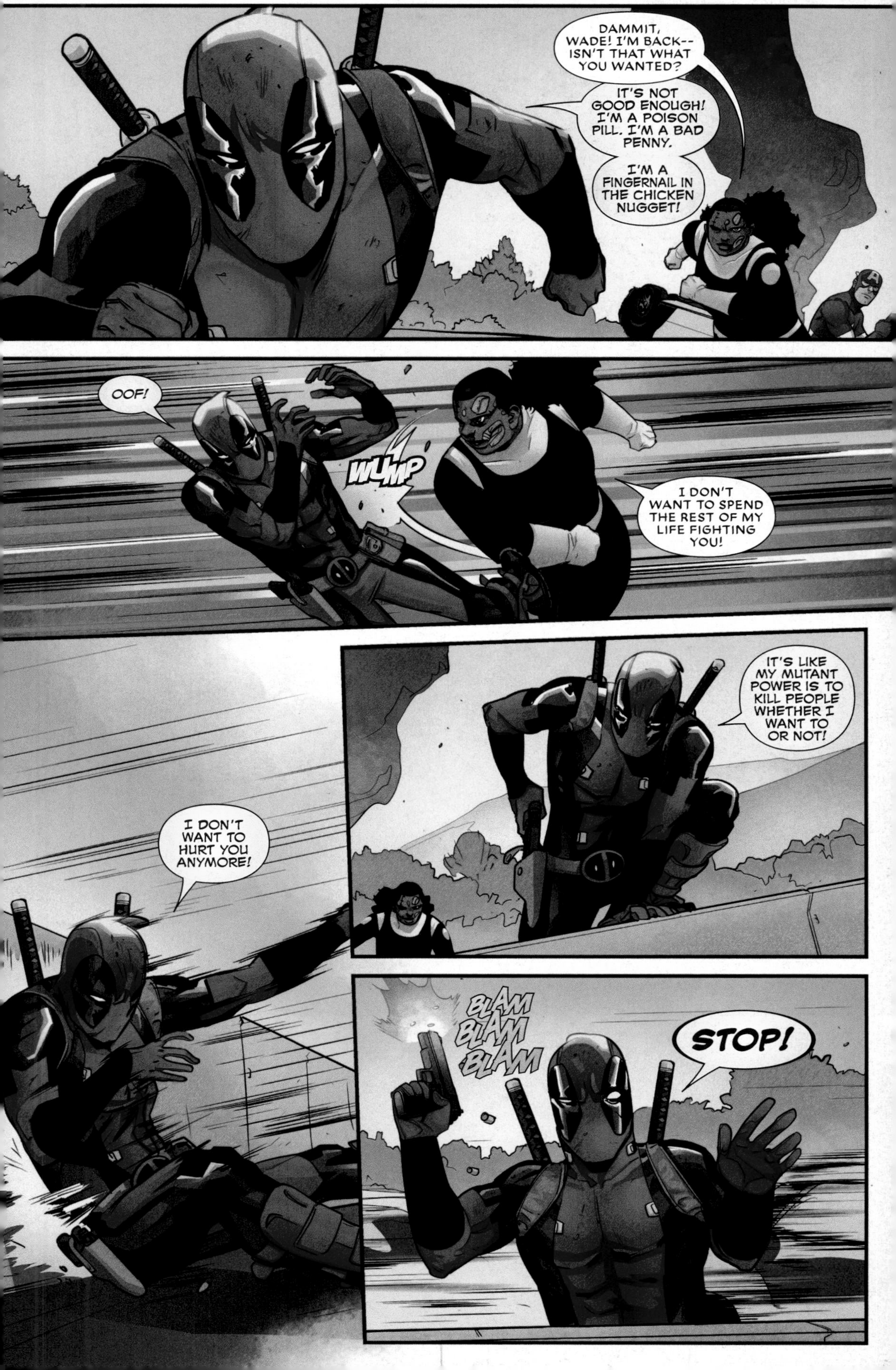

DAMMIT, WADE! I'M BACK-- ISN'T THAT WHAT YOU WANTED?
IT'S NOT GOOD ENOUGH! I'M A POISON PILL. I'M A BAD PENNY.
I'M A FINGERNAIL IN THE CHICKEN NUGGET!
OOF!
WUMP
I DON'T WANT TO SPEND THE REST OF MY LIFE FIGHTING YOU!
I DON'T WANT TO HURT YOU ANYMORE!
IT'S LIKE MY MUTANT POWER IS TO KILL PEOPLE WHETHER I WANT TO OR NOT!
BLAM BLAM BLAM
STOP!

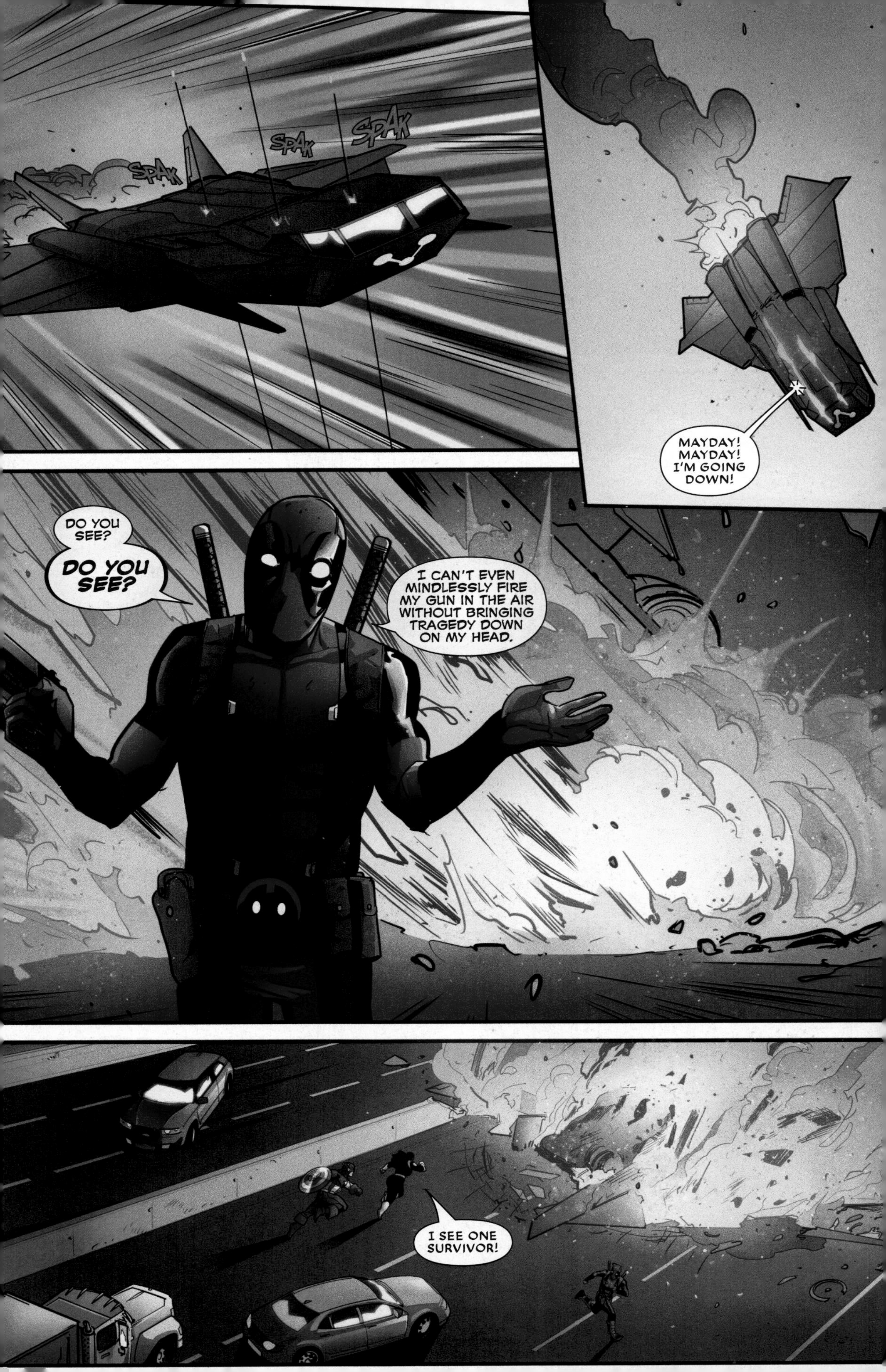
SPAK
SPAK
SPAK
MAYDAY! MAYDAY! I'M GOING DOWN!
DO YOU SEE?
DO YOU SEE?
I CAN'T EVEN MINDLESSLY FIRE MY GUN IN THE AIR WITHOUT BRINGING TRAGEDY DOWN ON MY HEAD.
I SEE ONE SURVIVOR!

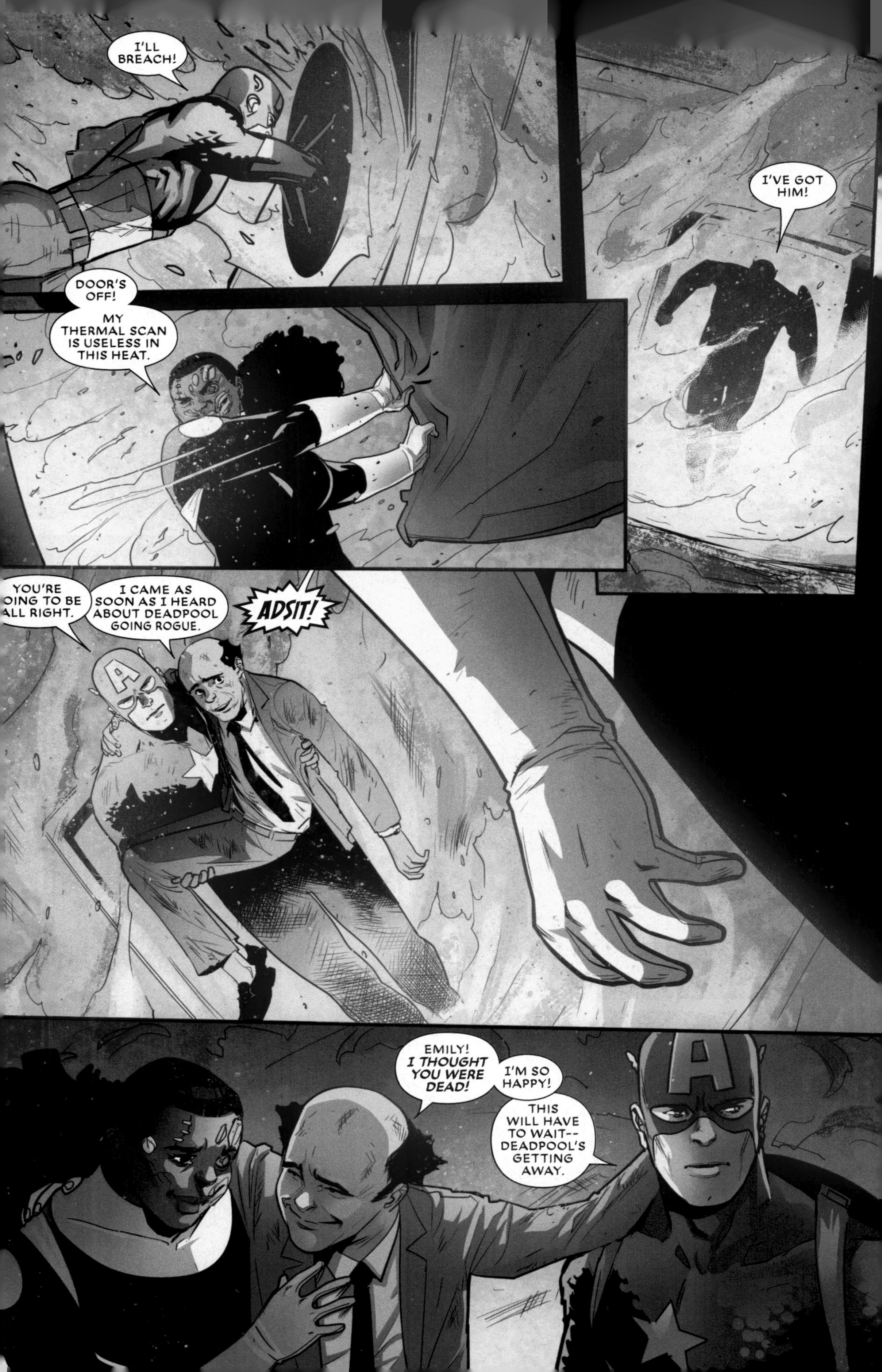
I'LL BREACH!
I'VE GOT HIM!
DOOR'S OFF!
MY THERMAL SCAN IS USELESS IN THIS HEAT.
YOU'RE GOING TO BE ALL RIGHT.
I CAME AS SOON AS I HEARD ABOUT DEADPOOL GOING ROGUE.
ADSIT!
EMILY! I THOUGHT YOU WERE DEAD!
I'M SO HAPPY!
THIS WILL HAVE TO WAIT-- DEADPOOL'S GETTING AWAY.

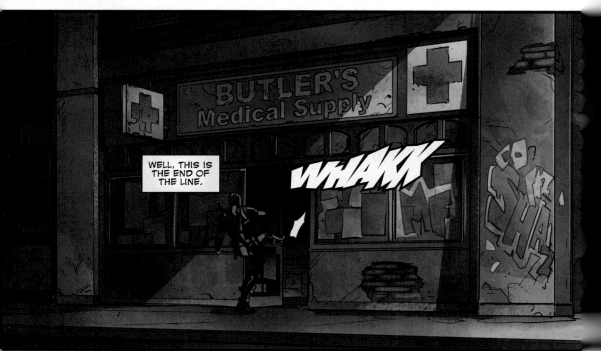

WELL, THIS IS THE END OF THE LINE.

WHAKK

HELLO, BUTLER.

OR UTLER, OR WHATEVER YOUR NAME WAS.

I DIDN'T @#$& EVERYTHING UP--

WHUOO

--YOU STAYED DEAD.

THE REMAI
YOUR SCI
EXPERIMEN
RIGHT WH

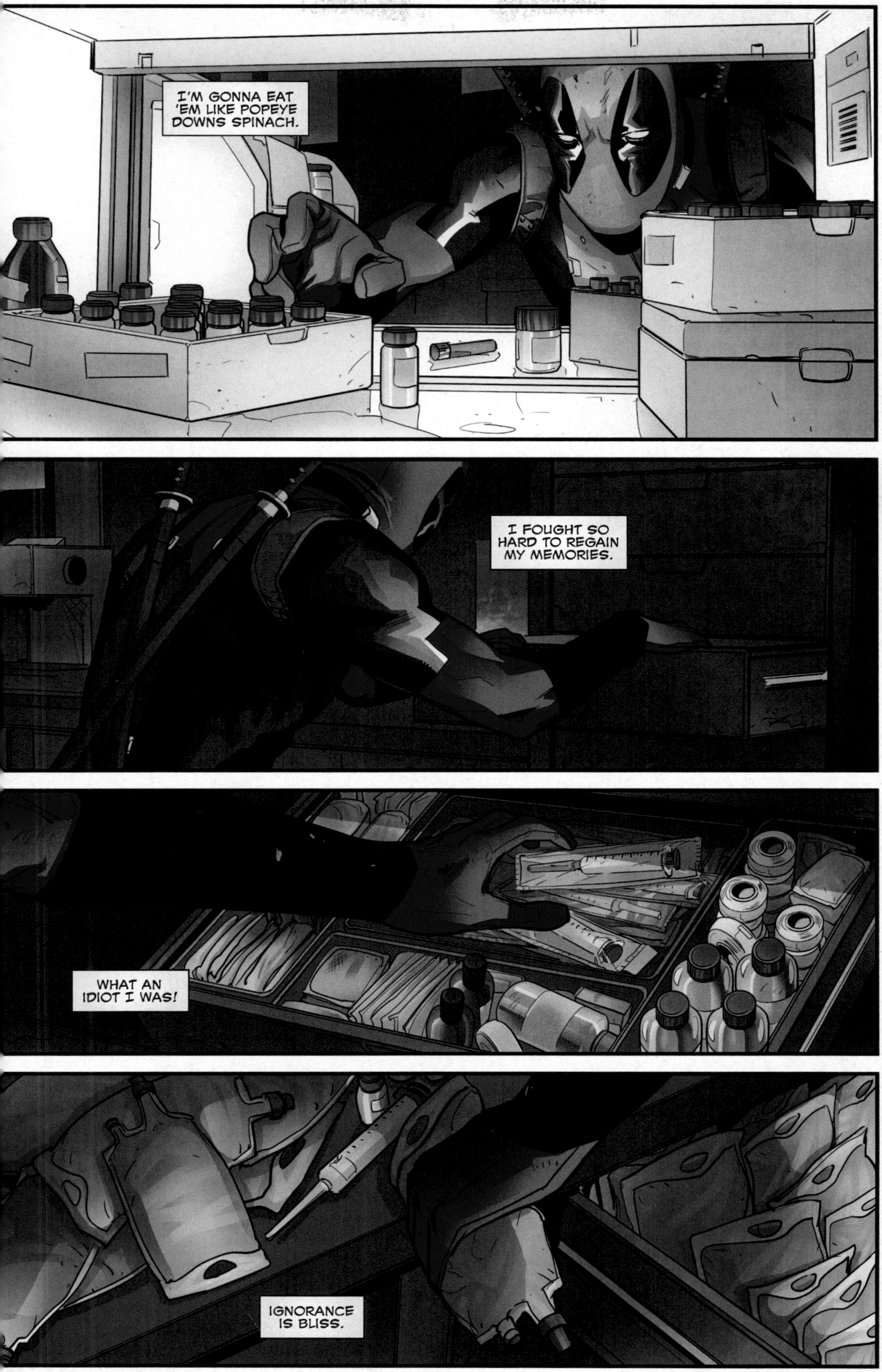
I'M GONNA EAT 'EM LIKE POPEYE DOWNS SPINACH.
I FOUGHT SO HARD TO REGAIN MY MEMORIES.
WHAT AN IDIOT I WAS!
IGNORANCE IS BLISS.

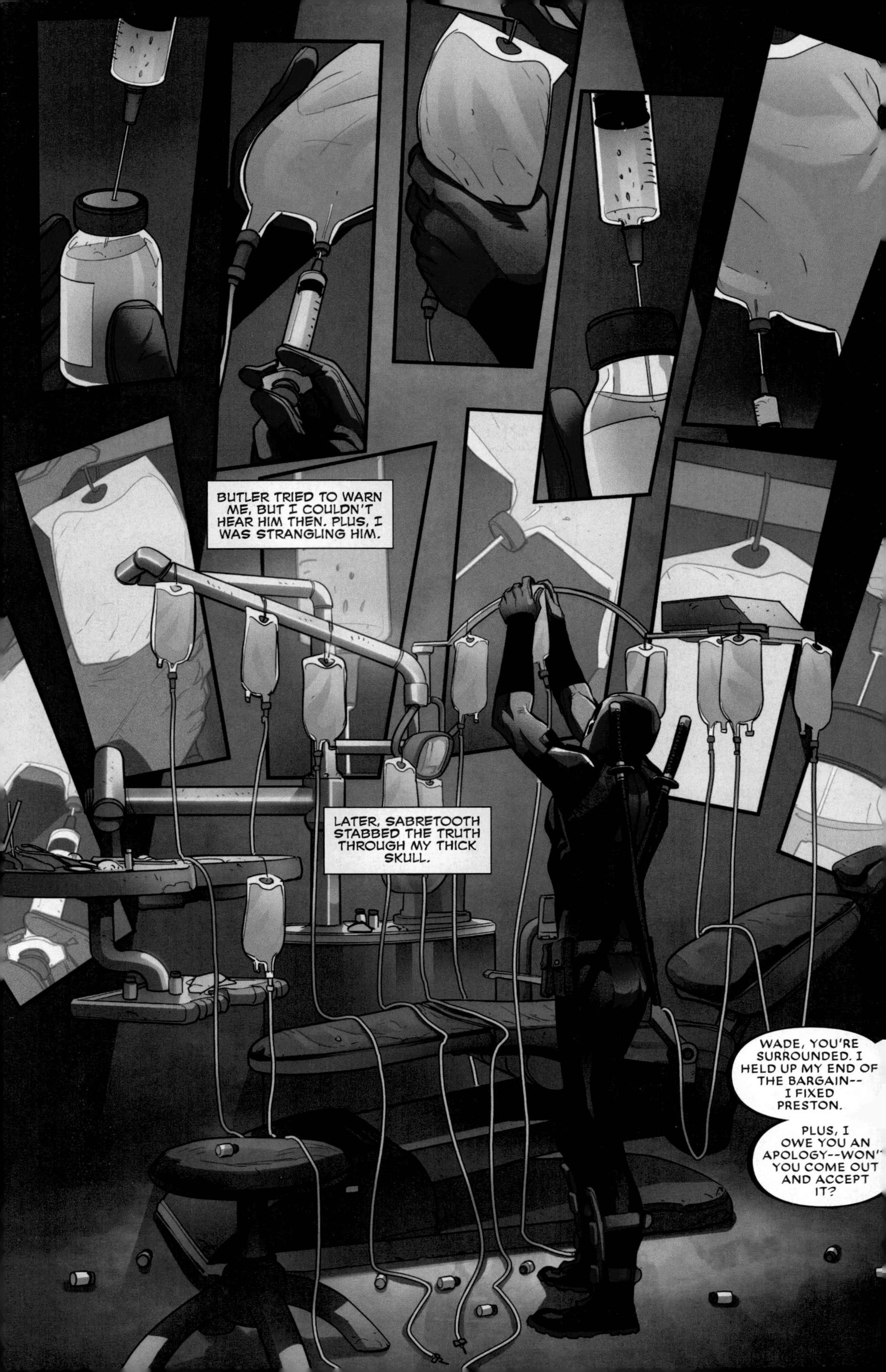
BUTLER TRIED TO WARN ME, BUT I COULDN'T HEAR HIM THEN. PLUS, I WAS STRANGLING HIM.
LATER, SABRETOOTH STABBED THE TRUTH THROUGH MY THICK SKULL.
WADE, YOU'RE SURROUNDED. I HELD UP MY END OF THE BARGAIN-- I FIXED PRESTON.
PLUS, I OWE YOU AN APOLOGY--WON'T YOU COME OUT AND ACCEPT IT?

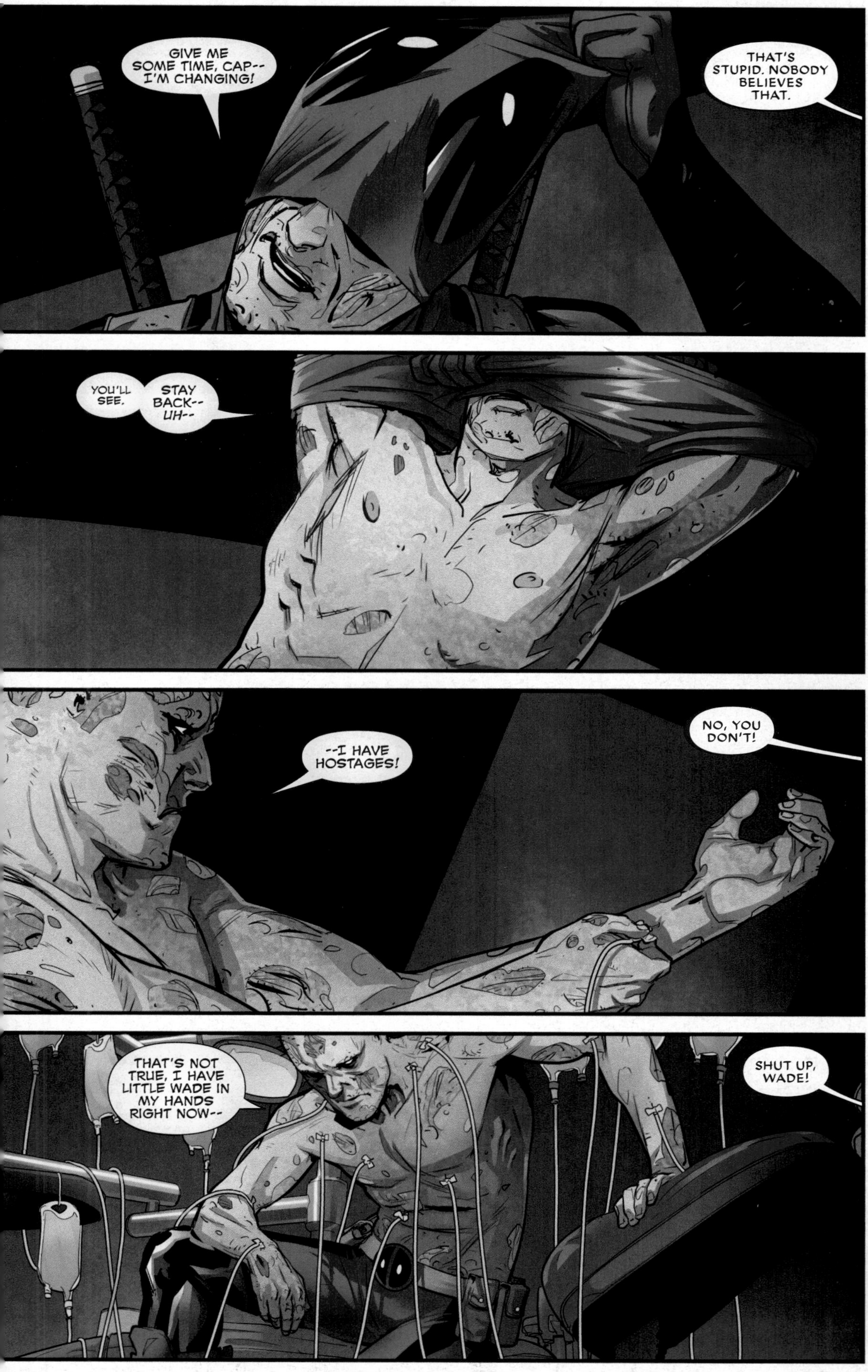
GIVE ME SOME TIME, CAP-- I'M CHANGING!
THAT'S STUPID. NOBODY BELIEVES THAT.
YOU'LL SEE.
STAY BACK-- UH--
--I HAVE HOSTAGES!
NO, YOU DON'T!
THAT'S NOT TRUE, I HAVE LITTLE WADE IN MY HANDS RIGHT NOW--
SHUT UP, WADE!

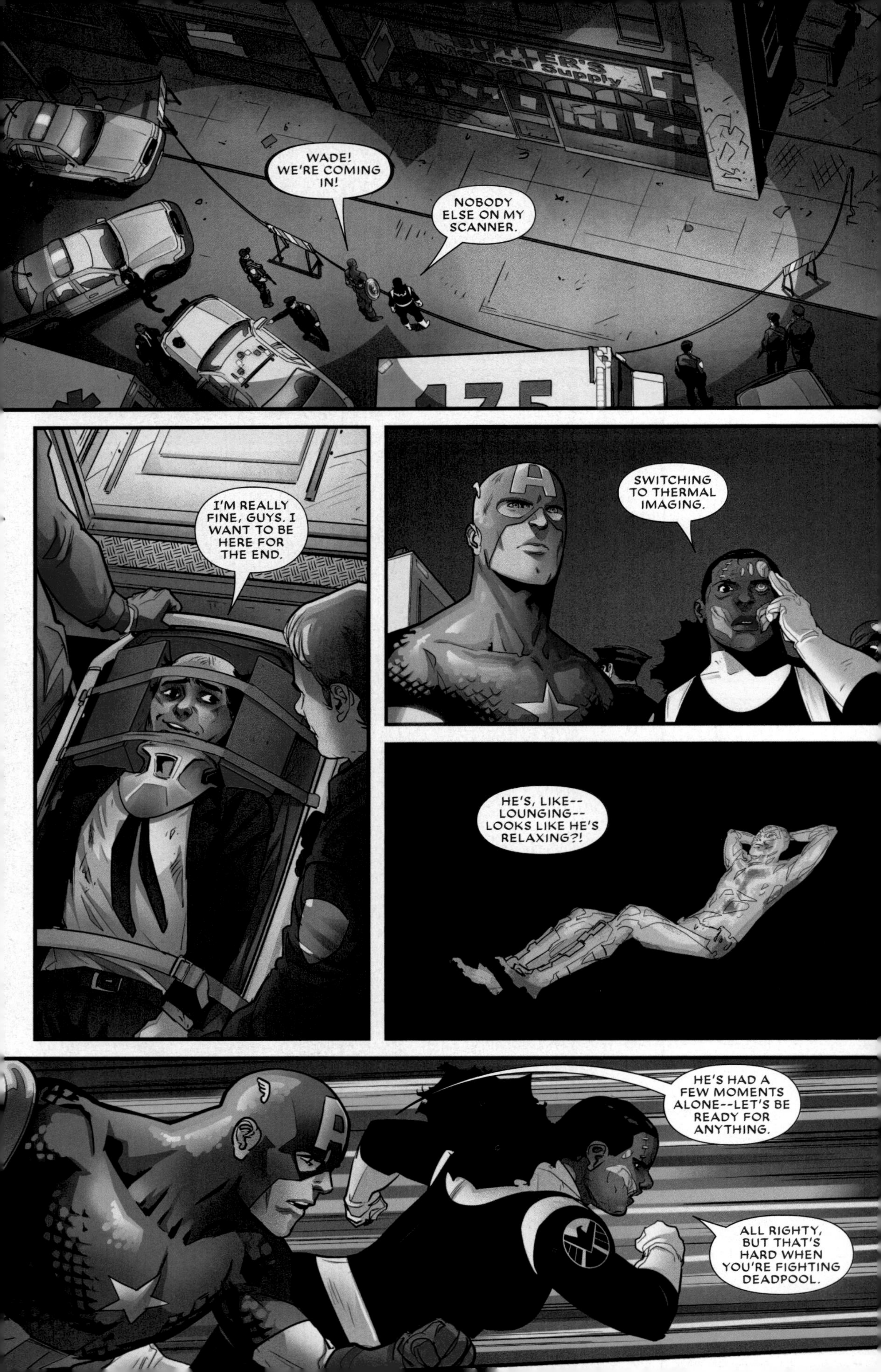
BUTLER'S Medical Supply
WADE! WE'RE COMING IN!
NOBODY ELSE ON MY SCANNER.
175
I'M REALLY FINE, GUYS. I WANT TO BE HERE FOR THE END.
SWITCHING TO THERMAL IMAGING.
HE'S, LIKE-- LOUNGING-- LOOKS LIKE HE'S RELAXING?!
HE'S HAD A FEW MOMENTS ALONE--LET'S BE READY FOR ANYTHING.
ALL RIGHTY, BUT THAT'S HARD WHEN YOU'RE FIGHTING DEADPOOL.

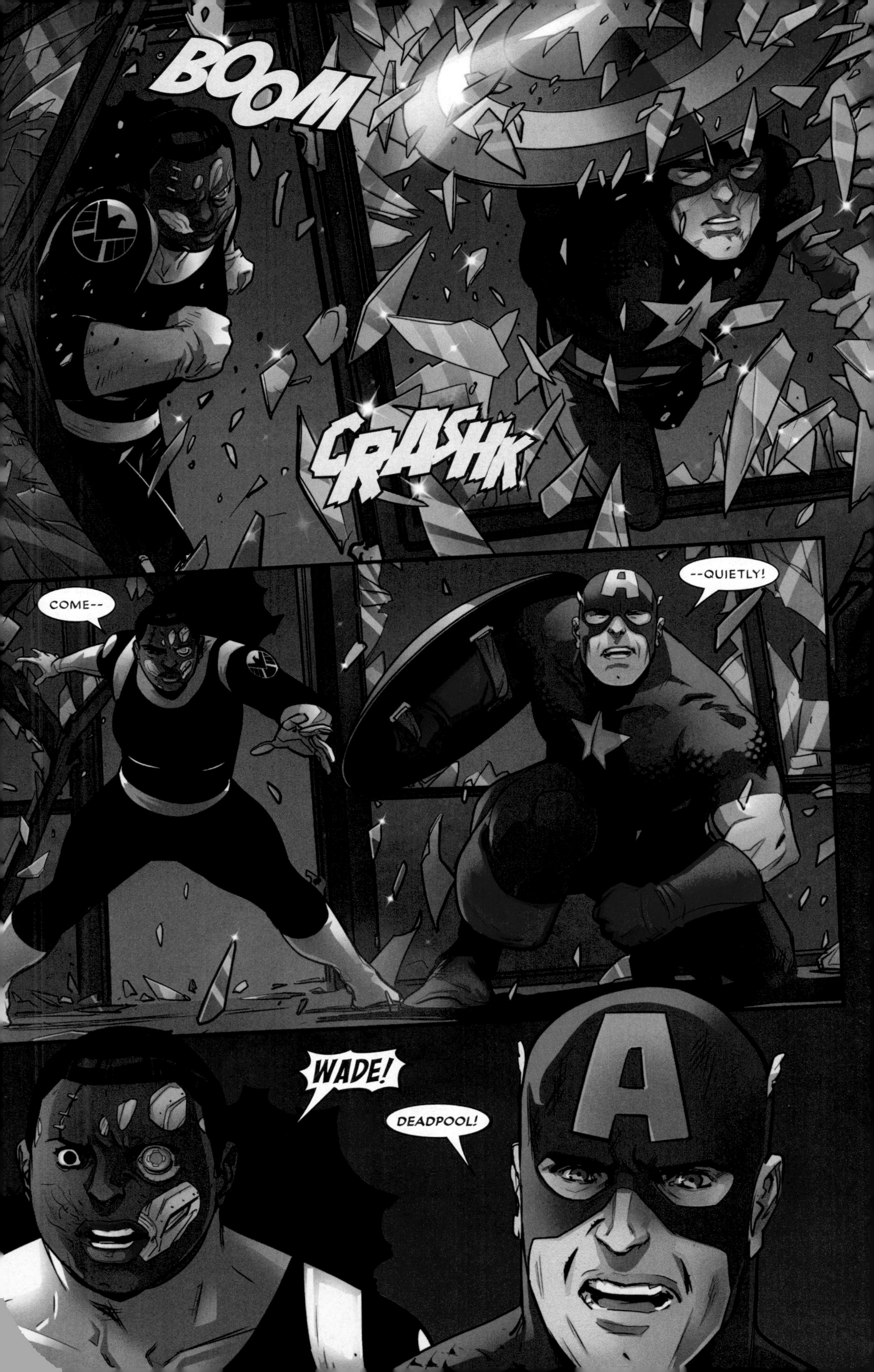
BOOM
CRASHK
COME--
--QUIETLY!
WADE!
DEADPOOL!

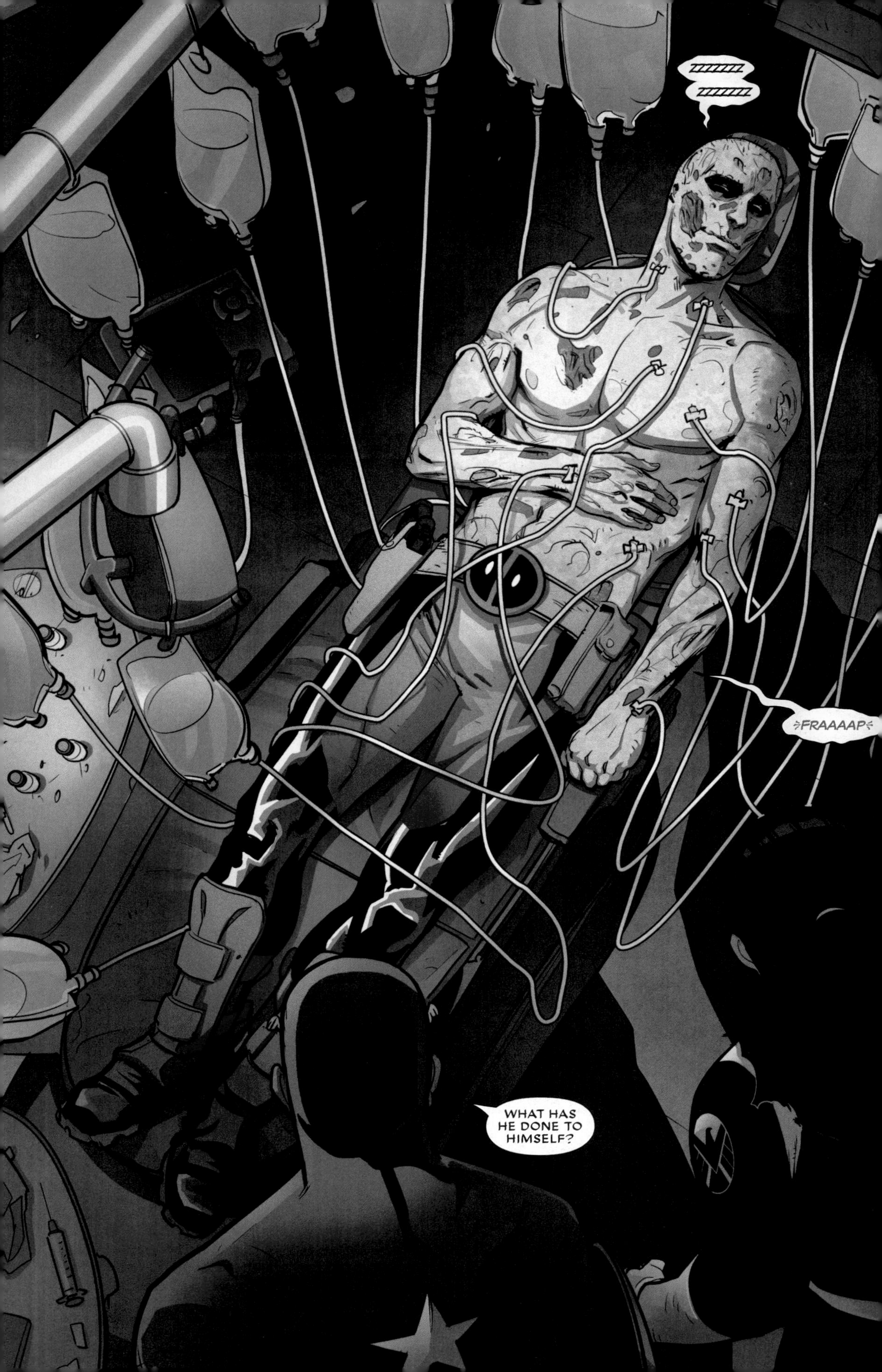
ZZZZZZZ
ZZZZZZZ
FRAAAAP
WHAT HAS HE DONE TO HIMSELF?

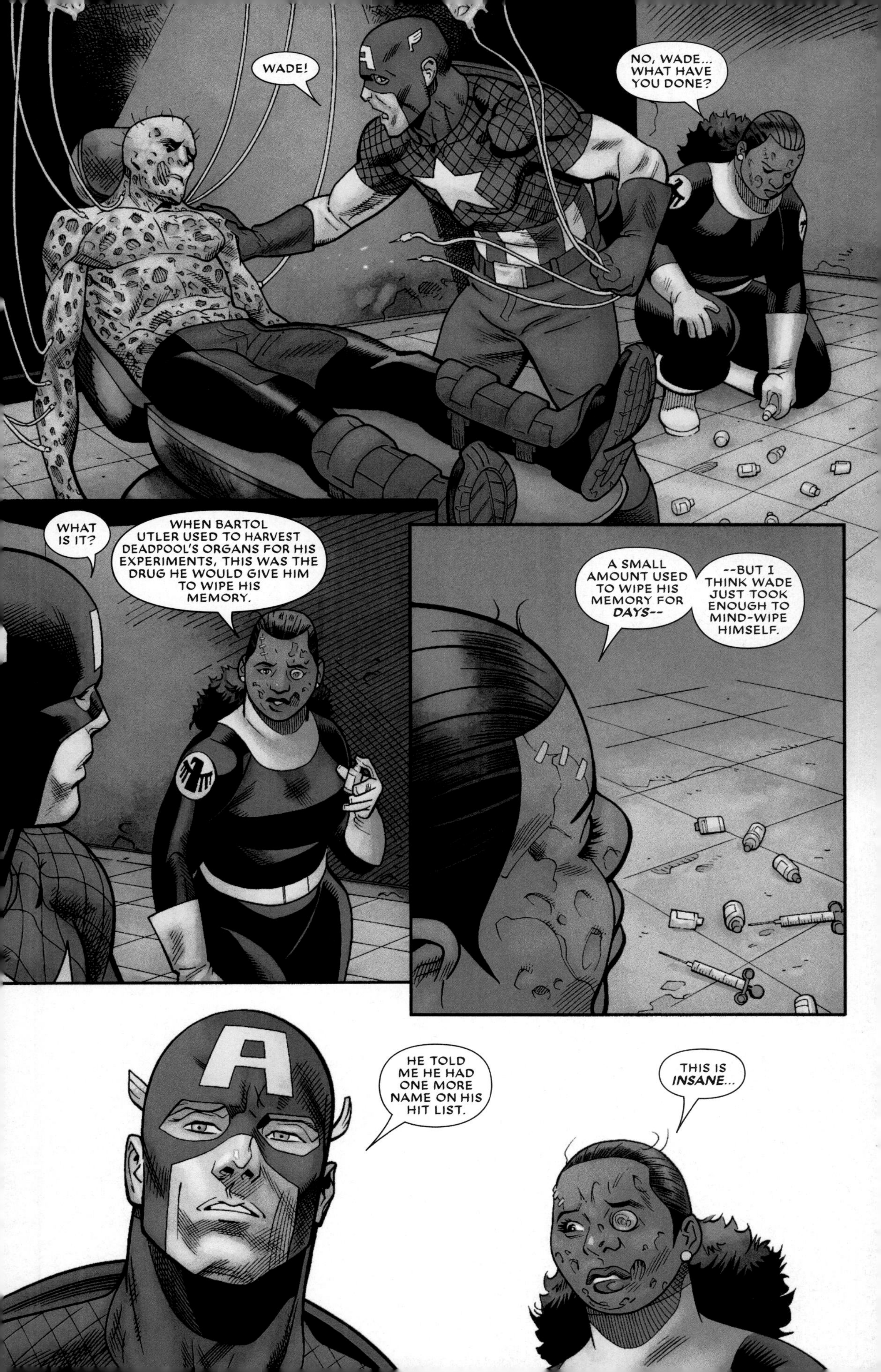
WADE!
NO, WADE... WHAT HAVE YOU DONE?
WHAT IS IT?
WHEN BARTOL UTLER USED TO HARVEST DEADPOOL'S ORGANS FOR HIS EXPERIMENTS, THIS WAS THE DRUG HE WOULD GIVE HIM TO WIPE HIS MEMORY.
A SMALL AMOUNT USED TO WIPE HIS MEMORY FOR DAYS--
--BUT I THINK WADE JUST TOOK ENOUGH TO MIND-WIPE HIMSELF.
HE TOLD ME HE HAD ONE MORE NAME ON HIS HIT LIST.
THIS IS INSANE...

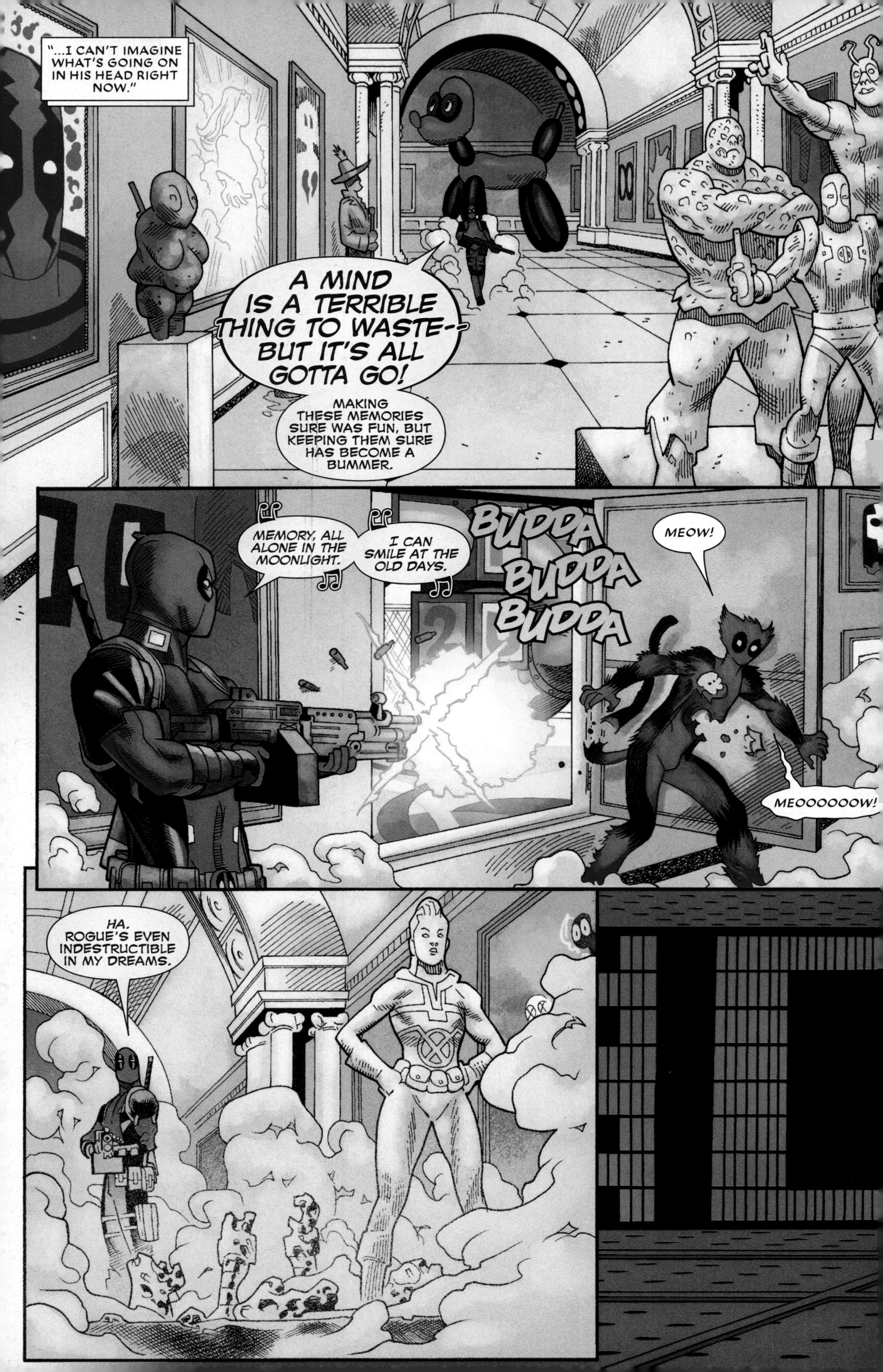
"...I CAN'T IMAGINE WHAT'S GOING ON IN HIS HEAD RIGHT NOW."
A MIND IS A TERRIBLE THING TO WASTE-- BUT IT'S ALL GOTTA GO!
MAKING THESE MEMORIES SURE WAS FUN, BUT KEEPING THEM SURE HAS BECOME A BUMMER.
MEMORY, ALL ALONE IN THE MOONLIGHT.
I CAN SMILE AT THE OLD DAYS.
BUDDA BUDDA BUDDA
MEOW!
MEOOOOOOW!
HA. ROGUE'S EVEN INDESTRUCTIBLE IN MY DREAMS.

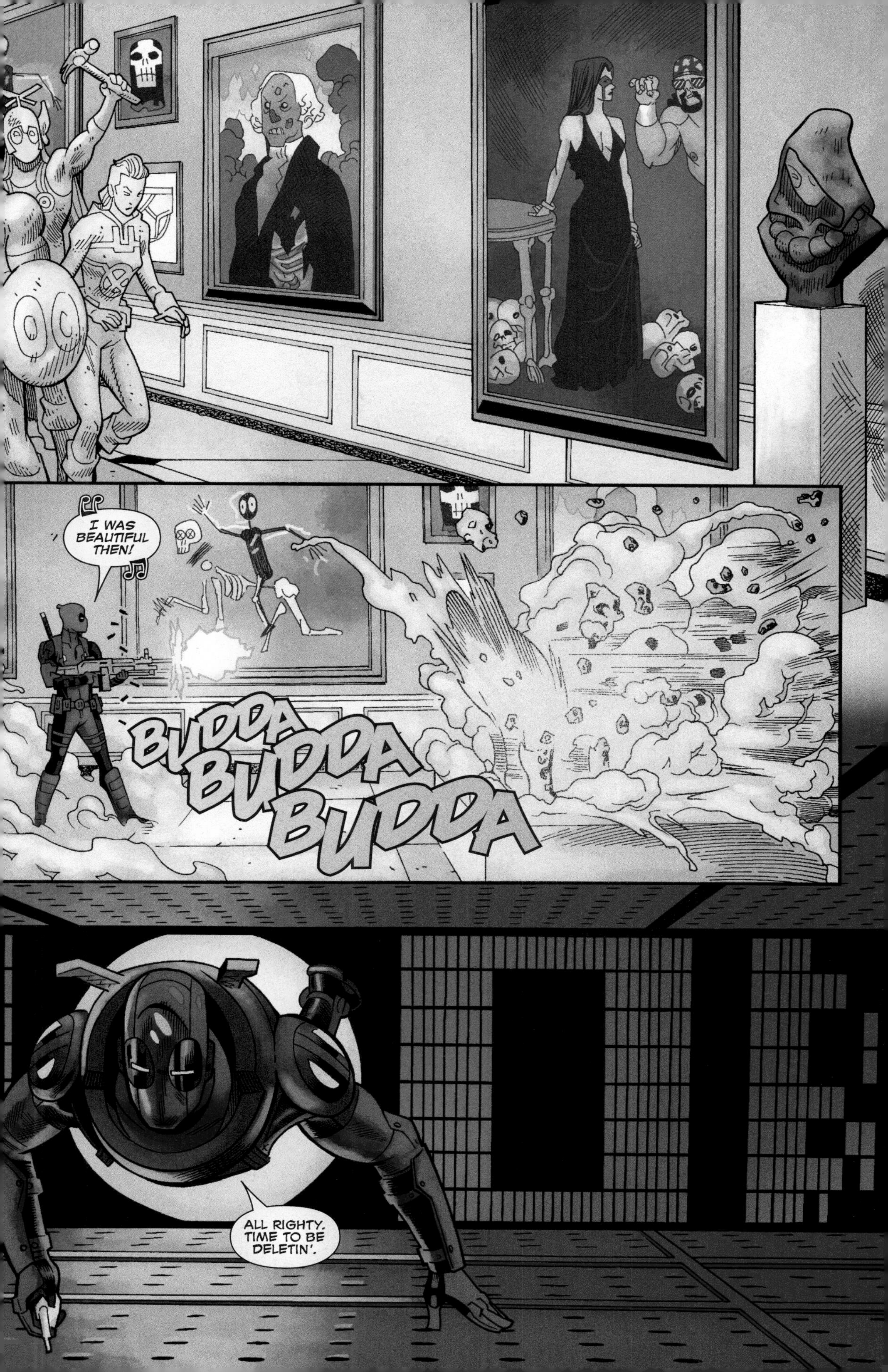
I WAS BEAUTIFUL THEN!
BUDDA BUDDA BUDDA
ALL RIGHTY. TIME TO BE DELETIN'.

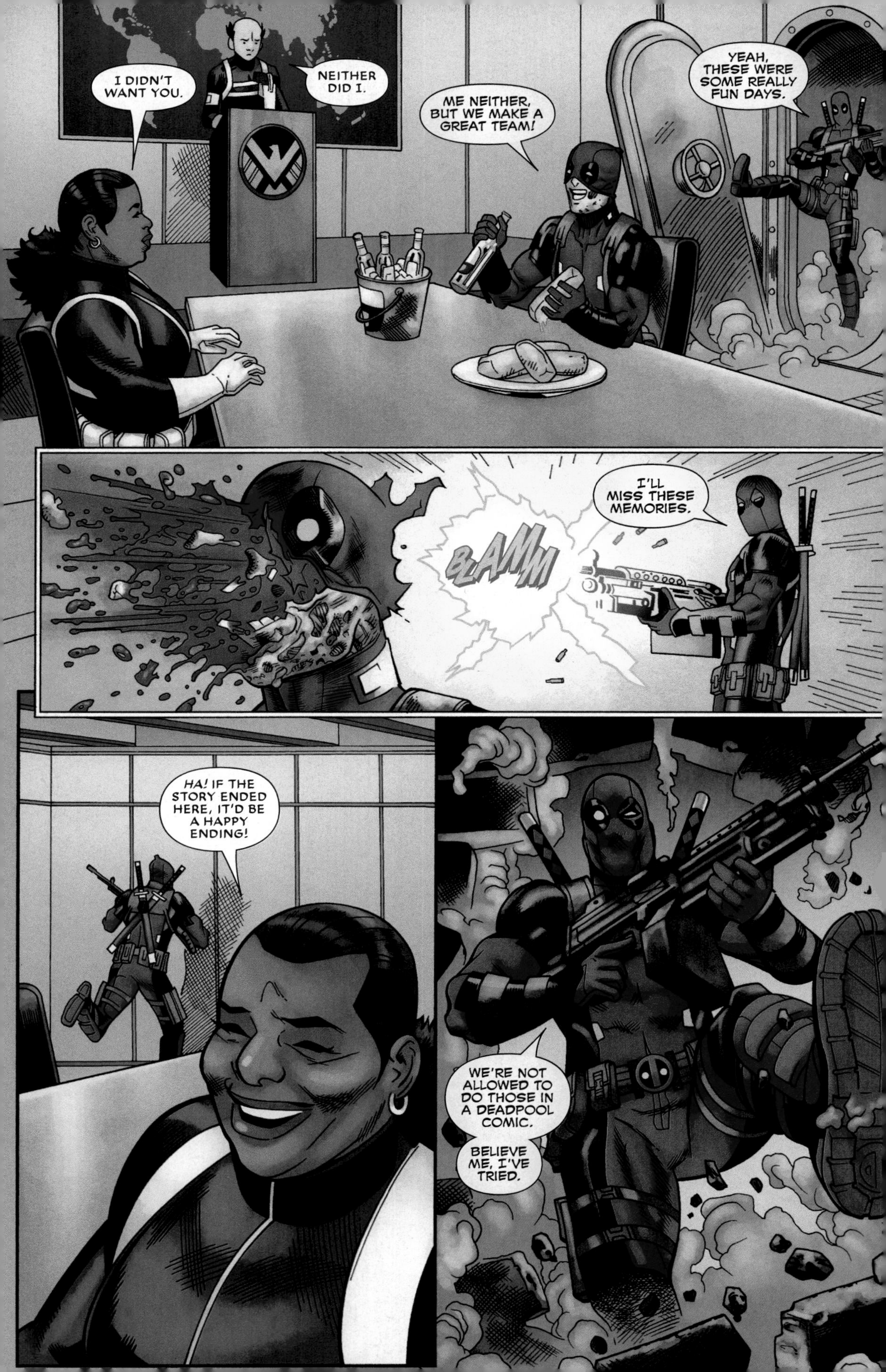
I DIDN'T WANT YOU.
NEITHER DID I.
ME NEITHER, BUT WE MAKE A GREAT TEAM!
YEAH, THESE WERE SOME REALLY FUN DAYS.
I'LL MISS THESE MEMORIES.
BLAMM
HA! IF THE STORY ENDED HERE, IT'D BE A HAPPY ENDING!
WE'RE NOT ALLOWED TO DO THOSE IN A DEADPOOL COMIC.
BELIEVE ME, I'VE TRIED.

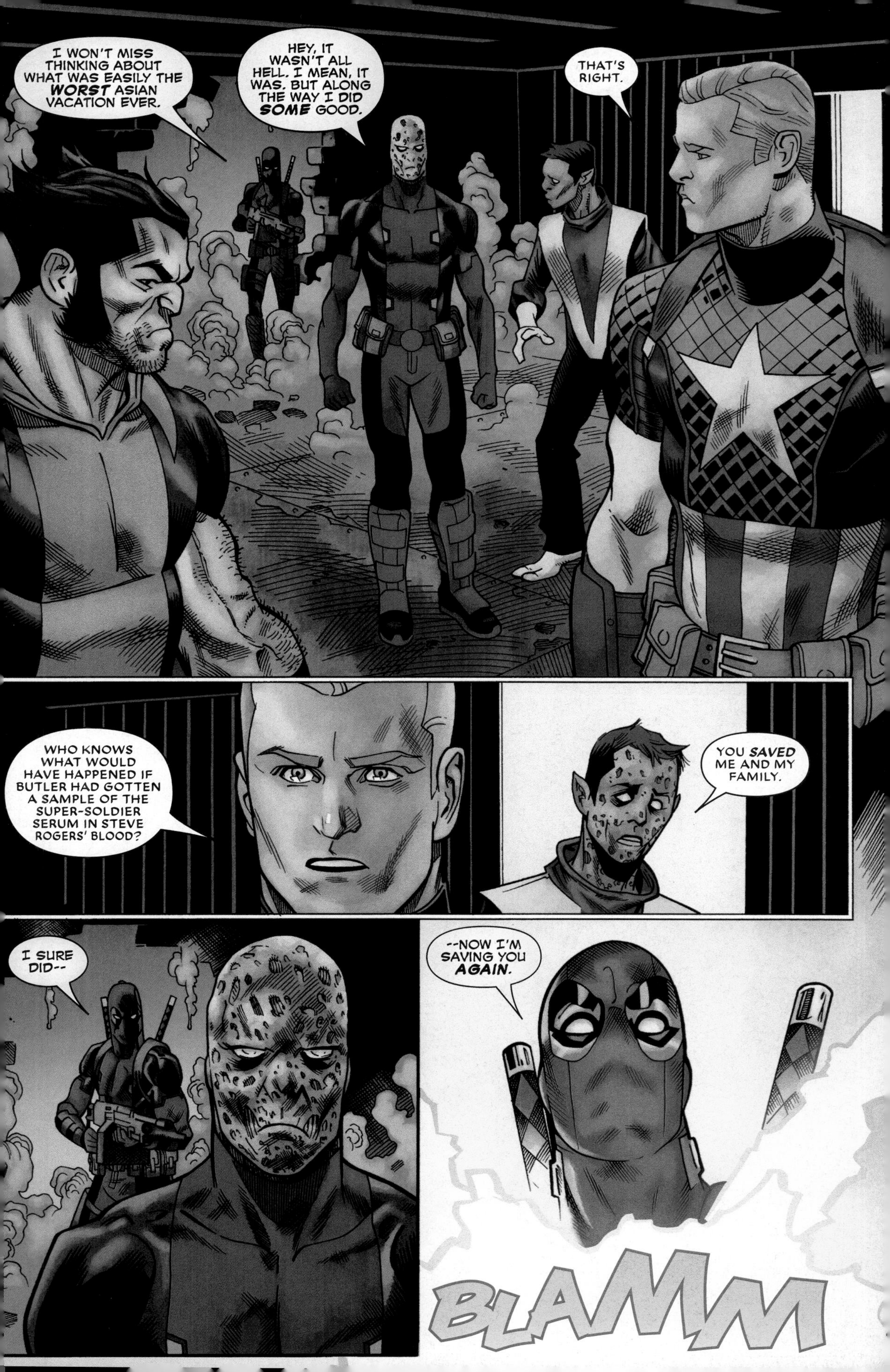
I WON'T MISS THINKING ABOUT WHAT WAS EASILY THE WORST ASIAN VACATION EVER.
HEY, IT WASN'T ALL HELL. I MEAN, IT WAS. BUT ALONG THE WAY I DID SOME GOOD.
THAT'S RIGHT.
WHO KNOWS WHAT WOULD HAVE HAPPENED IF BUTLER HAD GOTTEN A SAMPLE OF THE SUPER-SOLDIER SERUM IN STEVE ROGERS' BLOOD?
YOU SAVED ME AND MY FAMILY.
I SURE DID--
--NOW I'M SAVING YOU AGAIN.
BLAMM

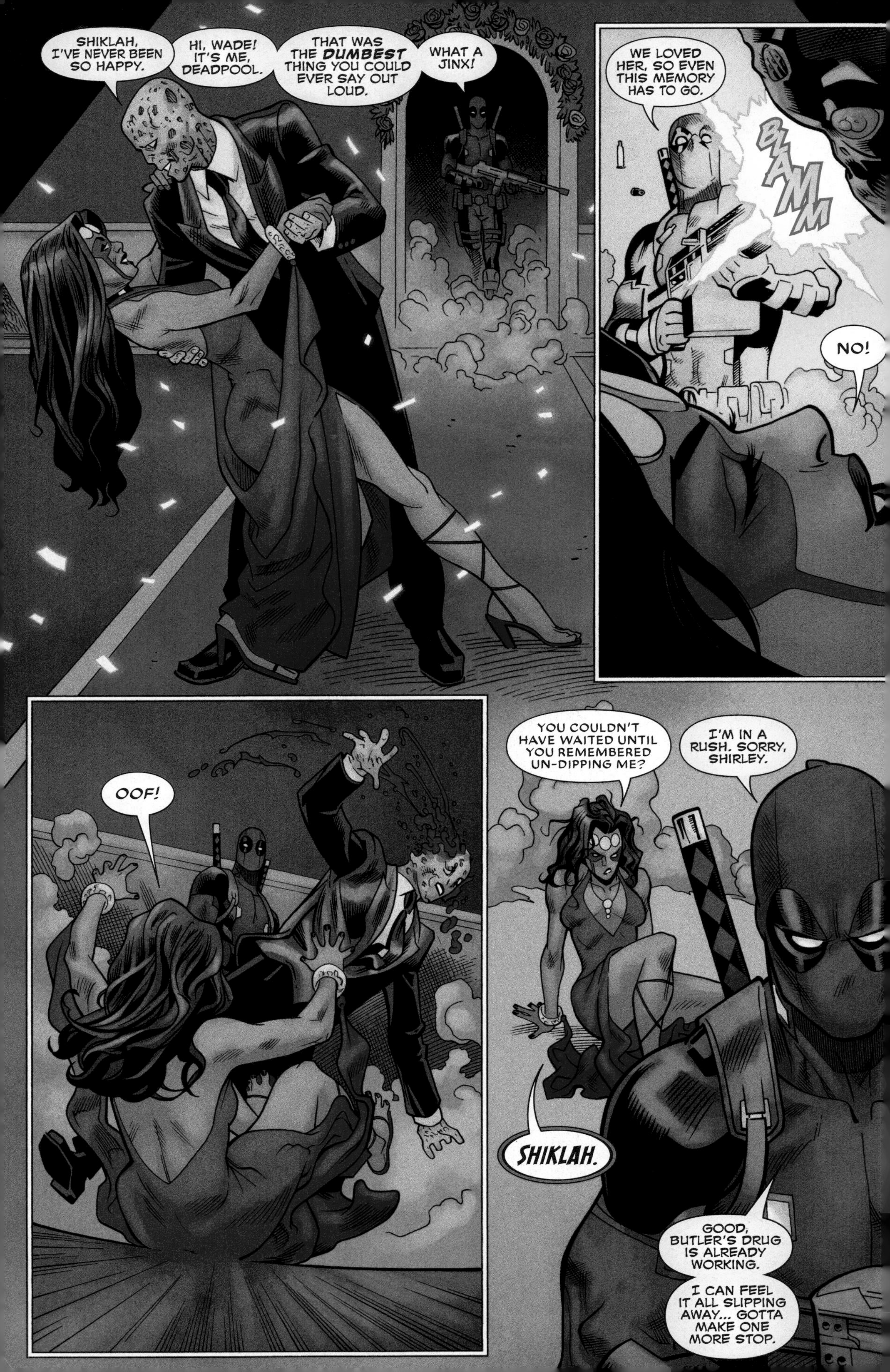

SHIKLAH, I'VE NEVER BEEN SO HAPPY.
HI, WADE! IT'S ME, DEADPOOL.
THAT WAS THE **DUMBEST** THING YOU COULD EVER SAY OUT LOUD.
WHAT A JINX!
WE LOVED HER, SO EVEN THIS MEMORY HAS TO GO.
BLAMM
NO!
OOF!
YOU COULDN'T HAVE WAITED UNTIL YOU REMEMBERED UN-DIPPING ME?
I'M IN A RUSH. SORRY, SHIRLEY.
SHIKLAH.
GOOD, BUTLER'S DRUG IS ALREADY WORKING.
I CAN FEEL IT ALL SLIPPING AWAY... GOTTA MAKE ONE MORE STOP.

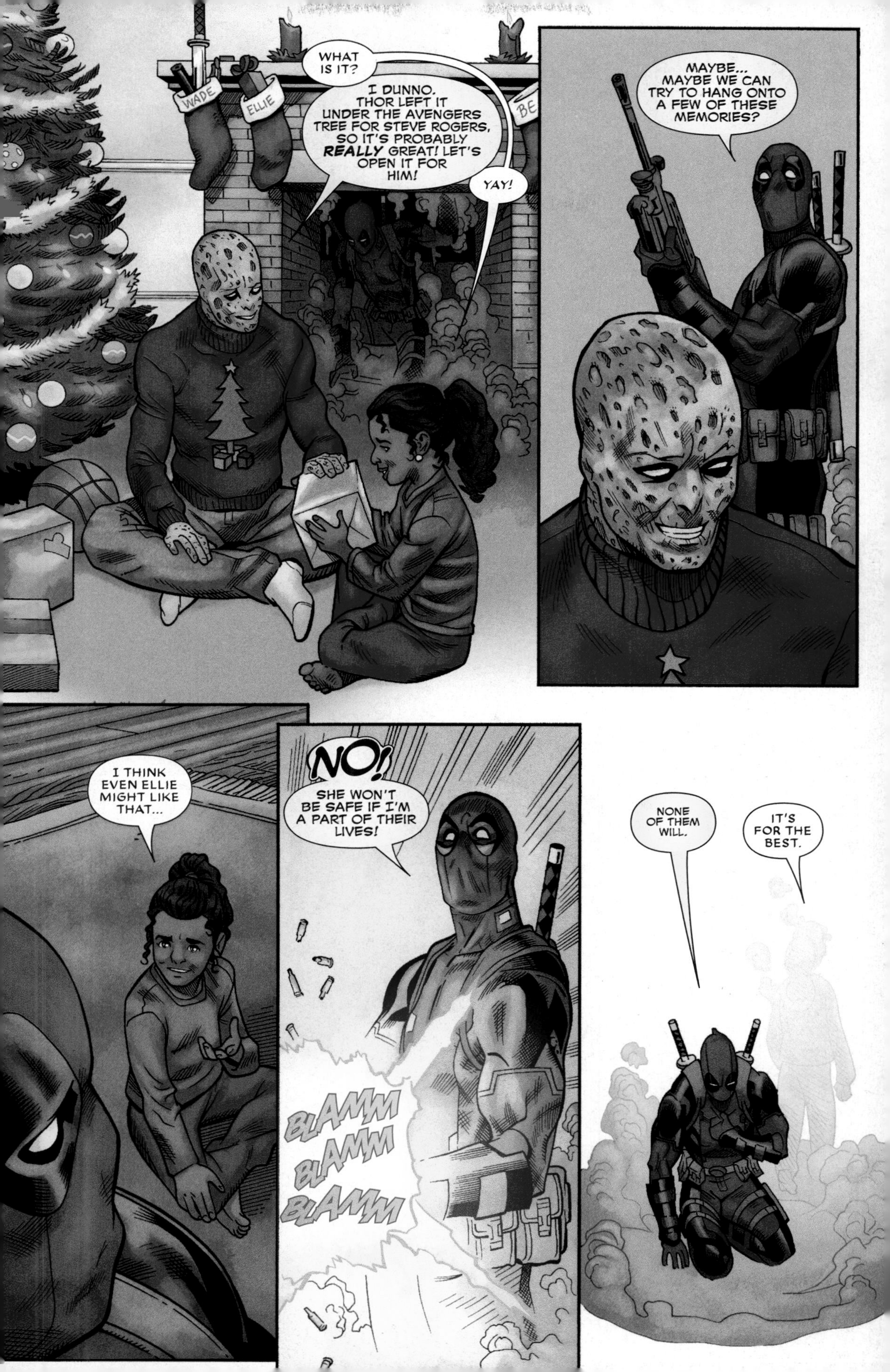
WHAT IS IT?
I DUNNO. THOR LEFT IT UNDER THE AVENGERS TREE FOR STEVE ROGERS, SO IT'S PROBABLY REALLY GREAT! LET'S OPEN IT FOR HIM!
YAY!
WADE
ELLIE
MAYBE... MAYBE WE CAN TRY TO HANG ONTO A FEW OF THESE MEMORIES?
I THINK EVEN ELLIE MIGHT LIKE THAT...
NO!
SHE WON'T BE SAFE IF I'M A PART OF THEIR LIVES!
BLAMM
BLAMM
BLAMM
BLAMM
NONE OF THEM WILL.
IT'S FOR THE BEST.

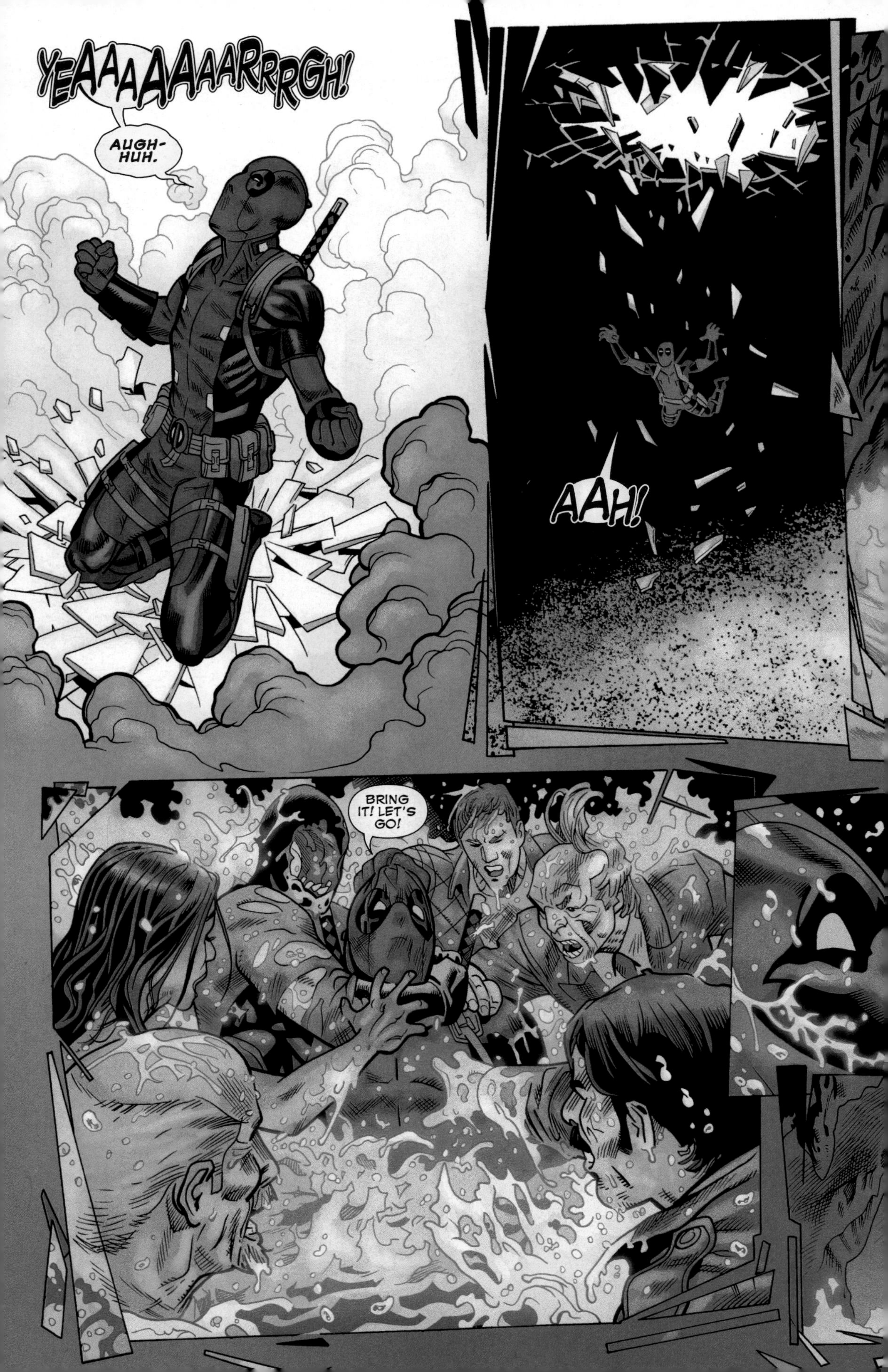
YEAAAAAAARRRGH!
AUGH-HUH.
AAH!
BRING IT! LET'S GO!

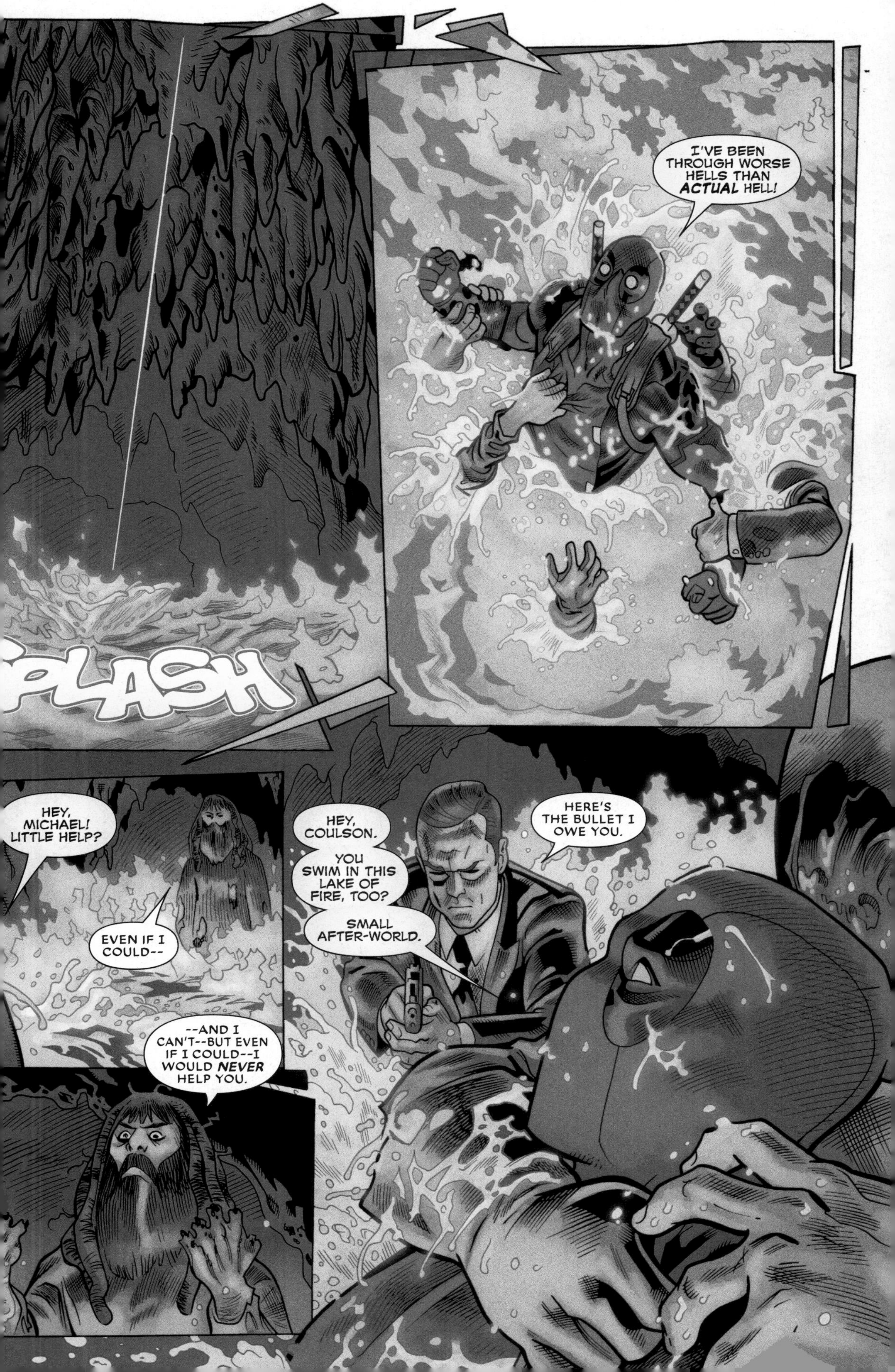
SPLASH
I'VE BEEN THROUGH WORSE HELLS THAN ACTUAL HELL!
HEY, MICHAEL! LITTLE HELP?
EVEN IF I COULD--
--AND I CAN'T--BUT EVEN IF I COULD--I WOULD NEVER HELP YOU.
HEY, COULSON.
YOU SWIM IN THIS LAKE OF FIRE, TOO?
SMALL AFTER-WORLD.
HERE'S THE BULLET I OWE YOU.

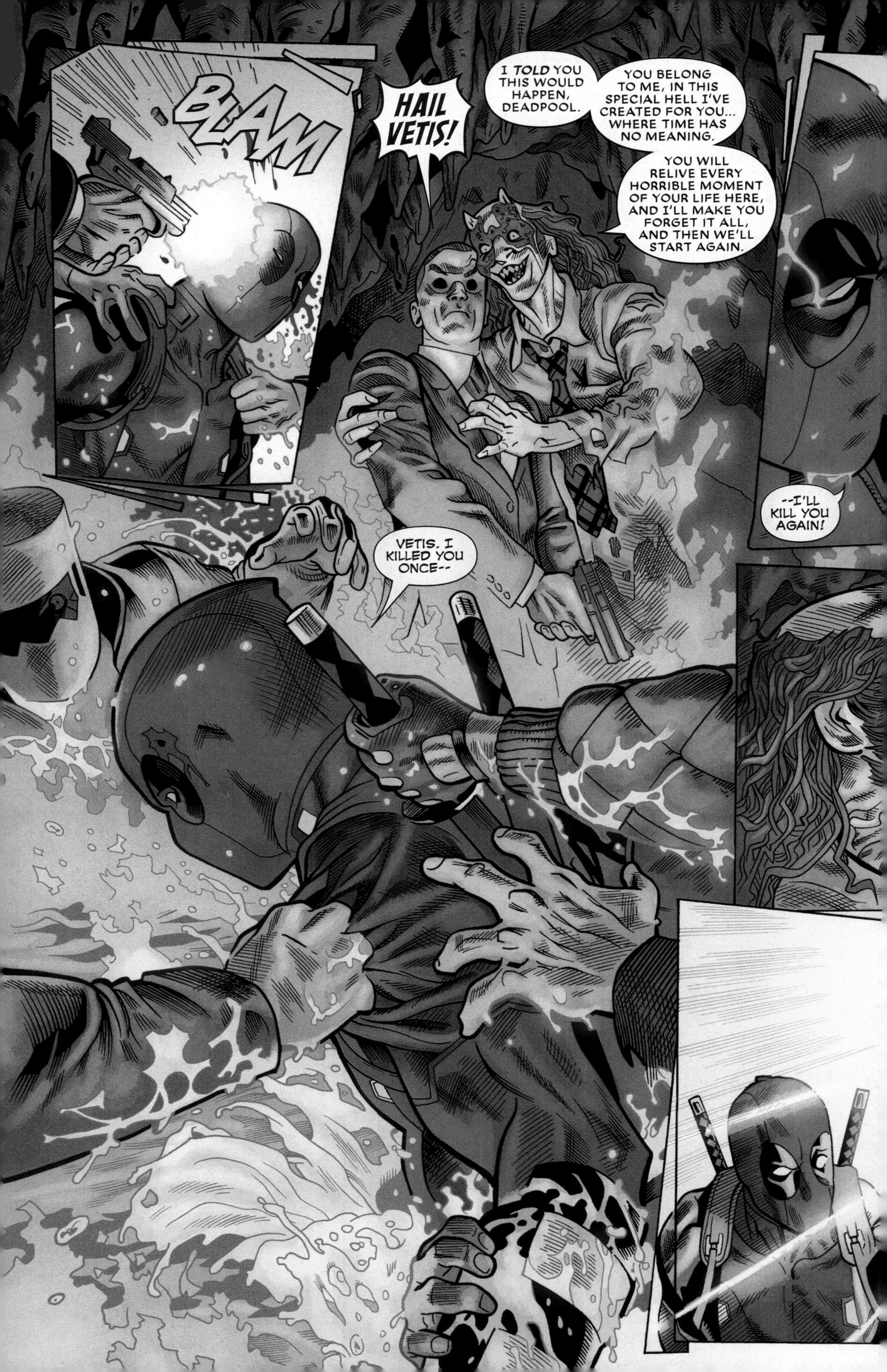
BLAM
HAIL VETIS!
I TOLD YOU THIS WOULD HAPPEN, DEADPOOL.
YOU BELONG TO ME, IN THIS SPECIAL HELL I'VE CREATED FOR YOU... WHERE TIME HAS NO MEANING.
YOU WILL RELIVE EVERY HORRIBLE MOMENT OF YOUR LIFE HERE, AND I'LL MAKE YOU FORGET IT ALL, AND THEN WE'LL START AGAIN.
VETIS. I KILLED YOU ONCE--
--I'LL KILL YOU AGAIN!

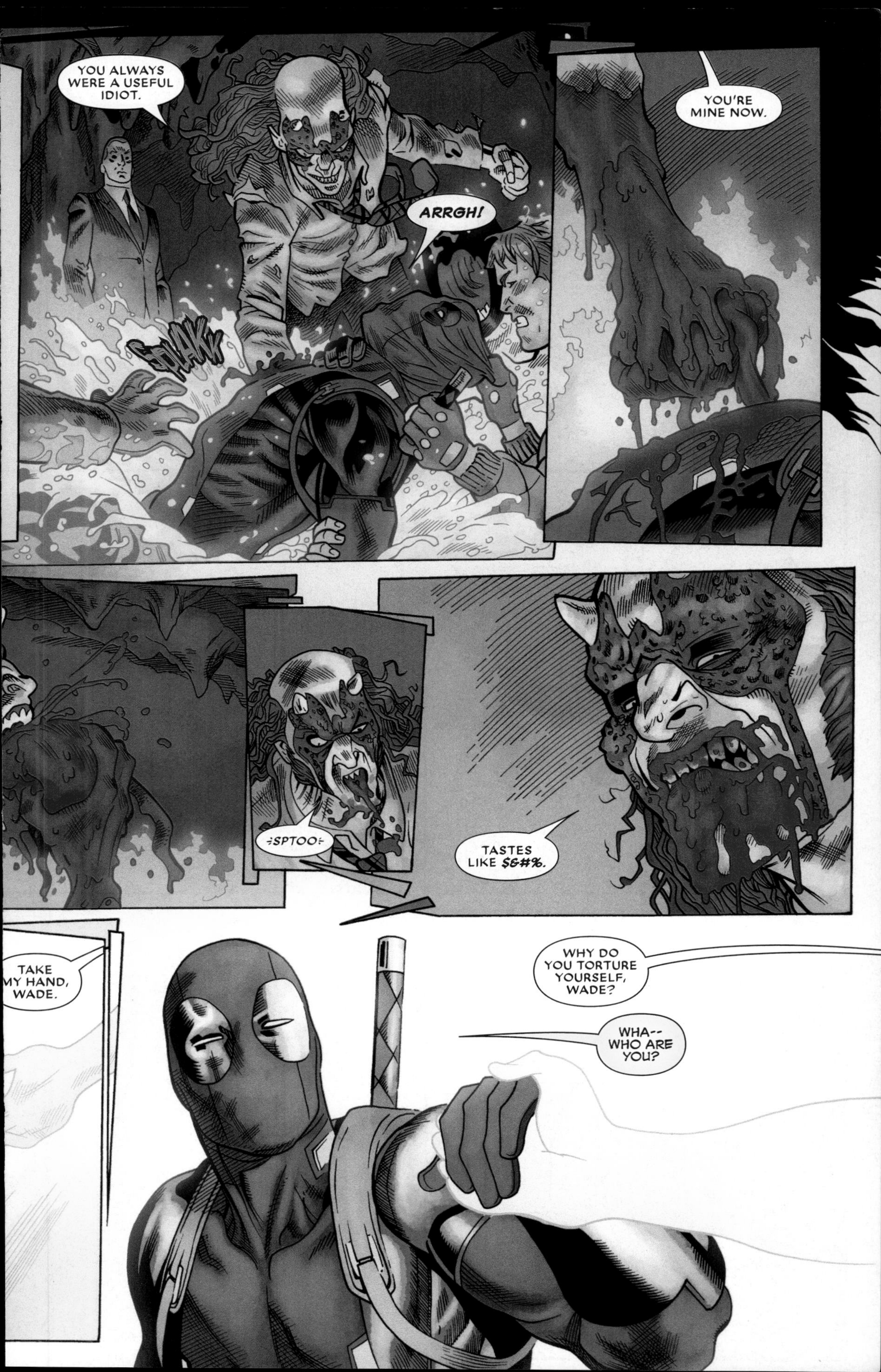
YOU ALWAYS WERE A USEFUL IDIOT.
ARRGH!
YOU'RE MINE NOW.
=SPTOO=
TASTES LIKE $&#%.
TAKE MY HAND, WADE.
WHY DO YOU TORTURE YOURSELF, WADE?
WHA-- WHO ARE YOU?

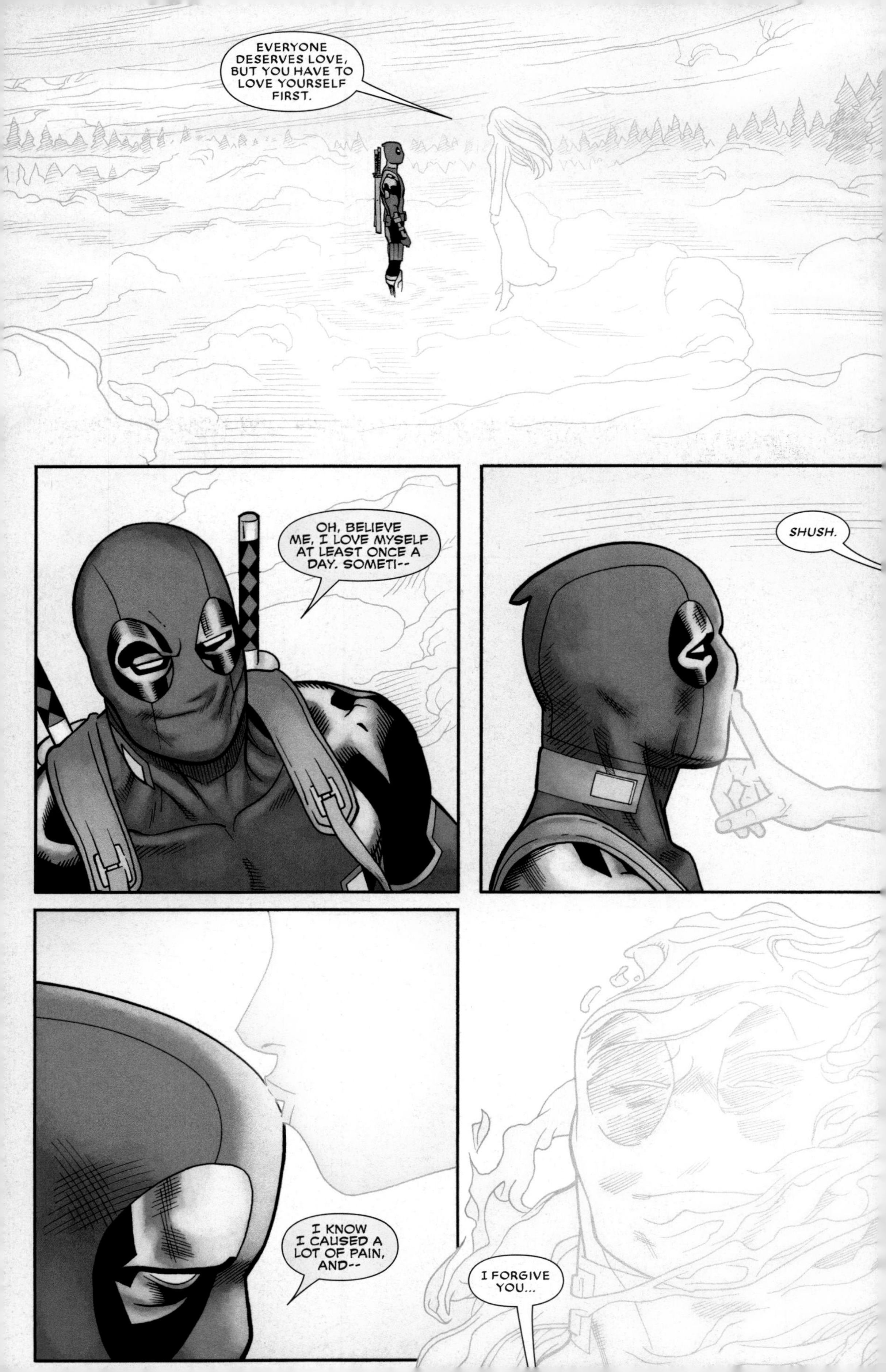
EVERYONE DESERVES LOVE, BUT YOU HAVE TO LOVE YOURSELF FIRST.
OH, BELIEVE ME, I LOVE MYSELF AT LEAST ONCE A DAY. SOMETI--
SHUSH.
I KNOW I CAUSED A LOT OF PAIN, AND--
I FORGIVE YOU...

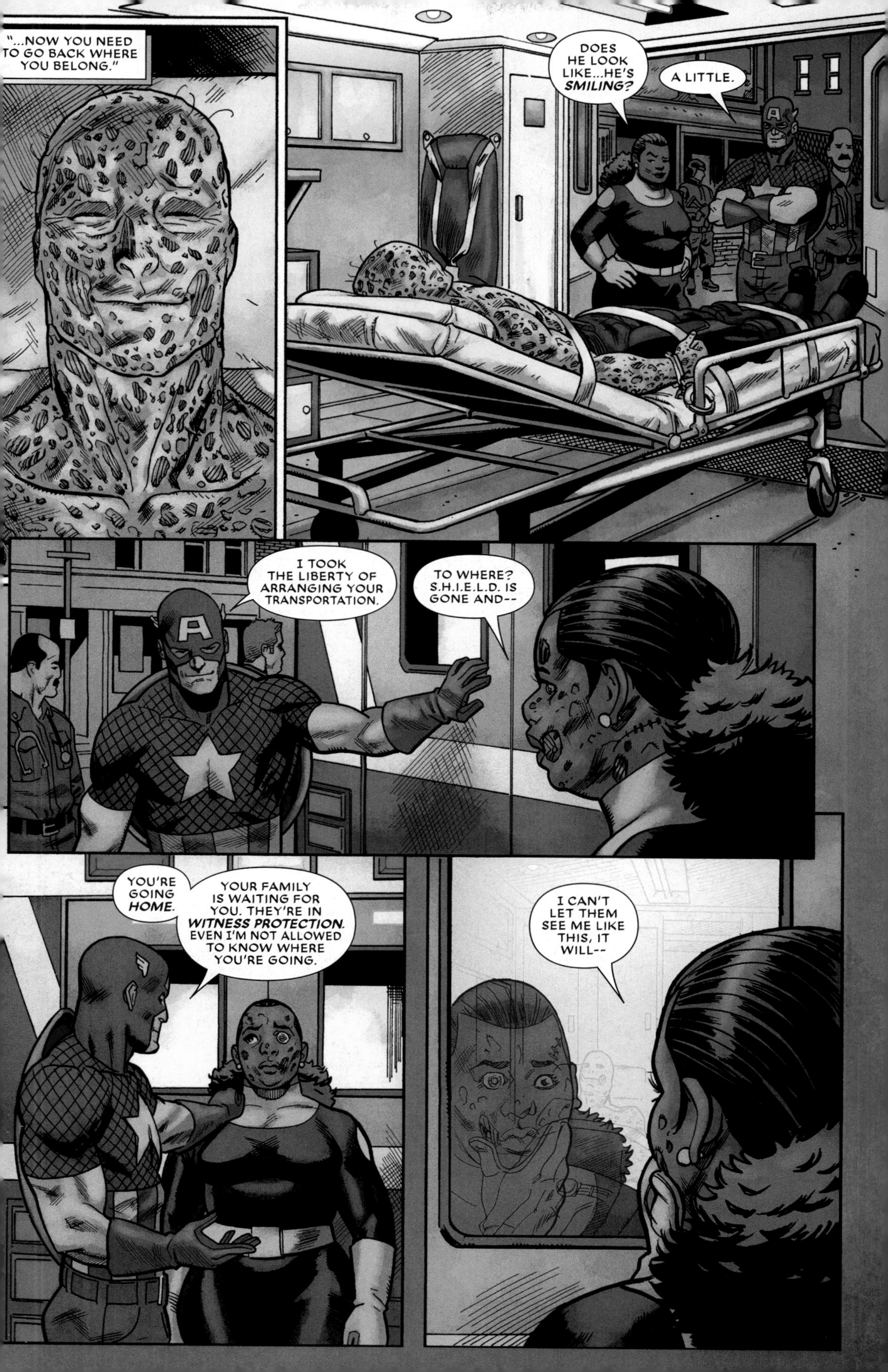
"...NOW YOU NEED TO GO BACK WHERE YOU BELONG."
DOES HE LOOK LIKE...HE'S *SMILING?*
A LITTLE.
I TOOK THE LIBERTY OF ARRANGING YOUR TRANSPORTATION.
TO WHERE? S.H.I.E.L.D. IS GONE AND--
YOU'RE GOING *HOME*.
YOUR FAMILY IS WAITING FOR YOU. THEY'RE IN *WITNESS PROTECTION.* EVEN I'M NOT ALLOWED TO KNOW WHERE YOU'RE GOING.
I CAN'T LET THEM SEE ME LIKE THIS, IT WILL--

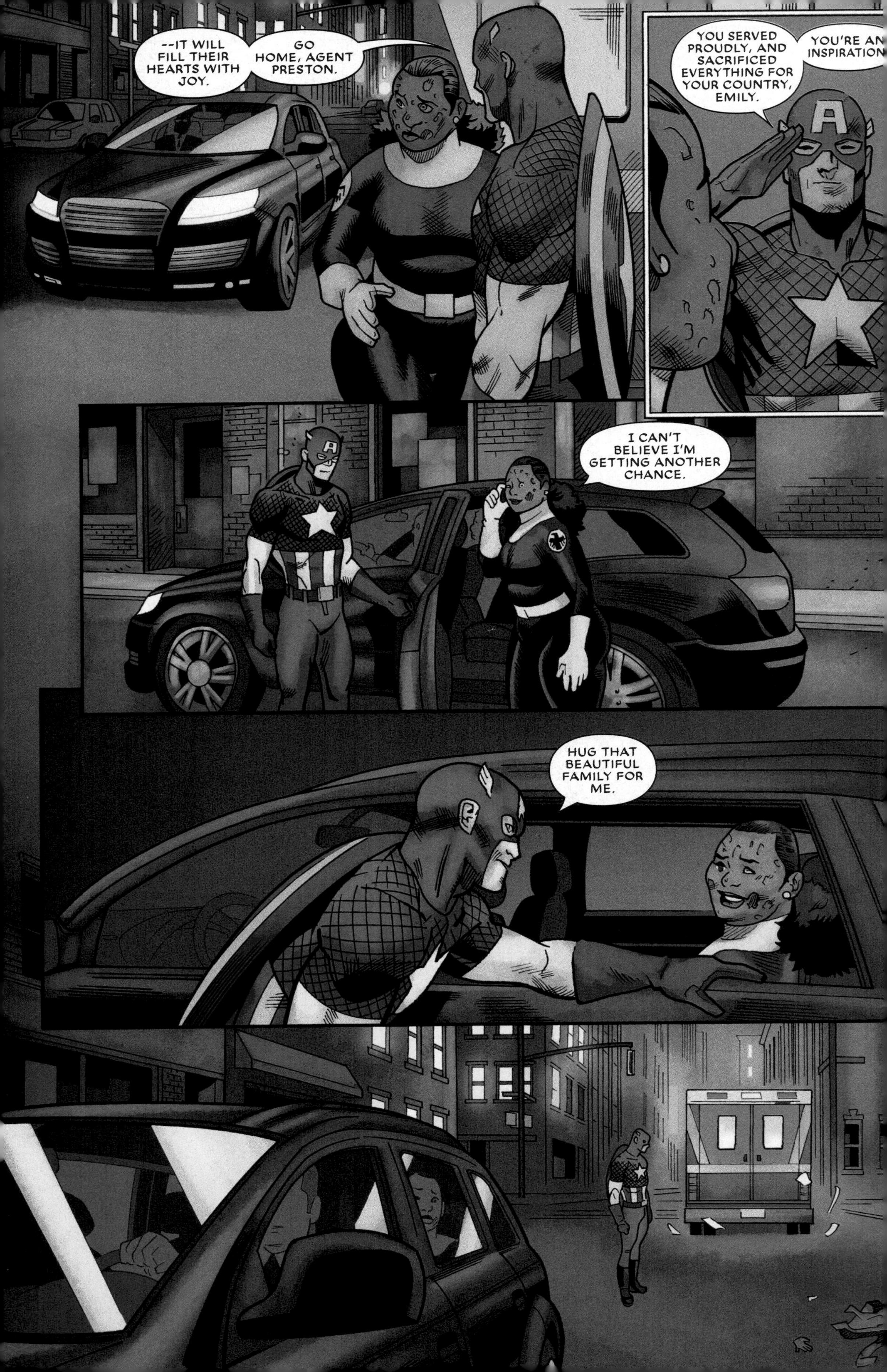
--IT WILL FILL THEIR HEARTS WITH JOY.
GO HOME, AGENT PRESTON.
YOU SERVED PROUDLY, AND SACRIFICED EVERYTHING FOR YOUR COUNTRY, EMILY.
YOU'RE AN INSPIRATION
I CAN'T BELIEVE I'M GETTING ANOTHER CHANCE.
HUG THAT BEAUTIFUL FAMILY FOR ME.

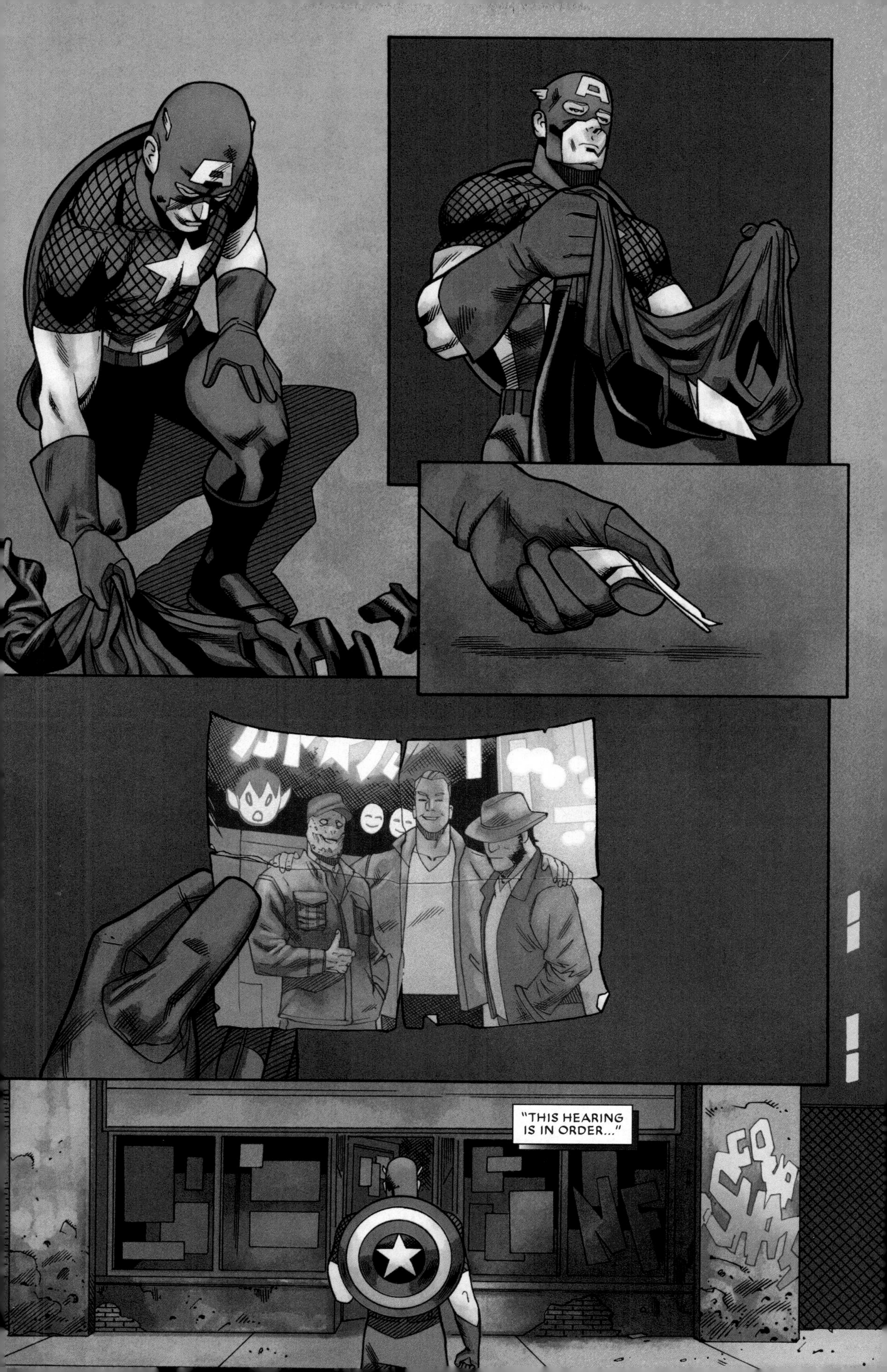
"THIS HEARING IS IN ORDER..."

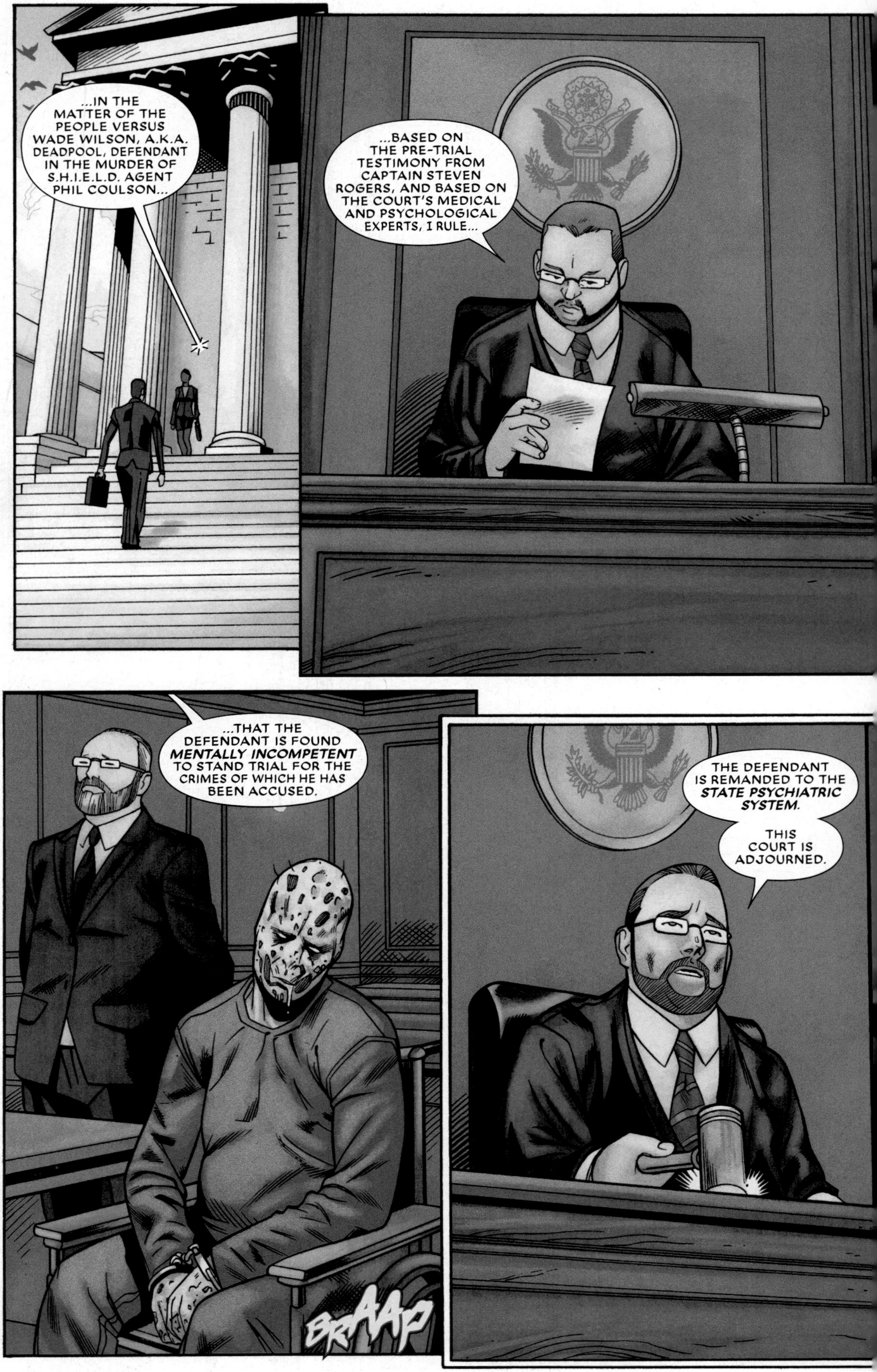
...IN THE MATTER OF THE PEOPLE VERSUS WADE WILSON, A.K.A. DEADPOOL, DEFENDANT IN THE MURDER OF S.H.I.E.L.D. AGENT PHIL COULSON...
...BASED ON THE PRE-TRIAL TESTIMONY FROM CAPTAIN STEVEN ROGERS, AND BASED ON THE COURT'S MEDICAL AND PSYCHOLOGICAL EXPERTS, I RULE...
...THAT THE DEFENDANT IS FOUND MENTALLY INCOMPETENT TO STAND TRIAL FOR THE CRIMES OF WHICH HE HAS BEEN ACCUSED.
BRAAAP
THE DEFENDANT IS REMANDED TO THE STATE PSYCHIATRIC SYSTEM.
THIS COURT IS ADJOURNED.

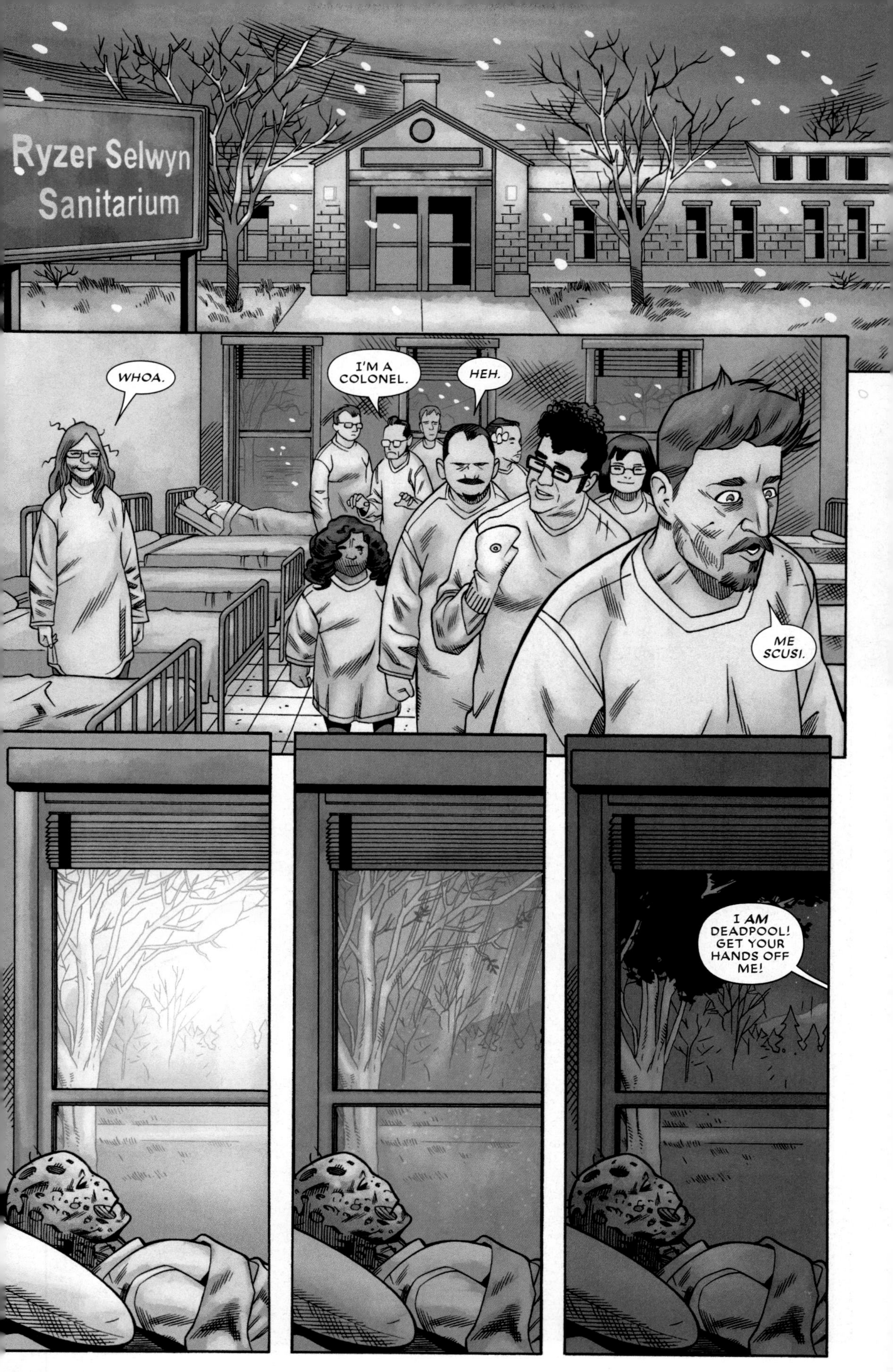
Ryzer Selwyn Sanitarium
WHOA.
I'M A COLONEL.
HEH.
ME SCUSI.
I AM DEADPOOL! GET YOUR HANDS OFF ME!

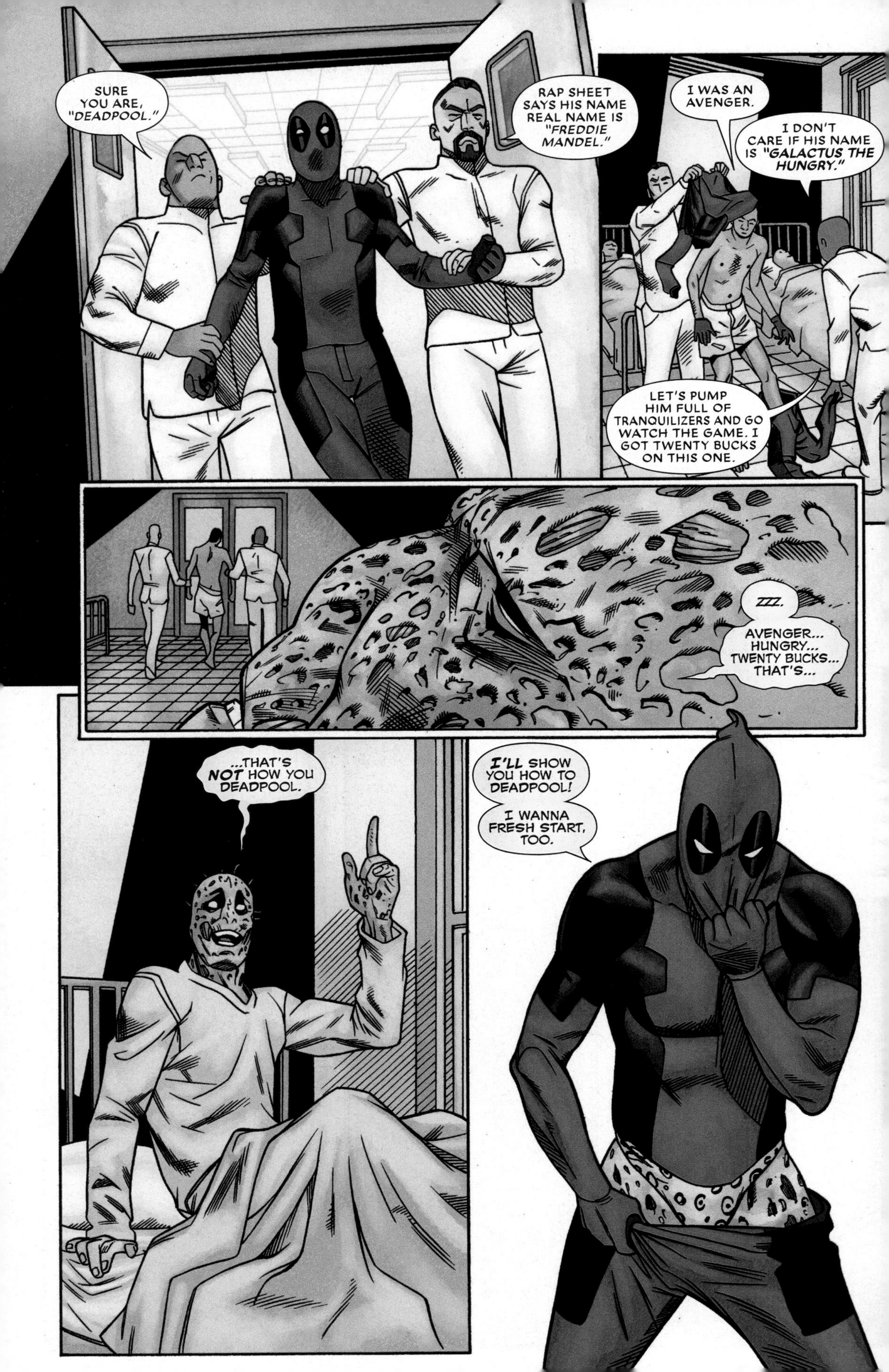
SURE YOU ARE, "DEADPOOL."
RAP SHEET SAYS HIS NAME REAL NAME IS "FREDDIE MANDEL."
I WAS AN AVENGER.
I DON'T CARE IF HIS NAME IS "GALACTUS THE HUNGRY."
LET'S PUMP HIM FULL OF TRANQUILIZERS AND GO WATCH THE GAME. I GOT TWENTY BUCKS ON THIS ONE.
ZZZ.
AVENGER... HUNGRY... TWENTY BUCKS... THAT'S...
...THAT'S NOT HOW YOU DEADPOOL.
I'LL SHOW YOU HOW TO DEADPOOL!
I WANNA FRESH START, TOO.

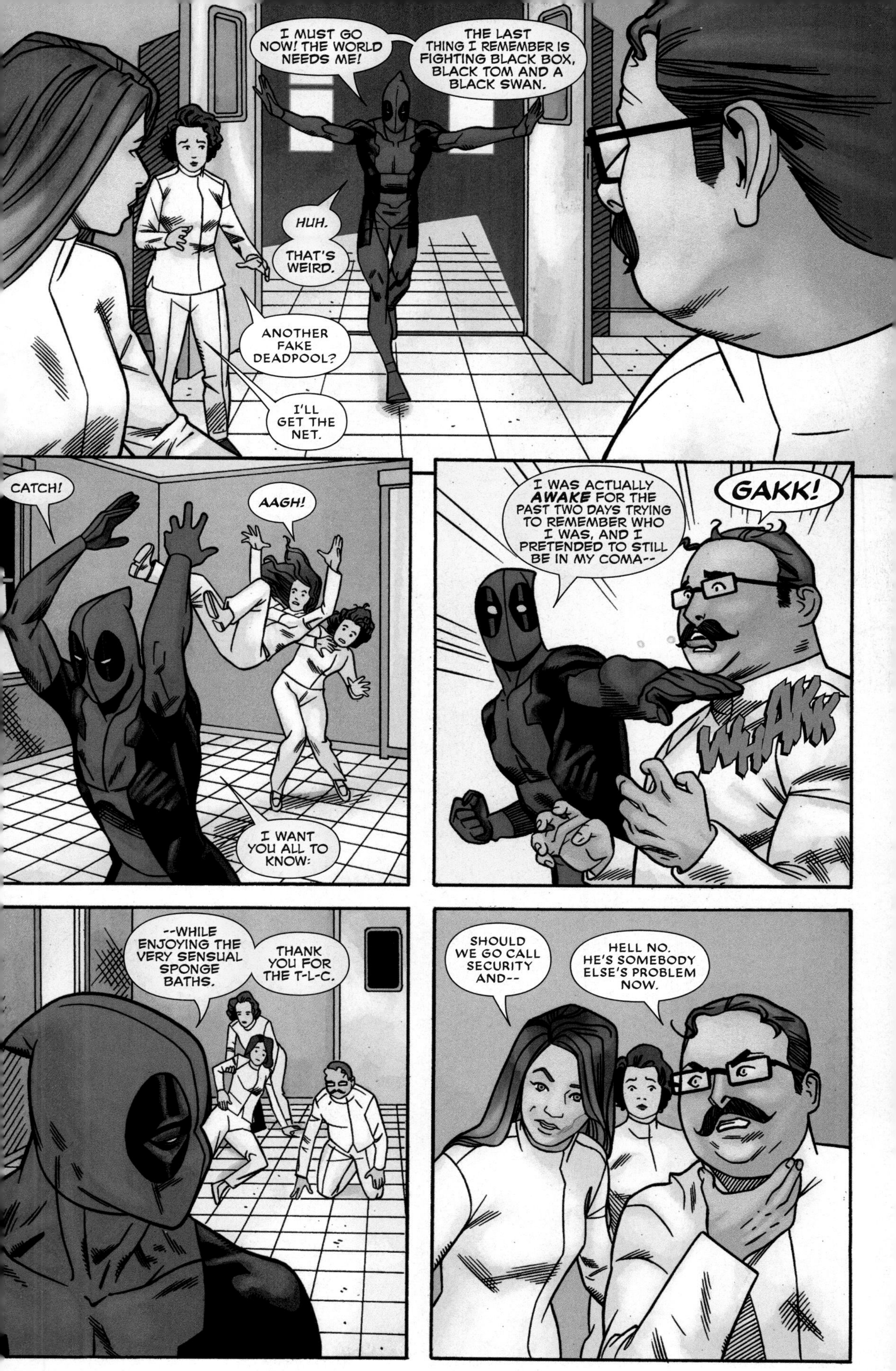
I MUST GO NOW! THE WORLD NEEDS ME!
THE LAST THING I REMEMBER IS FIGHTING BLACK BOX, BLACK TOM AND A BLACK SWAN.
HUH.
THAT'S WEIRD.
ANOTHER FAKE DEADPOOL?
I'LL GET THE NET.
CATCH!
AAGH!
I WANT YOU ALL TO KNOW:
I WAS ACTUALLY AWAKE FOR THE PAST TWO DAYS TRYING TO REMEMBER WHO I WAS, AND I PRETENDED TO STILL BE IN MY COMA--
GAKK!
WHAKK
--WHILE ENJOYING THE VERY SENSUAL SPONGE BATHS.
THANK YOU FOR THE T-L-C.
SHOULD WE GO CALL SECURITY AND--
HELL NO. HE'S SOMEBODY ELSE'S PROBLEM NOW.

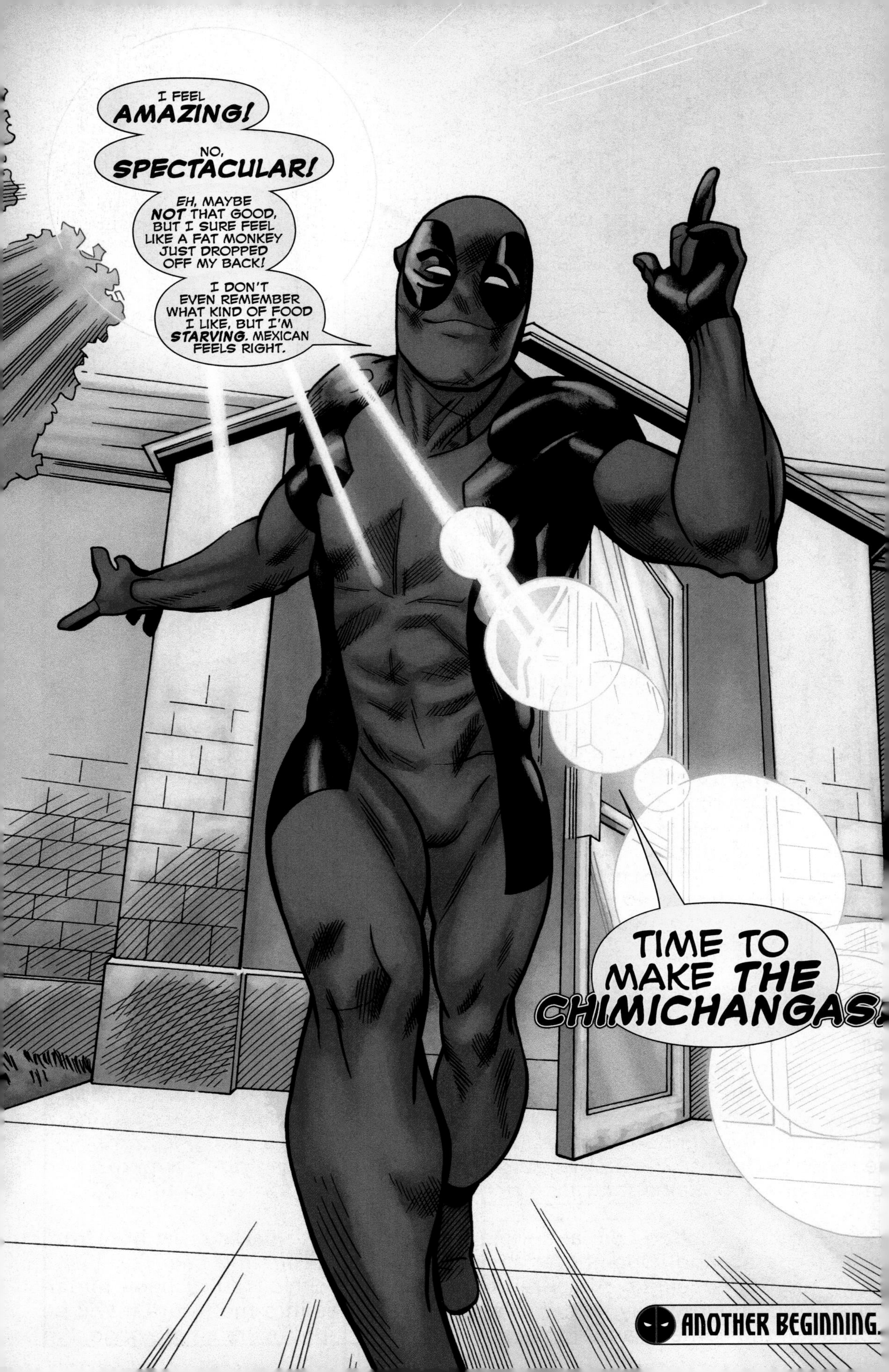
I FEEL **AMAZING!**
NO, **SPECTACULAR!**
EH, MAYBE ***NOT*** THAT GOOD, BUT I SURE FEEL LIKE A FAT MONKEY JUST DROPPED OFF MY BACK!
I DON'T EVEN REMEMBER WHAT KIND OF FOOD I LIKE, BUT I'M ***STARVING.*** MEXICAN FEELS RIGHT.
TIME TO MAKE ***THE CHIMICHANGAS!***
ANOTHER BEGINNING.

Adios, Friendos.

When I was a kid, every Thanksgiving my uncle Victor used to make everyone go around the table and name what we were thankful for. He was an immigrant to this country, and he worked like hell to start a new life in a new world. The wisdom of naming what you're thankful for rubbed off on me, and now on my first Thanksgiving as a former DEADPOOL writer I wanted to tell you what or rather who I am thankful for.

For the past several years it has been my privilege to collaborate on some of the most fun comics I'll ever get to make. Deadpool came into my life and I thought we'd wash out pretty quickly. I'm thankful I got to inherit the character for a while. Sorry we made it rough on you, Wade.

I'm sincerely grateful for every penciler, inker, cover artist, colorist, flatter, editor, assistant editor and everyone involved behind the scenes at Marvel for contributing to DEADPOOL for the last five years. Thanks to all the retailers, fans and especially those of you that had us on your pull lists. I'm thankful for that.

Brian Posehn, thanks for writing some of my favorite Deadpool stories ever, and for putting up with a difficult writing partner. Thanks to Axel Alonso, Nick Lowe, Tom Brevoort, C.B. Cebulski and all the folks that let us be us. Thanks to the Marvel writers that vouched for us on the way in the door: Bendis, Brubaker, Fraction and especially Rick Remender, who literally handed Axel Alonso a comic about Santa Claus after the apocalypse and said we could work at Marvel. And thanks to all the men and women in the editorial retreats for making our stories better. I left every room in much better shape than when I walked in.

There's a danger that these Deadpool comics might be referred to as "Duggan's Deadpool" and that wouldn't be fair. It's not false modesty to say that this book has belonged to the artists from the very first page. It's been a murderers' row beginning with Tony Moore agreeing to design our Deadpool and drawing the first arc. The good luck and great timing continued throughout including Declan [Shalvey] and Jordie [Bellaire] coming into our lives at just the right moment for the right story. Then John Lucas and every other guest artist hit the notes perfectly. Joe Sabino has lettered every issue going back to our first number one. I'm thankful for the good luck in collaborators every time out.

Scott Koblish, Matteo Lolli and Mike Hawthorne, your backs must hurt from carrying me around. Opening emails from you guys for the past few years has been such a delight. You three have put on a clinic. You've been under-appreciated in every way, and if this work resonates into the future it will be because of the comedy and tragedy you crammed into every single page. I'm

so thankful to call you my friends and collaborators. Let's all take a moment t
really appreciate Mike Hawthorne. He's not just one of the best artists working
but he's also leaving having drawn the most Deadpool pages in the histor
of the character. He makes Deadpool look good no matter how awful he'
behaving.

Last, and never least, I'm thankful for our editors. There have been many alon
the way that helped get these comics to the printer. Heather Antos, Annalis
Bissa and especially Jordan D. White deserve to be called out. They all mad
it look easy. It was not. I'm thankful for their joke pitches that made me loo
funny and their story ideas that made me look smart.

Jordan's been editing DEADPOOL since Dan Way was on the book, and thi
issue is his last for now as well. In the best of times he and I have operated a
a married couple, and at the worst of times, and old married couple. Some c
your favorite Deadpool moments sprung from Jordan's mind. I'm thankful I g
Jordan's credit.

I've written more Deadpool comics than anyone to date, and that's enough t
last a lifetime. Having done this a while, I can tell you how special it is to get t
write the words "The End" in a comic and see it roll off the printer. Your drear
job doesn't always end the way you want. The success of this run is due to har
work of the teams that built Deadpool up and made him popular before w
ever began. Some of them didn't know when they would have to wrap up. I'r
thankful I got to enjoy the fruits of their labor, and finally - I'm grateful to leav
before I started repeating myself.

The best days are ahead for Deadpool. More films, cartoons, toys...and bes
of all: a lot more comic books. I can't wait to see what Skottie Young, Nic Klein
Jake Thomas and their collaborators are cooking up. I'm grateful to return t
Deadpool as a reader.

I hope I've been as good to Wade Wilson as he has been to me. I'll leave yo
with a story about my relationship with Wade. I was in need of a quick gag on
day, and decided to ruin the Harry Potter novels for him. Wade would have hi
revenge, hunting down and killing the unnamed character that spoiled the book
for him in the pages of our comic, but Wade would also have his revenge on me
My son snuck the finished issue from the spinner rack in my office and proceede
to have Harry Potter ruined for him. My wife is still furious with me. You're neve
safe from Deadpool, no matter how many walls you're hiding behind.

Thank you all for the suppor

G
Los Angeles, Thanksgiving Night, November 201

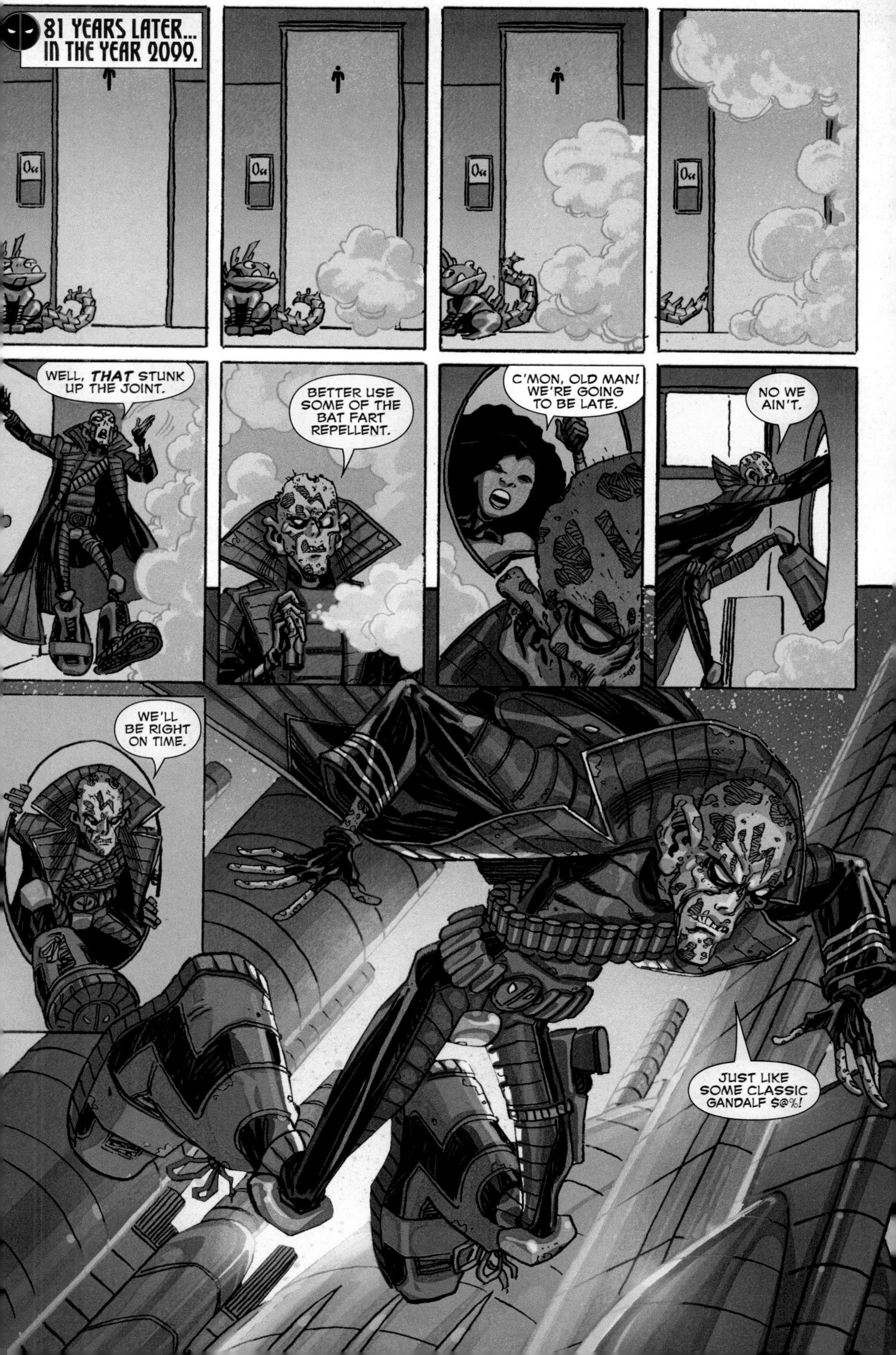

81 YEARS LATER... IN THE YEAR 2099.
WELL, THAT STUNK UP THE JOINT.
BETTER USE SOME OF THE BAT FART REPELLENT.
C'MON, OLD MAN! WE'RE GOING TO BE LATE.
NO WE AIN'T.
WE'LL BE RIGHT ON TIME.
JUST LIKE SOME CLASSIC GANDALF $@%!

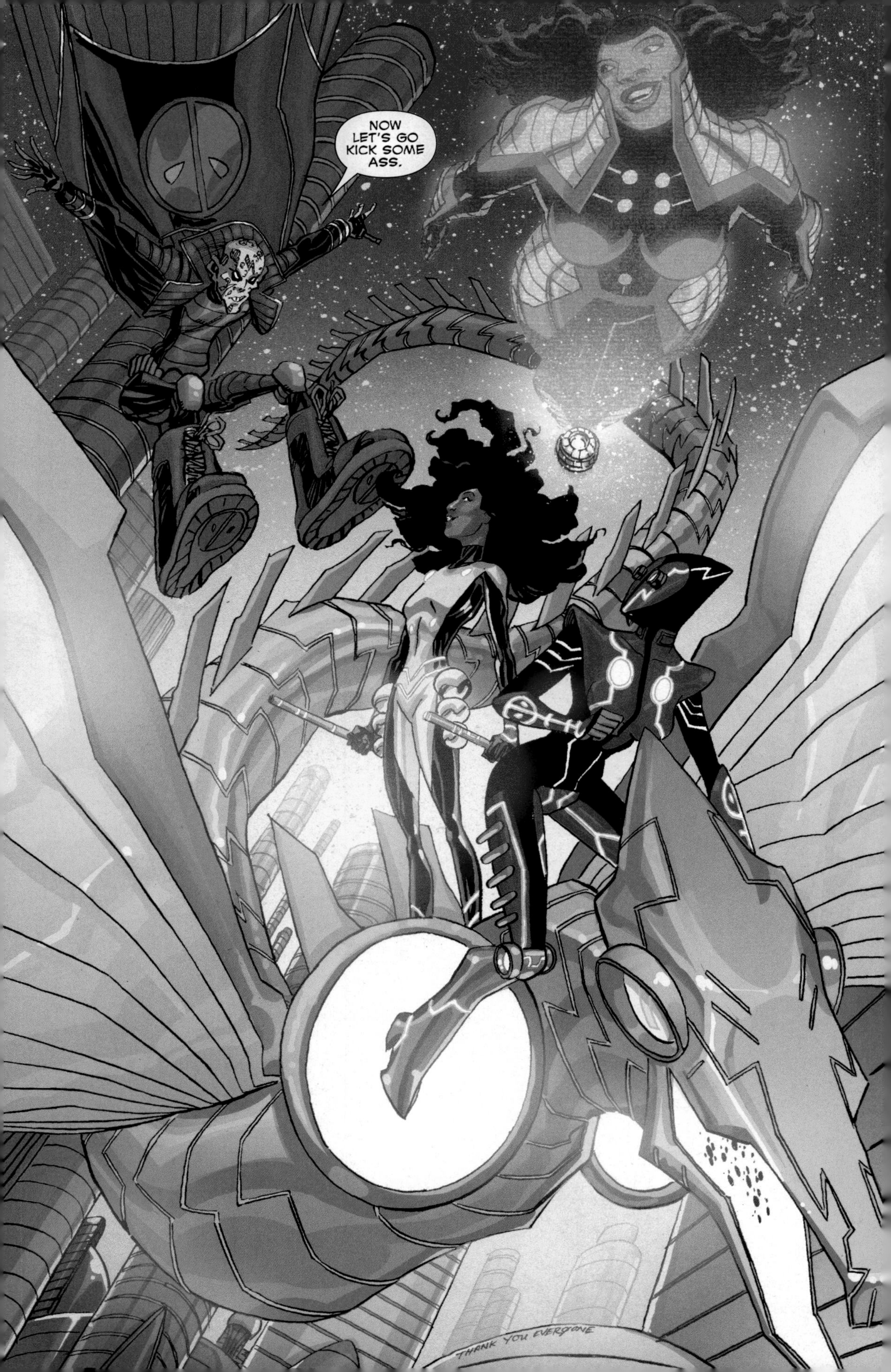
NOW LET'S GO KICK SOME ASS.
THANK YOU EVERYONE

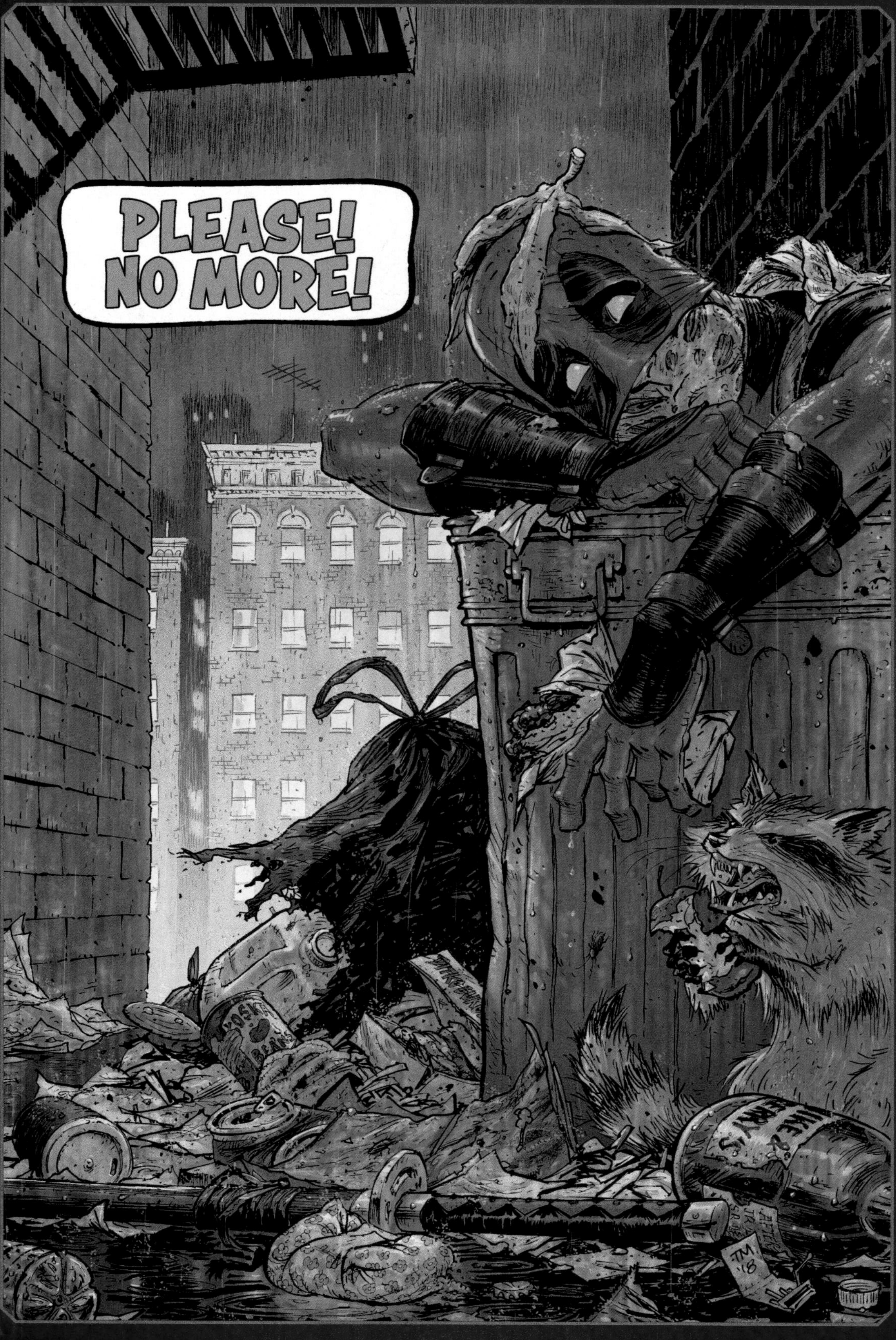
PLEASE! NO MORE!

#300 VARIANT BY **TONY MOORE**

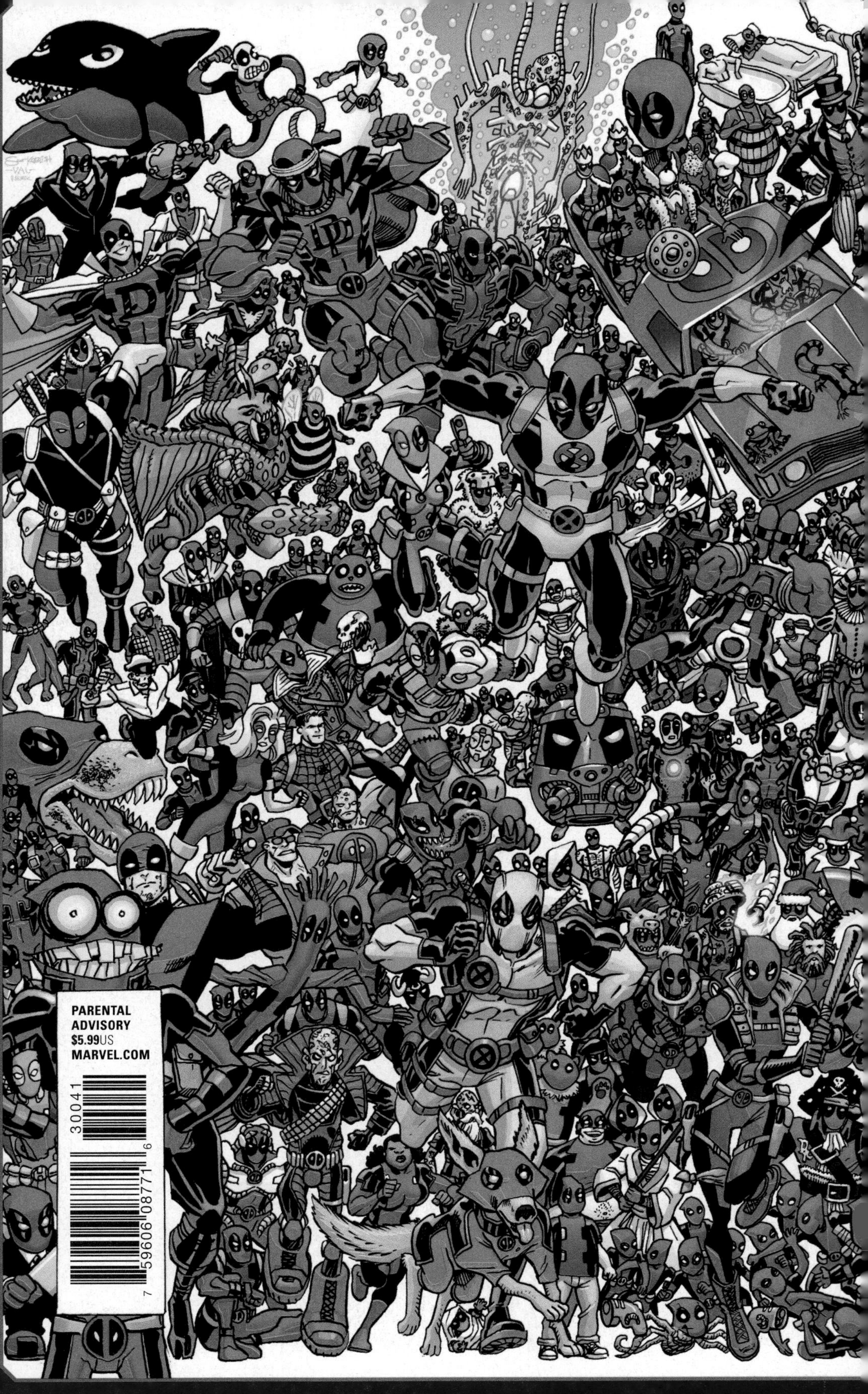

PARENTAL
ADVISORY
$5.99US
MARVEL.COM

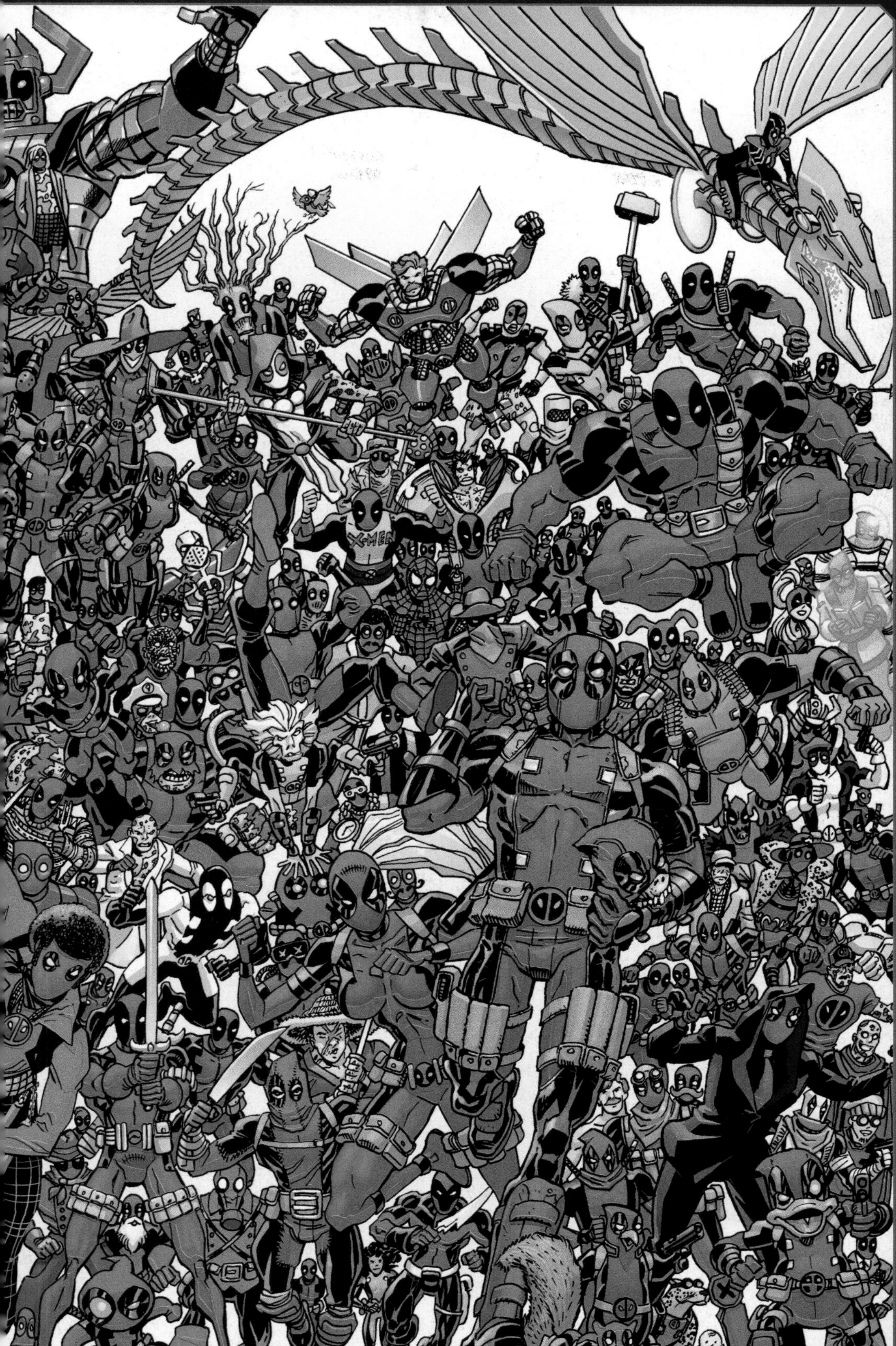
X-MEN

#300 VARIANT BY SCOTT KOBLISH & VAL STAPLES

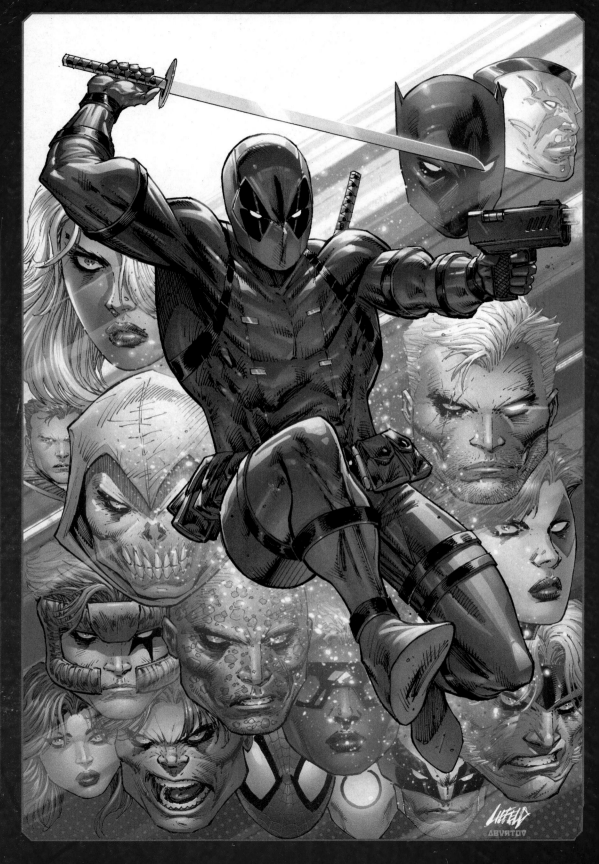

#300 VARIANT BY **ROB LIEFELD** & **JESUS ABURTOV**